UNLAWFUL KILLINGS

Life, Love and Murder:
Trials at the Old Bailey

HER HONOUR
WENDY JOSEPH KC

PENGUIN BOOKS

TRANSWORLD PUBLISHERS
Penguin Random House, One Embassy Gardens,
8 Viaduct Gardens, London SW11 7BW
www.penguin.co.uk

Transworld is part of the Penguin Random House group of companies
whose addresses can be found at global.penguinrandomhouse.com

First published in Great Britain in 2022 by Doubleday
an imprint of Transworld Publishers
Penguin paperback edition published 2023

A CIP catalogue record for this book
is available from the British Library.

ISBN
9781804990902

Text design by Couper Street Type Co.
Typeset in Adobe Minion Pro by Jouve (UK), Milton Keynes.
Printed and bound in Great Britain by Clays Ltd, Elcograf S.p.A.

The authorized representative in the EEA is Penguin Random House Ireland,
Morrison Chambers, 32 Nassau Street, Dublin D02 YH68.

Penguin Random House is committed to a sustainable
future for our business, our readers and our planet. This book
is made from Forest Stewardship Council® certified paper.

To my sister Elizabeth, always my first,
always my best and kindest reader.
With love and gratitude.

CONTENTS

Preface   xi

Introduction: Interested Parties   1

TRIAL ONE: The Fiery Furnace   23

TRIAL TWO: Amid the Alien Corn   63

TRIAL THREE: In the Vale of Tears   107

TRIAL FOUR: The Offering   147

TRIAL FIVE: The Good Soldier   187

TRIAL SIX: Vengeance Is Mine   231

Conclusions   275

Appendices   281

Acknowledgements   313

UNLAWFUL KILLINGS

PREFACE

BETWEEN 2000 AND 2018, roughly half a million people died each year in the UK. The vast majority lost their lives from illness or accident, but a significant number were neither ill nor unlucky – they were unlawfully killed.

Exact figures are harder to come by than you might think. What looks like murder isn't if the jury decides a defendant acted in self-defence. What might be manslaughter isn't if the jury says it was an accident. But whatever the exact figures, every day in the UK lives are suddenly, brutally, wickedly taken away. Victims are shot or stabbed. Less often they are strangled or suffocated or beaten to death. Rarely they are poisoned, pushed off high buildings, drowned or set alight. Then there are the many who are killed by dangerous drivers, or corporate gross negligence.

There are a lot of ways you can kill someone. I know because I've seen most of them at close quarters.

I see them day in, day out because it's my job to preside over the trials that follow. It's my job to sit on the Bench at the Old Bailey and ensure there is a careful, clinical sifting of the evidence in each case that comes before me; a rational and considered examination of who killed this person, how, and why. It's my job to bring dispassionate focus to the most terrible situations in which human beings manage to get entangled. Every unlawful death tells a story. Every trial involves characters to be understood, motives to be unravelled, plans and methodology to be exposed. It involves human good and human bad. Sometimes very bad.

You may think all this – all that is going on around us – is nothing to do with you, that it's stuff to do with other people, with other lives a long way from yours. But the ways in which each of us can be touched by these killings are many and subtle. The increasing number of gang-related killings, drug-related killings, knife-killings, the increasing number of killers only fifteen or sixteen years old, or with mental health problems or from backgrounds that have marginalized them, is a reflection of the society in which we live. You and me. In fact, it's surprising how many of us are involved with the lives of these people who kill and are killed.

There are obvious ways we might be involved. Any one of us could be the victim. It could be our body on the mortuary table. We could be the lone jogger targeted by a knifeman, the one who wakes to find a violent burglar in our sleeping home, the sufferer of domestic abuse or the person shot in mistake for another as we sit in a park. We could be the parent whose child is stabbed by a class mate outside the school gates. We could be the parent of the stabber. We could be the bereaved, or the bemused and horrified family of the defendant. But every suspect accused of homicide who is brought before the court involves many, many more of us than this, because each killing drops into our world like a stone into a deep, dark pool. The ripples widen and widen.

Of course, if you work in the world of law and order, all this will be your daily fare. So it is for the police, the pathologists, the forensic scientists, the telephone analysts and psychologists and other experts. So it is for the prison officers and the probation officers, the court clerks and ushers and administrative staff, the lawyers, the judges and many more. Then, each year, tens of thousands of us see a crime or something relevant to a crime that may make us witnesses. Each year, hundreds of thousands of us receive a summons to do jury service so that we must become intimately involved in a court case. And each day we hear about things that make us shake our heads in disbelief at what people do to each other. One way or another, huge numbers of us are touched by the stories unfolding in a trial, especially where the subject of that trial is the death of a fellow human being.

Why write this book now? Because now we're in trouble. Real trouble. Because, with the ability of the criminal courts so compromised by Covid-19 and remanded prisoners seeing their trial dates receding into the unknowable future, we have the chance to focus. In the Covid-induced pauses that have put on hold so much, we have all been able to stand back and take in where we are going. Even before the pandemic, the fracture lines driving through our society were harder and harder to ignore; and now, we do so at our peril.

Of course, we should have paid more attention before, to the many people who were waving the red flag for danger. We never should have let it get to this stage. We all should have asked louder, more often, more determinedly, 'What is wrong with our society?' As well as punishing people after they have killed, we should have demanded clearer analysis of and better answers to *why* people kill. We should have been asking not only how can we deter, but how can we deflect. We should have wondered why we didn't offer help while there was time, before it came to this – to the cold body on the cold mortuary slab. We should have recognized that killers are not aliens landing from another planet. They are part of our society. We have nurtured them.

So, what is actually happening? Some things are obvious. Although mental illness makes increasing numbers of us vulnerable, both as the victims and the perpetrators of crime, there is less and less help available for the sick. The internet allows those with perverted ideas about sexual contact with children to put those ideas into practice, and the dark web is out of our control. Drug dealing breeds violence, greed breeds drug dealers, and the constant pressure of our society to accumulate and flaunt breeds greed. We have constructed a set of rules by which we expect the people of this country to live, and a terrifying number of young people are opting out of it, disaffected, signing up to an alternative. The gang. And in the world of the gang, they are creating their own language, their own rules, their own way of life which brings them into direct conflict with ours.

I'm well positioned to write this book because I've seen more murder trials than the average person. In fact, I've seen more murder trials than the average judge. As a barrister I practised in the criminal courts for thirty-two years, nearly ten of them as a KC. During those years I both defended and prosecuted in many homicide cases. In 2007 I became a judge, sitting first in one of the biggest and busiest Crown Courts in the country; and, since 2012, at the Central Criminal Court, the Old Bailey. Only a small proportion of judges are licensed to try murder cases. Of those who are, most will try no more than a few a year. Of all the Crown Courts in the country, only at the Old Bailey is murder part of the daily judicial diet. I know how the system works. I have seen it produce justice and, arguably, injustice. I have seen the guilty and the not guilty, the excellent jurors and the frankly awful ones. I have heard great advocacy and plenty of pitiful stuff too. It's all in the job.

Side by side with this 'day job', I have, for many years, had another role. Since 2012 I have been a Diversity and Community Relations Judge. This is a 'post' given to at least one judge in each Crown Court and it brings with it the responsibility not only of promoting diversity on the Bench, but a wider remit to reach out into the community, especially to those who want to understand or be understood by the criminal justice system. So, for example, I speak a lot to schoolchildren and older students. I will engage with those representing the mentally ill, ex-prisoners and the families of prisoners, those who feel they are unfairly dealt with by the law because of their background, their race or religion or sexual orientation or identity, in fact any group that is concerned about their relationship with the law and has the patience to bother with me.

The purpose of the DCRJ is to try to bridge the gap between the community and the judiciary. Sometimes that gap feels like a dark chasm, but it shouldn't be. There should be nothing mysterious about the way the courts work, and nothing frightening – unless you happen to be guilty of a crime. Everything is meant to be transparent. The business of the courtrooms in every Crown Court is almost always open to the public and the press. If members of the public still find proceedings confusing, rules unclear, sentences baffling, this is wrong and it is unnecessary. So, in this book I lift the curtain and let in the light of day. I show what it's like to be in the courtroom, and what it's like to be the judge who sits there as the story, the characters, the crime unfolds in front of you. I describe what it is like to watch the suffering of the bereaved and the family of defendants, to watch the struggles of witnesses and jurors, to look into the eyes of a child and send him to prison for life.

I do this by telling the stories of different trials and the characters involved in them. It would be wrong as well as hurtful to identify particular individuals as they appeared in actual cases. I haven't done that, so it would be pointless to try to identify anything in this book with any case I have sat on. Rather, I have taken aspects of what I have seen over decades – the people, the events and issues – and mixed them together to create for you a representation of what really can and does happen in a courtroom like mine. And just what it is like to be the judge.

INTRODUCTION:

Interested Parties

LET ME INTRODUCE YOU to the Central Criminal Court, known – from the name of the little street on which it stands – as the Old Bailey. It is here that some of the most serious cases in the country are tried. The building has eighteen functioning courtrooms, but if we want a flavour of the place, Court One is where to go. Trials have been held here for well over a hundred years and it is probably the most famous courtroom in the world. Heinous criminals of the last century have sat in its dock. Famous advocates have spoken from its counsel's rows. If I'm to describe to you what it feels like to walk in here, one of the best ways to do that is through the eyes of those who, like you, aren't actually engaged in its activities.

Court One is where I'm presiding over a murder trial one late afternoon in May. The weather outside is lovely, so my usher tells me. I have to take her word for it because the courtrooms in the Old Bailey have no windows. No one inside looks out. No one outside looks in. We are a world apart. It's five o'clock and my trial was adjourned half an hour ago. The defendants accused of murder have been taken down to the cells, from where they will be put in vans and sent back to prison for the night. The jury are heading home on tubes and buses. The barristers have gone to their Chambers to prepare for the next day's work. Clerks and ushers are deep in the administrative tasks that have to be done at the end of a court session. No one is left but me. I'm still sitting where I've sat all day – in the judge's chair on the judge's Bench. I'm waiting for a group of Year Nine schoolchildren to arrive. Apparently I'm part of their Citizenship Course. I fit into this term's 'Playing a Full and Active Part in Society'. The syllabus isn't clear about how I do it, but if the children are willing to give it a go, so am I.

As well as the day job – sitting on trials, ruling on the law, passing sentences on the guilty – I do quite a lot of this additional activity as a Diversity and Community Relations Judge. Not only with schools and universities, but in discussion sessions with anyone who has the patience and inclination to listen to me. I talk to any group that is concerned about its relationship with the law, which feels its members are unfairly dealt with, not given a fair hearing, shut out, or who just want to understand more. I also try to encourage into the Bar (and ultimately into the judiciary) bright youngsters from diverse backgrounds. And who knows, it might work. Every Lord Chief Justice must have been in Year Nine once upon a time.

The children should have been here half an hour ago, but there's no sign of them so I sit listening to the emptiness of the court and the faint echo of what happened there during the day. After a while I'm aware that the echo has deepened, and turned into the shuffle of uncoordinated feet. Two voices drift through the open door. The first expresses what is clearly a considered and concluded opinion. It says, 'Fucking waste of time, Sir.'

The second says, 'You are entitled to your view, Shane, but you will express it without the adjectival intensifier.'

I'm impressed. I had no idea that 'fucking' was an adjectival intensifier.

Shane is impressed too. He modifies his language to 'Sod it, Sir.'

I hear more feet. 'Sir' is gathering his troops. I hear him hissing instructions: 'Do not take anything. Not anything. Not even a pencil. Do not damage or destroy anything. Do not carve your names into anything. Especially not that because they'll know who did it.'

'How, Sir?' says someone.

'Gorm,' says someone else.

Sir's head appears round the door. He looks about the courtroom and sees me perched high on the Bench. He takes in the black gown and waistcoat, the crisp white bands at my neck, the wig which I've taken off and put beside me. He takes in my expression.

'Hello,' he says with a determined cheerfulness. 'I hope we haven't kept you waiting.'

'No,' I lie. I've been working on papers since 7 a.m. I've been in court since 10 a.m. I have at least another three hours' reading to do before the day is over. I can't begin on that until I've dealt with the school visit. It would have been nice if they had been on time. He reads the situation perfectly.

'I really am sorry we're late,' he says, 'but one of the girls was sick on the bus.' He speaks with resignation, as if barely a day passes but one of his charges is sick on something.

I reflect that there are, after all, worse things than sitting in an airy courtroom, waiting.

Behind him, faces are peering in.

'Welcome,' I say. 'Come in. Come in, all of you.' The class of fourteen-year-olds elbows its way through the door. 'It's a great pleasure to have you here.' Perhaps I'm overstating it. 'Come in and find yourselves a seat, quickly and quietly, please.'

They come in, but they do it neither quickly nor quietly. They push and jostle into the rows that an hour before had been occupied by barristers and solicitors. I wonder if I dare add an adjectival intensifier. I decide against it. They reach for the bundles of trial papers which counsel have left there. In the trial, our afternoon has been spent examining photographs of the scene of a murder. I had warned counsel that a party of schoolchildren was coming, and that their papers should be left tied up and in neat piles. It would have been unkind of them to leave the bundles untied or with the photographs loose on the top.

'Please don't touch any of the papers, if you can help it,' I say. It seems they can't help it. They reach. They pull at pink ribbon. They open files and turn pages. They wish they hadn't. It's really surprising how much blood a human body can produce. I hope the girl who was sick has been left on the bus. Still, the desired effect is achieved. They fall silent.

In the course of a year, lots of schools come to the Central Criminal Court. Some – like this group – come as part of the curriculum. Others bring pupils who are thinking about a career in the law. Some are dragged here because their teachers think it will do them good to see what happens if they push the rules too far. The ones who arrive in expensive uniforms, in a private coach, with a list of carefully prepared and earnest questions, are pretty much wasting their time and mine because they can learn all they want to know from their parents or their parents' friends or their schools' expensive networking systems. It's the Shanes of this world who it's worth getting into the Old Bailey. It's the Shanes that might get something out of the visit. And it's from the Shanes that I will learn something too.

'Thank you for coming,' I say. I tell them my name and that I'm a judge here at the Old Bailey. I tell them they are sitting in Court One, one of the most famous courtrooms in the world. They look up at me. Some – a few – are interested. Some are suspending judgement. Some are frankly hostile. I wonder which one is Shane.

'I'm guessing,' I say, 'that some of you think this is a waste of your time.'

Polite titters from the few who think no such thing. Murmurs of assent from the many who do.

'You probably think this place has no part to play in your life and never will.'

A small boy with large spectacles puts up his hand. Good grief, he puts up his hand! I didn't think they did that any more. Except in the schools with expensive uniforms and private coaches. I focus on the boy. His spectacles really are very large and he really is very small. Either puberty is playing a cheap trick on him, or he has a brain whose rocket-power has shot him up the school ahead of his years. He says he thinks the courtroom will play a very big part in his life on account of his intending to be a barrister. This is clearly a boy who doesn't need to use adjectival intensifiers. Someone sitting behind him says, 'Sheeesh.' I have sympathy with this, but aspiration must be encouraged so I turn from Spectacles to Sheeesh.

'Do you see yourself as a barrister?' I ask. This is a stupid question. Really stupid.

'You taking the piss?' says the boy, then, judging that I am not, explains, 'I was thinking of being the defendant.'

'Good.'

He stares.

'Without a defendant, I'm out of a job.' I say it with a smile. There's always one joker. Then I look at him again and think, 'He isn't joking.' The boy next to him doesn't think he's joking either. Boy number two says he is Sheeesh's Mate-Unto-Death (that isn't quite how he puts it), and if his mate is the D he confidently expects to be the co-D. One of these two must surely be Shane.

'Excellent,' I say. 'We have two defendants. Go and sit in the dock, please.'

Sheeesh and Mate-Unto-Death look surprised. They look at each other. Sheeesh says he thinks that's an adjectivally intensified stupid idea. But Sir thinks it has merit and chivvies them along. The dock in Court One is a large square wooden affair raised above the floor of the court so that defendants sitting there look straight into the face of the judge. And vice versa. Sheeesh and his Mate-Unto-Death are staring at me.

I tell them, 'You're sitting where some of the most notorious murderers in England have sat. You're sitting where George Joseph Smith sat.'

'What did he do?' asks Sheeesh.

'He married three times and drowned each of his wives in the bath.'

'Shit,' says Mate-Unto-Death.

'And you're sitting where Dr Crippen sat. He poisoned his wife and cut up her body. The head and limbs were never found, but her torso was discovered under the floorboards.'

While the rest of the class are digesting this, Spectacles shoots to his feet. His brow is wrinkled with forensic thought.

'Please, Miss' – a nice touch, I think – 'if her hands had gone so they couldn't fingerprint her, and her face had gone so they couldn't identify her, how did they know it was her under the floorboards?'

I think about saying that if a woman disappears from her home and a torso appears under the floor, there's a reasonable correlative inference to be drawn. Instead I tell him the truth. 'There was a scar on the abdomen of the torso,' I say solemnly, 'and it was exactly where Mrs Crippen had a scar. The skin was removed and put in a soup bowl and passed around the jury.'

Spectacles swallows so hard I can hear it from the Bench. Still, if he is to have a successful career at the Bar, he can't start facing reality too early.

'Also in that very dock have sat the Yorkshire Ripper, the Soham murderer and the Kray twins.' Sheeesh and Mate-Unto-Death shift uncomfortably. 'Does anyone else see themselves sitting in that dock in years to come? Anyone else want to join our two defendants?' I wonder if I have gone too far, but Sir is grinning, which I take as a good sign. 'Right,' I say. 'So I have my defendants, and I have . . .' I pause and eye Spectacles. 'I take it you are happy to prosecute?' Spectacles nods solemnly. 'So I have counsel for the Crown. Now, does anyone see themselves as barrister for a defendant? It's a goodish sort of life . . . very interesting, reasonably well paid if you are successful, nice colleagues, the opportunity to make good friends . . .'

Two girls who had earlier made a show of taking the seats next to Spectacles now look at each other, then at him. One says, 'Can a defence barrister be friends with a prosecution barrister?'

'Certainly,' I say. 'They change in the same Robing Room, eat in the same Bar Mess, often work from the same Chambers ... it's a small and close-knit world.'

The girls look at each other again. They look at Spectacles. They announce that both have been thinking of a career in the law for some time. I regard the boy with new respect. If this is the effect he is having already, heaven only knows what will happen when puberty catches up with him. I turn to Sir.

'What an aspirational lot you have,' I say.

'They never cease to surprise me,' he replies.

'So five of you see the possibility of a future that might bring you into this courtroom. What about the rest of you? Does anyone see themselves as a prison officer?'

A series of 'No way's and 'Uncool's rise through the air. Sheeesh and Mate-Unto-Death look smug. 'No one's going to lock us up,' says Sheeesh with a smirk. But two boys I hadn't noticed before are on their feet. I double-check what I think I am seeing because although there are clearly two boys, they have only one face between them. Twins so identical I can no more distinguish one from the other than I could Bill from Ben. Bill (or it might be Ben) says they do not rule out the possibility that in the future they might become prison officers and would like to give it a try. I am surprised to find there are young people interested in this area of work. I wonder aloud if members of their family are prison officers. Ben (or it might be Bill) says no. It turns out their dad is currently inside and it occurs to them that life might be easier for him if they were the ones with the keys. They could provide a mobile phone so their mum could talk to him. They could get a little cannabis to him to help him pass the time. They are full of good and unlawful ideas along these lines. But there are no other takers for the job so I send them to sit one each side of the defendants and am gratified to see they take a stern line with Mate-Unto-Death, who is picking his nose and attempting to attach the result to the glass pane on the front of the dock.

One by one parts are assigned and players dispatched to their place in the courtroom. I appoint an usher, a clerk, a probation officer, a solicitor, a representative for the Crown Prosecution Service and some detectives. This latter is interesting, since no one wants to be a uniformed police officer but a surprising number volunteer for plain-clothes work. I don't ask why. I count those left. Thirteen. Perfect.

'Twelve of you will be my jurors,' I say, 'and one will be the witness.'

Slowly, a heavy boy gets to his feet. His face is tough. He crosses his arms in front of his chest. I think I am in for trouble but the expression on Sir's face hasn't changed as he says, 'What are you volunteering for, Shane?'

'Witness,' says Shane. 'I'll be the fucking witness. I'll be the one with the balls to stand up and say what happened. I won't be fright-ened out of it by any of you bastards.' He is staring at the dock. I worry how Sheeesh and Mate-Unto-Death will react to this but they are not taking offence. They only look away as if they understand this is not personal. It is Sir who says, quietly, 'Shane's brother was stabbed to death in a gang-fight last year. There were lots of people who saw it happen but so far no one has come forward to say who did it.'

The session goes well. Spectacles shows an innate grasp of forensic advocacy and I make a note to tell Sir that, if he wishes, I will have the boy back to spend a day with me in court at the end of the year. Shane is brilliant and brave. The jury are engaged and frequently ask better questions than the girls defending. They wrangle, heads locked together, over their verdicts, but in the end they convict. It clearly goes against their grain to condemn anyone for committing any crime, but they have each taken an oath to bring in a true verdict in accordance with the evidence, and they are taking it seriously. The foreman of the jury delivers the verdicts solemnly. A small girl on the back row bursts into tears and between hiccuping sobs asks, 'What's the sentence, Miss? Will they go to prison?'

'They will.'

'For long?'

I pause. 'If they were adults, I would be thinking of sentences in the region of four years.'

A silence.

'They only do half of it,' says Bill (or Ben) knowledgeably.

The silence becomes reflective.

'They'll miss the end-of-term party,' says one of the two defence barristers. Presumably Spectacles can only take one of them, and the other might have had hopes of being partnered by Sheeesh.

'Ah, well,' says the jury's foreman. 'Let's get on with it. Let's take them down to the cells.'

It takes Sir and I a goodish while to explain that this is not part of the event, and the teacher is expected to leave with the same number of pupils he brought in.

'It's the rule,' I say apologetically.

'There's always rules for us,' says the foreman.

'There's rules for everyone.'

'Not for you, I bet.'

I smile. But he's wrong. There are rules for everyone, including me. Especially me. My job is all rules. From the start of my working day to the end of it I have to apply rules – the Statutes, the Criminal Procedure Rules, the Sentencing Council's Guidelines, the Practice Directions, and these are only the thin end of a very thick wedge. A judge has little free will, and even where there is a judicial discretion it must be exercised within strict limits. Day in, day out I pass sentences I might prefer not to pass and make decisions I might prefer not to make, because that's the job. That's the law. Law Rules – and that's not always OK.

CAST LIST

In Interested Parties so far, I've shown you what some of the characters in the courtroom look like from the point of view of an outsider. Now let me show you what they look like from where I sit on the Bench.

The Defendant

When I said to Sheeesh and Mate-Unto-Death 'Without a defendant, I'm out of a job', I meant it. In a criminal court, if you haven't got someone accused of crime, you don't need a judge. Nor do you need barristers, solicitors for the prosecution or the defence, jury or witnesses. You don't need clerks or ushers, computer technicians, or officers to keep order in the dock. You can get rid of all the forensic scientists and forensic pathologists. You can empty the Old Bailey of cell staff and probation officers and mental health nurses. The security staff, cleaners, telephone operators, list officers, court manager and administrative staff, together with the catering staff for the judges' dining room, the jury canteen, the Bar Mess and the public cafeteria – all are redundant. And this is before you even look at the many dedicated volunteers, such as those in witness support. When the Central Criminal Court functions at full capacity, it has a footfall of up to 2,000 people a day. Some are the feet of visitors but mostly they belong to people who work there. On one view, a defendant is a one-man (or -woman) job creation scheme.

So who are they, these defendants? At the Central Criminal Court, most cases have a dead body in them. Or a nearly dead body. The majority of those who stand in the dock face a charge of murder or attempted murder or conspiracy to murder, or manslaughter or causing grievous bodily harm, or causing death by dangerous or careless driving. There are often associated charges of possession of firearms and ammunition and knives. Especially knives. Often they are Rambo knives and combat knives and hunting knives, but a vegetable knife can kill easily enough and does so surprisingly often. Of course we get lots of young men charged with these offences against a background of gangs and drugs, but to think that represents all defendants is plain wrong. I have, in the relatively recent past, had before me an elderly headmistress (causing the death of a pedestrian by careless driving), a teenage girl of impeccable character and promise (causing the death of her sister by dangerous driving) and a teenage cycling enthusiast (causing a death by wanton and furious driving of his pedal cycle). Among those I have recently sentenced are the son of a barrister, a respectable man who ran a small business, and a family of apparently decent and hard-working people who slaughtered their son's rival-in-young-love. All were guilty of serious offences which they had committed in circumstances that, by the time they came into my courtroom, they themselves could barely comprehend. There is no one incapable of doing things that could bring them into the dock at the Old Bailey. No one.

The Solicitors

Suspects, once arrested, are taken to a police station where they are given their 'rights'. These include the right to free and independent legal advice – enter the defence solicitor. If after interview and investigation the police have a case against the suspect, they will refer the matter to their lawyers – enter the CPS or Crown Prosecution Service . . . the prosecuting solicitors.

Who – or what – are solicitors? The legal profession has two main branches: solicitors and barristers. Solicitors provide advice to clients in every area of law from commerce and property to crime, family, personal injury and a dozen others. They may work in a law firm or the legal department of an organization, for government or in other settings. There are around 136,000 practising solicitors in England and Wales. They function primarily away from the courtroom though they are permitted to appear in the lower courts and may qualify for rights of audience in higher courts. But in any case in which the trial involves serious criminal offences, both prosecuting and defending solicitors are likely to instruct barristers to appear on their behalf in court. The two sorts of lawyers will then work together. The Crown Prosecution Service has its own budget, while defence solicitors (and barristers) are paid either privately by the client or out of the public Legal Aid Fund. Once the solicitor has instructed counsel, the former will do the 'foot work', often under the guidance and advice of the barrister.

The Barristers

Barristers (often called counsel) are principally courtroom advocates specializing in particular areas of law. To become a barrister you must join one of the four ancient Inns of Court (Middle Temple, Inner Temple, Gray's Inn and Lincoln's Inn). Since medieval times the Inns have been places where those established in the profession have educated aspiring barristers, and when the student has reached an appropriate level of expertise, 'called' him (and since 1922, her) 'to the Bar'. These days, the newly qualified barrister may enter employment in any number of settings, or may practise independently of an employer by taking a 'tenancy' in a set of chambers where a group of barristers with similar specialisms share the cost of premises, clerking etc. There are around 16,000 practising barristers in England and Wales. At the Criminal Bar, many both prosecute and defend. No matter how old they are, barristers are all known as 'junior counsel' unless and until they are recognized as having outstanding abilities by being appointed as Queen's Counsel (KC).* Then they are often known as 'silks' because the elevation means they set aside the traditional 'stuff' gown and wear, instead, the lovely silk one.

The Judge

There is no 'Judge School'. There is no MA (Judge). You cannot elect to study judgeship at any formal level. You can only be appointed to hold a salaried judicial appointment after open competition for the position. The competitions are held by the Judicial Appointments Commission (JAC), and one of the critical criteria they are looking for is experience. You are only eligible to apply after you have already been a lawyer for a considerable number of years. So being a judge in the Crown Court is strictly a second career after you have been a barrister or sometimes a solicitor for a long time. It follows that as a group, we Crown Court judges – we who sit on jury trials – appear weirdly old. We also appear unnaturally white and, until recently, worryingly male. A lot of work is being done to improve diversity. A lot more remains to be done.

The Witnesses

They come in three main flavours – eye-witnesses, professional witnesses and experts. As flavours do, they can leach into one

* Or, when there is a king on the throne, King's Counsel (KC).

another – a professional witness such as a police officer may also be an eye-witness – but the distinctions are useful.

Eye-witnesses may equally well be called ear- or nose-witnesses. They are the people who saw or heard or smelled something happen and can give a first-hand account of it. They are the neighbours who say, 'I heard screams at 10 p.m. and saw the blood seeping under the front door at 10.15 p.m. and I knew it would happen one day because I'd heard him threaten to slit her throat a dozen times before.'

Professional witnesses are a species of eye-witness but usually involved after the event. For example, they may be officers who comb the area around the scene and find the blood-stained knife, the discarded jacket, the Oyster card or mobile phone which an extraordinary number of defendants carelessly drop as they flee from the crime.

Expert witnesses are a thing unto themselves. They are not there to say what they saw or heard, but to express their opinion. They are the only witnesses allowed to do so. They provide the jury with evidence of findings and the conclusions that can be drawn from those findings, in areas of science which are a mystery to the rest of us. Experts cover a vast variety of disciplines. There's pathology, toxicology, blood spatter, biological analysis, ballistics and gunshot residue. There's mobile phones, CCTV imagery, psychiatry and psychology. There's handwriting, fibres, fingerprints and myriad others. Experts generally come from well-founded and well-governed professional bodies. But there are always newer ones coming to the party, for example face-mapping, voice and gait. Although there's always a place for new knowledge which will assist juries, before the courts will recognize any type of expertise the technique or science must be appropriately accredited. It must be shown to have been tested, with peer review, publication, use and acceptance and the establishment of a set of standards. Anything less can undermine the safety of a conviction. For those interested in how it can go right or wrong, identification-by-ear-print might prove a fruitful field.

Clerks and Ushers

The clerk manages the courtroom, and the judge, and without him or her, nothing would function. We don't even sit until the clerk turns on DARTS – the recording device that has with heartless efficiency replaced our stenographers – and brings before me all those with an interest in the matter by 'calling on the case'. It's the clerk who accurately and promptly records pleas and verdicts, jury notes, judges' rulings, orders and sentences; who sets up the telephone and video links with prisons etc. for the short preparatory hearings which these days are conducted 'remotely'; who sits in front of me with a barrage of technical equipment, turning knobs, shoving back loose wires and generally making the system work.

The usher makes everything else work. It's the usher who opens up the courtroom and calls for defendants to be brought up, barristers to come down, witnesses to come in. The usher administers oaths to jurors and witnesses, labels exhibits, and looks after the jury once they have 'retired' to their deliberating room to consider their verdicts. It's the usher who makes sure I don't walk into court without my wig, and who 'knocks me in' at the beginning of the day and takes me out at the end of it.

The Jury

And so to the jury – the essence of almost all Crown Court trials, and deserving of a section to itself. The origin of the English jury isn't clear, but the usual suspects are the Danes. They came around AD 793 with their longboats and their language and their law-men, twelve of whom ran a local district. In due course, under the Unready leadership of Ethelred, the law-men segued into twelve thegns, and then under Henry II into a jury of twelve free men who reported crimes to a peripatetic judge. I use the terms 'judge' and 'jury' loosely because the jury did little beyond accuse, and the judge did little at all. Trial was by Combat (think Bishop Wulfstan v. Abbot Walter 1077) or by Ordeal (think water and fire). God was called upon to decide the outcome. As a system of justice, it was tidy and cheap but it had the disadvantage of leading to palpably unjust results which gave God a bad name, and in the end the Church disapproved the whole business. Thus came Magna Carta, which says (in Latin) that 'No free man shall be captured or imprisoned or disseised of his freehold or of his liberties, or of his free customs . . . but by the lawful judgment of his peers or by the law of the land.' And so the way was opened for juries of twelve men to provide verdicts as well as accusations, and the rest – as they say – is history. Historically, though, only men could sit as jurors, and they had to satisfy a property qualification, for example owning a freehold with an annual value of at least £10, or a tenancy for at least twenty-one years with an annual income of at least £20. By 1920, however, the men-only rule had gone; and with the Juries Act 1974, the property qualification went too. Now, by your mere act of registering to vote in elections, you enter a ballot to be a juror.

If you haven't received a jury summons, you probably know someone who has. It doesn't make you a juror. Not yet. But it does give you a shot at it. When potential jurors roll into the Old Bailey on a Monday tide from all places within the M25, they bring with them their different lives, and their jury summons. They received it through the post some months before together with an accompanying guide. The guide states that 'Jury service is one of the most important civic duties that anyone can be asked to perform.' It doesn't say, 'This isn't such a big deal since the other principal civic duties are to pay taxes and obey the law.' Still, the guide tells you useful things. It says you may be barred from jury service if you have insufficient English to follow a trial (or, I suppose, to follow the guide). It says that, if called, you must do your service provided you have reached the age of eighteen, haven't reached the age of seventy-six and are registered to vote. If you think you can avoid jury service by removing yourself from the electoral roll, I should point out you also qualify if you have lived in the UK for a period of five years since you were thirteen. If you are thinking you might move to the Channel Islands or Isle of Man, they are included too. There are uninhabited rocks around the coastline where the writ doesn't run, but actually why not just do your jury service? You'll find it more interesting than you think.

The guide next tells you when you cannot serve. There is a list of those excluded, with the penalties for putting yourself forward when you shouldn't, for example if you lack mental capacity, or are liable to be detained under the Mental Health Act 1983 or similar (though no one can stop you voting in these circumstances). You are also excluded if you have, for example, ever been sentenced to an inde-terminate prison sentence* or one of five years or more, or been convicted in the last ten years of pretty much anything except speeding or not paying your TV licence. Really, it's surprising there are enough jurors left to go round.

If you have received a jury summons and your English is suffi-cient to have read and understood it, and you are not excluded by age, lunacy or criminal inclination, you will arrive at court and pass through security into the embrace of the jury bailiffs who organize and look after the jurors. You will be made to look at a video which explains your duties and the perils of failing to fulfil them. You will be fed into a computer and in due course you will be spat out as part of a jury panel and sent down to one of the eighteen courtrooms. But

---

* A sentence without a minimum length but no fixed length.

even though you have o'er-leapt hurdles of age, mental incapacity and criminal background, even though you have been selected by computer and not got lost on the way from the lavatory, even so you may fall, for there are fences yet to jump. While all this has been happening to you, in the courtroom counsel and judge will have decided who else besides lunatics and criminals will not be allowed to sit on their jury.

Every juror must come to the trial unprejudiced by preconceptions about it. There's a limit to how much objectivity you can ask of a human being, so the judge will try to filter out those who live too close to the scene of crime, or who know people involved, or who may have close sympathies with one side or the other. Given the large number of jurors and the very wide area from which they come, you might think it next to impossible that a potential juror is the neighbour of the defendant or went to school with the dead man or works for the chief prosecution witness; but you would be wrong. I have seen all these things happen.

So when you emerge as part of the panel, blinking in the unfamiliarity of my courtroom, I will ask prosecuting counsel to tell you in a sentence what the case is about and to read out the names of those involved. I will ask you, if your name is called, to let me know if you have an association in any way with the case. Then I will tell you how long the trial is expected to last. Most trials at the Old Bailey last three weeks or more. When I get to this bit, I will see anxious glances among the panel. If the trial is due to last more than a month, foreheads will frown, heads will shake. At five weeks, I will see a handkerchief pulled out, the back of a neck mopped, eyes will roll. More than six weeks and faces will say as clear as words: 'She wants me to do *what*?'

I never cease to marvel at the generosity with which jurors give up many weeks of their lives, leaving behind their own problems to sort out other people's. I never cease to be thankful for how seriously they take this duty and the care and attention most give to it. I never cease to be amazed at the few who try every trick in their book to get out of it. But once the trial begins they will all be engaged. Most will be engrossed because the unfolding of the story, the gradual revelations, the ravelling and unravelling of the lives of others is, after all, truly engrossing. And the chance to play a part in this is not only a public duty and a public service. It is a private privilege.

So my clerk will take the cards with the names on – perhaps as many as sixty for a long trial – give them a shuffle and begin the selection process. Unlike in the USA, this is a swift and unintrusive process. Counsel will ask no personal questions about a potential juror's private life or interests or affiliations. Random means random. They get what they get. It is only if the juror raises an issue, or if there is other good reason such as the defendant or counsel knowing the juror, that questions are asked or challenges made.

Once selected, the juror sits in the jury-box. There's one in almost every courtroom of every Crown Court. The judge has a chair behind a long bench, counsel have their rows; there's a dock and a place for the press and another for the public; but the iconic piece of furniture which makes a criminal court so different from almost all others is the 'box' where the jury sits.

A jury is a living thing. It comes into being at the start of the trial and dies at the end of it. Twelve people* are called randomly to sit in the box's twelve seats, and when they speak the words of the oath or affirmation, lo, the twelve-headed creature is born. After the verdicts are delivered, it fades into nothingness or, as legal scholars say, it is 'functus' (don't ask – we're not supposed to use Latin any more).

---

* In longer trials we take fourteen to sit through the prosecution's opening – hearing more facts – in case anyone in the original twelve discovers they can't, after all, sit on the case.

Whether a trial lasts days or months, the focus of everyone's attention is always the jurors because it is they (save in the rarest of exceptions) who decide whether or not the defendant is guilty.

A jury is supposed to represent the community from which it comes. It is supposed to be a way of achieving trial by a defendant's peers with freedom to act in accordance with their collective conscience. Put another way, twelve people with twelve sets of life experiences really should be better at finding the right verdict than one judge from one background with one life. It is a system admired around the world but not always imitated because it has disadvantages too. For one thing, it's cumbersome and expensive. For another, a jury is only as good as the jurors on it. Mostly they are brilliant, but in any random selection, from time to time you are bound to get some who are not good. I've had a young woman who, discovering she couldn't take her mobile phone into the jury room, became irremediably hysterical. I've had an elderly gentleman who, when required to vote, retired to the loo in tears. I've had a woman who screamed at other jurors that they would never sleep again if they convicted anyone of anything. I've had a young man of bohemian bent who declined on a point of uncertain principle to take part in any discussion whatsoever with his fellow jurors. The system allows for this and for more natural dissent by permitting a majority verdict; that is, one on which at least ten out of the twelve agree. If the jury can't reach even this level of agreement, it is 'hung' and must be discharged. A retrial may follow,* with all the public expense and private grief that entails.

On a daily basis, up and down the country, we send jurors into small locked rooms to sit round a table and make findings of fact

---

* If the first jury is 'hung', the prosecution may have one retrial as of right. If a second jury is 'hung', the Crown generally offers no further evidence and a verdict of 'not guilty' is recorded. However, these days, in limited circumstances, it is possible for the Crown to seek a 3rd and even a 4th trial.

about what happened between people they barely know, whose lives they can only imagine, in places they have never been; and then to apply those facts to the law. We ask them to do it without training or experience. It's a very big ask. It can be gruelling. It says much for the integrity of the average juror that mostly sensible verdicts are reached. But I can't think of any good reason why we don't help them. Why don't we teach all schoolchildren to discuss problems in groups of ten or twelve – to express a reasoned view, to listen to others, and to modify their thoughts as different ideas emerge? With a little training, encouragement and practice, Shane and his class mates could learn to do it. I daresay there are schools where it is done, but I have never had one visit the Old Bailey.

Hopefully, one day, Shane and Sheeesh and Spectacles and all their class mates will sit on juries. They will bring their particular knowledge and experience of life to the courtroom. They will leave behind their own problems to try to sort out those of other people. Each of them will work with eleven strangers over days, weeks – perhaps months – to do justice. I expect they will make a very good job of it.

TRIAL ONE:

The Fiery Furnace

ONE LATE SUMMER'S day, when the sun was shining and the pavements hot to walk on, four boys were out and about in the area of a high street in north London. One of them was Daniel.

He was working in a chicken shop – a Saturday job, his first, and he liked it. He liked the money. He liked the chicken. He liked his life. Before he left home, he kissed his grandma goodbye. At fifteen he reckoned himself too old to kiss anyone except his girlfriend, but he made an exception for his nan. He wore a new white T-shirt. Beneath it, his fifteen-year-old body was muscular, not yet broadened into manhood but promising to do so soon. Inside his chest, his fifteen-year-old heart beat strongly. Eleven o'clock. A slackening in trade before the lunchtime rush.

'Time for your break, Daniel,' called his boss.

Daniel grinned and took off his overall. 'Can I have some fries?'

'Sure.' The boss watched him shovelling chips into a carton. 'Don't take the lot.'

Daniel grinned again. 'See you in twenty . . .'

He lied. He won't see his boss in twenty minutes. He won't ever see his boss again. Less than two minutes later he will run into a little alley off the high street. He will be chased there by someone holding a knife. Never run into a blind alley, Daniel. Never, never do that. You'll be trapped. You'll be caught. And what will happen then? Then the blade of a knife will press against the outer layer of your skin, pushing hard because the skin is tougher than you might think. It's difficult for the blade to get through your skin, but once it has, there's no stopping it. It will slip through the thin layer of your fat, your youthful muscle, between your ribs, into your heart. It will be the end.

1

THE END FOR DANIEL. The end for Daniel's grandma and his mother. But for three other boys, accused of Daniel's murder, it will be a new and terrible beginning. They have lost their lives too, in a way – certainly they have lost the lives they had before. In the life before, the law meant police on the street – maybe a difficult conversation if they were caught with weed or stolen trainers, maybe a visit to the police station or even a caution. No big deal, relatively. Now, though, the law means magistrates and doors slamming on them, a Young Offender Institution, a time when things move too fast and then too slowly. It means a cage in a prison van and then, down in the bowels of the Old Bailey, a cell barely big enough to squeeze in a decent-sized Jersey cow. It means my courtroom. It means me.

There isn't a week at the Old Bailey when we aren't trying boys like these three, accused of murder by stabbing. They fill our Young Offender Institutions and, because the sentences mean they will be locked up well into adulthood, our prisons too. The courts seem powerless to stop it. All a judge can do is apply the law. That law's declared purposes are to punish, to rehabilitate, to keep dangerous people locked up and to deter others. With murderers, the locking up goes on for a long time. The Criminal Justice Act 2003 and its subsequent amendments means the time murderers must serve before release has become markedly longer. The starting point for how long an adult convicted of murder by stabbing must serve before applying for release has gone up from an average of about fifteen years to twenty-five years. The increase in sentences was meant to deter people from carrying knives and using them, but the number of knife murders has not gone down. In recent years it has been quite the reverse.

If the three boys I am about to try are convicted of Daniel's murder, they will join what will eventually be thousands of prisoners who must, in some far future, emerge back into society having spent over half their lives locked up. Rehabilitative work will have been done with them, but they will be men who for all their adulthood have lived in male institutions, without normal interaction with women or children, taking no real responsibility for organizing their days or making their own decisions. Many of them while 'inside' will have found solace in illicit drugs, and safety under the wings of stronger offenders. If we think they are going to come out and slip seamlessly back into society, we are wrong. We may be stoking up a power of trouble for ourselves.

I first see these three boys – let's call them Shadrach, Meshach and Abednego – nearly six months after Daniel's death, when they stumble through the green leather door into the dock of Court Eight. Behind that door is flight after flight of stone stairs leading to the cells far below. The boys stand blinking uncertainly in the bright light. Shadrach is a tall, rather plump eighteen-year-old of mixed race. Abednego is a black boy, only fifteen. Meshach is white and has just had his sixteenth birthday in the Young Offender Institution. Many happy returns, Meshach. Each has the usual number of features and limbs, each is dressed in the regulation tracksuit. It's just another Monday morning at the Central Criminal Court. Just another murder with another set of faces. The same story in so many respects. Except that it never is the same because each dead body is the end of a life different from any other. Each defendant, each grieving relative, is different too. And each juror and witness who lives through a murder trial leaves it changed for ever.

Shadrach stares around the courtroom as if it bewilders him. His eyes take in the press-box (full), the jury-box (empty), the public gallery with faces that are familiar and not familiar to him. He stares at the backs of the lawyers in the well of the court. His gaze rises over my clerk, my usher, up and up to me where I sit on the Bench. He puts the tip of his thumb in his mouth and bites it gently. Meshach and Abednego look at him, then at each other. They sit a couple of seats away from Shadrach, heads together. A dock officer moves them apart. Meshach waves to the public gallery and smirks. Remember, I tell myself, he's a child. Remember, before long that smirk will be wiped off his face. Very soon this boy, like all defendants, will be very frightened. Or should be. His life will be decided by strangers. And that's enough to frighten any sensible person.

Whatever crime a remanded defendant has – or hasn't – committed, he has lost almost all power over his own life. His choices are few. He can come out of his cell or refuse to. He can plead guilty or not guilty. He can give evidence or stay silent, lie or tell the truth. Sometimes he may feel he can't even tell the truth in case it brings down retribution from others on him and his family. And that's beyond his control too. You might say it serves him right – he chose to join the gang, to use the drugs, to carry the knife, to run with the pack. Let him shake with fear, you might say, as he made his victim do. But still, from the defendant's point of view it's a terrifying position to be in; and from ours, it can be wiser to withhold judgement until all the facts are clear.

My conduit to these three, as to almost all defendants, is through their lawyers. Although I can speak directly to defendants in the dock, I will mostly deal with them through their barrister or solicitor. On a charge of murder, each defendant will have a leader (a Queen's Counsel*) and a junior. There is, of course, another pair for the

---

* A Queen's Counsel is part of an elite group of acknowledged experts in the field of advocacy. Each year a limited number of barristers are promoted to this enviable position after open competition.

Crown. So in this trial there are eight barristers. They are advocates – they 'ad vocate' (to refer to the Latin), or speak to their cause. In plain English, they fight their corner. It's what they are there for. Unlike the Continental 'inquisitorial' system where the judge enquires into the facts, we have an 'adversarial' system, and the adversaries are there to do battle. It's a little like a war game with the judge as referee.

I scan the battle lines. From a judge's point of view, the smoothness with which a trial runs depends in no small part on the lawyers involved. It takes only one from the Awkward Squad to turn a case into a nightmare – to raise difficulties where none exist, to argue unarguable points of law, to cause bad feeling between counsel that undermines sensible and productive compromise. There aren't too many in that squad and other judges have drawn the short straws today. Good. Of my eight, the mix is typical – only one woman leader and two women juniors. Among them all there is one non-Caucasian face. He leads for Abednego. Abednego is lucky. He has a good man in Jeremiah Paul KC.

These four Queen's Counsel know each other well. They are respectful, even friendly, towards each other. But their wigs are grey with experience, and under those wigs, wily brains are at work. Everything they do will be designed to persuade the jury to favour their client, because advocacy is, above all, the art of persuasion. If they get the result they seek, they 'win'. If they don't, they 'lose'. This is the language of their job. No defending barrister says 'I won the case' when his client is lawfully and rightly convicted. No prosecutor says 'I won' when a defendant is properly acquitted.

So here we are. Three defendants, eight barristers and a judge. 'Are we ready for trial?' I ask brightly. After all, this could be the rare case when there are no problems.

Two KCs rise to their feet. Ah, well, there was no harm in hoping. 'Yes, Mr Larch?'

'My Lady, I represent the first defendant.' The order of defendants is determined by how the prosecution chose to charge them on the indictment. First is Shadrach. 'I'm sorry,' says Mr Larch, 'but . . .'

This 'but' means he has a problem. 'Sorry' means he doesn't have a solution.

'My Lady, I am concerned . . .' He stops. Words are the tools of this man's trade, and now he's lost for them. Lionel Larch KC is experienced and has a deal of common sense. If he is concerned, I must be too. He tries again. 'Shadrach is the oldest of the defendants in years but . . .' He looks round at his client. So do we all. Shadrach is gazing at a flickering ceiling light. 'He seems unable to focus on the proceedings. It wasn't apparent when I saw him in conference but now . . .'

I close my eyes briefly but it doesn't help. Now Shadrach is staring intently at his left thumb as if it's a thing of great interest. Perhaps it is. 'Are you suggesting your client isn't fit to stand trial, Mr Larch?'

The KC shakes his head. 'I hope that's not what I'm saying,' he says.

I hope not too. Issues of 'fitness to plead' are complicated and require a different process from that of a trial. It involves deciding whether a defendant's mental state is such that he or she may not be able to understand and participate in the trial process. It needs psychiatric or other expert evidence. It's a tricky business. 'Do you want some time to consider this and, if necessary, get help?'

From the back of the court Meshach says, quite audibly, 'Shadrach's thick as shit, and you can't get help for that.'

As it happens, Meshach is wrong. There is help for both witnesses and defendants who have difficulty following the complexities of the courtroom. For those whose first language isn't English or who are deaf, I can appoint an interpreter. For the very young and the intellectually impaired I can appoint an intermediary. Interpreters and intermediaries can sit with a defendant or witness at all or any stages of the trial, whenever they are needed to ensure he or she understands what is being said, and to facilitate communication. In addition, I can control the way the court runs. When dealing with the very young or the mentally impaired I can require counsel to use simple language and sentence structure. No idioms (the attacker may have been a big man but a four-year-old witness doesn't get 'big as a house'). No 'tag' questions ('He hit you hard, isn't that right?' will elicit from the same four-year-old the answer 'no' since hitting him hard plainly isn't right). I used to have a matron – the cuts saw an end to that – but (lucky me, lucky Shadrach) there is still a mental health nurse in the building. I pause. I reflect. I send for the nurse.

Meanwhile, I turn to the other silk who had wanted to speak. Simon Barrington KC is tall with an aquiline nose, reddened at its significant tip. His grey brows arch over grey eyes. 'My junior has an application to make,' he says. His shrug speaks volumes: this is her idea, it says, don't blame me.

His junior shoots to her feet. Her gown is unfrayed. Her wig is very white. She is young, new, keen. Her client has probably appeared in court more often than she has. However, this is her moment and she isn't going to waste it. She has set out in writing her arguments of law, and hands my clerk beautifully prepared copies, enough for everyone who might have even a remote interest in the matter. There are coloured tags marking out the sections where she has attached every piece of earlier case law or 'authority' which she has been able to dig up. She looks as if she is about to address the Supreme Court. I'm prepared to put money on her doing just that someday. But not yet.

'Meshach's human rights, My Lady, are at the heart of my submissions.'

'I bet they are,' mutters someone in counsel's row. I frown in their direction but all the barristers are gazing with rapt interest at their copies of Miss Whittall-Blythe's document.

She explains eloquently why her client should not be in the dock but sitting beside her so she can guide him through the trauma of trial. He is, after all, but sixteen years old.

'Abednego is only fifteen,' I point out.

'I'm sure his counsel will join me in this submission,' says Miss Whittall-Blythe.

We all look at counsel-for-Abednego, who is studying the water jug. Miss Whittall-Blythe may one day appear in the Supreme Court, and she's a nice sort of girl, but not even for this will Jeremiah Paul make a fool of himself.

'Apparently not,' I say gently. 'But don't let that stop you.'

She doesn't. In the next ten minutes I learn a lot about her expectations of the law on human rights. Then the mental health nurse arrives. I indicate I have understood all her arguments. I turn to the prosecutor.

'Miss Wright, I needn't trouble you to respond. Miss Whittall-Blythe, thank you very much for your very complete submissions, but I fear I am against you. All three of these defendants will cope perfectly well with the trial process, sitting in the dock in the usual way. Security within the courtroom may well be compromised if one of them is out of the dock. And to treat one differently from the others is to risk the jury perceiving one differently from the others when there is no justification for that.'

Miss Whittall-Blythe, to her credit, takes it well.

I ask the nurse to see Shadrach and his legal team. Half an hour later Mr Larch reports that Shadrach will cope, as long as we have regular breaks and avoid Latin.

All this before I get a sniff of a jury. So far, so usual. Here's something else that's usual too. In the dock are boys of school age. In other situations, we'd call them children, but here they are 'the defendants'. Prosecuting counsel likes to call them by their surnames, dignified by the addition of 'Mr' or, for the very young, 'Master'. Truly. Defence counsel likes to invoke a human touch with first names. But mostly they are just 'the defendants'. If it's easy to lose sight of the reality of the three in the dock, it is even easier to lose the reality of the dead child.

Daniel too was only fifteen when he went out and didn't come home and will never come home again. In the courtroom the closest we will get to seeing him is in exhibit one, the graphics bundle. Page one shows photographs of four young faces. Those of the defendants were taken on arrest. It isn't surprising that they look frightened, sullen, bewildered, guilty. That of Daniel has been sourced from his grieving family. It isn't surprising that he looks happy. His eyes shine as he smiles into the future he wasn't allowed to have. In the 'scene photographs', his butchered body is pixelated so as not to upset the jurors. The clinical abuse of the post-mortem (necessary, for how else is Daniel to get justice?) is sanitized in graphics. The jury will never see his ribs cut open where a medical team reached inside him in a fruitless attempt to restart his heart. They won't see that heart skewered by a knife. They will see computer-produced images of a generic male with reproductions of Daniel's wounds; but they won't feel the blood, warm at first then cooling rapidly, that poured into his chest cavity and compressed the already fluttering, failing heart. They won't taste the iron tang of it as he must have in the minute when, after the stabbing, he was still able to move, to shout, to wonder what was happening to him, to grasp vaguely then with increasing intensity the fact that he was dying, he was a dead man walking, he was done. It's easy for most people in the courtroom to lose sight of the reality of Daniel, but not for me. Because, once the trial starts, I will have full in my eye-line not only the boys in the dock but also, out of sight of the jury, Daniel's mother and his grandmother, who will sit there listening intently to every heart-breaking step of the way their boy was taken from them.

Back in the courtroom I try again. 'Are we ready for a jury panel now?'

Miss Wright says she certainly is. She says it in a tone that suggests she has been ready for a long time and would be grateful if the defence could say the same. Finally, Miss Whittall-Blythe blushes.

'Are you ready, Mr Larch?'

Does he mutter, 'As I'll ever be'? Shadrach is staring at his thumb again. Still, ready is ready, so I send my usher up to the floor of the Old Bailey where the jury bailiffs look after potential jurors. There, the jury bailiffs will select at random a panel of thirty and bring them down to my court. From them, my clerk will then call, equally at random, twelve to try this case.

2

When the thirty of them have shuffled in and are standing uncomfortably at the side of the court, I begin the usual procedure. I explain that it's essential every juror comes to the case free from prejudice. Miss Wright neatly summarizes the time and place of the incident, its nature, and the names of the deceased, defendants and witnesses. I ask if any of them have a personal link to this case. Thirty heads shake. Good.

I tell them this trial is expected to last four weeks, explain the very limited circumstances in which I can excuse them from sitting, and that if they have a genuine problem with this, they should let me know.

I nod to my clerk. Today it is Angelique. She rises, a beautiful and statuesque woman, balances the jury cards in her firm hands, and looks squarely at the panel, daring them to make difficulties for her judge. The first name she calls is Mr St John Forbes.

A man walks briskly towards me. I take in the cut of his jacket (admirable) and his tie (who comes to court wearing a tie these days?). I recognize the tie. I recognize the type. I know what's coming. He takes the few steps up to the Bench with a certain stiffness of the knees which I suspect bespeaks years of aggressive squash. It turns out – did I ever doubt it? – that Mr Forbes has a Very Important Job. He cannot be away from it for four weeks. The very thought is intolerable to Mr Forbes.

'Are you a one-man business?' I ask.

He looks at me as if I'm mad. 'I am in charge of international contracts in a corporation that functions on the worldwide stage,' he says loudly. Among the rest of the panel, eyes roll. Mr Forbes hasn't, it seems, made himself popular with his fellow panellists.

'If your employer is a worldwide company, they will have plenty of staff to stand in for you as you perform this vital public service.'

He stares, aghast. 'I cannot be spared.'

'Mr Forbes, there are circumstances where people must be excused jury service. For example, if you were a single mum without childcare, a surgeon with a list of life-saving operations, or were caring for your dying partner, you really couldn't be spared.'

He flushes very red. 'The jury summons says "up to two weeks".'

I try to soften my tone. 'The jury summons says "usually up to two weeks" but at the Old Bailey nothing is usual. Take your seat, please.' I indicate the jury-box and watch him walk stiffly – let's hope it's the squash knee and not outrage – to seat number one.

The owners of the next three names take their seats without difficulty. Then Angelique calls a name to which there is no response. She tries again. At her third attempt, a small, elderly lady shuffles towards me. She is clutching a large black bag which she heaves on to the Bench. She nods vigorously and taps the bag. When I stare stupidly, she tuts at my slowness, and opens it. Together we gaze into the dark interior where there's enough medication to stock a small pharmacy.

'You are unwell?' I ask.

She reaches in and pulls out a box of tablets. I read 'one daily for raised blood pressure – for Mr K. Silva'. She reaches in again and produces a tube of cream for lactating nipples. She can see this isn't going well and piles up in quick succession liver pills, migraine tablets and an asthma inhaler, each for a different patient, none of them her. I do my best to adopt a stern face and say, 'None of this medication seems to be prescribed for you.'

The frown disappears. She beams. 'Wednesday,' she says.

'I beg your pardon?'

'Blue,' she says. Or possibly 'Blew'. Or even 'Bloo'.

Life is too short. 'This juror is excused.'

Shadrach's thumb has his full attention but Meshach and Abednego are staring at me as if it is somehow my fault. Perhaps it is.

After this, things go smoothly enough. I also excuse a teacher whose absence from her job for more than a fortnight would cause real hardship for others; and at length there is only one seat – number twelve – left to fill.

'David Rosenblum,' calls Angelique.

A man who must be in his thirties but somehow looks younger comes towards me.

'Yes, Mr Rosenblum. What's the problem?'

'Is there much blood?' he asks.

I pause. 'In what sense?'

'In the sense that I'm not very good with blood.'

I don't say, 'For heaven's sake, man, pull yourself together. It's a murder, you have to expect a modicum of body fluids.' Instead I say, 'You will not be asked to look at any post-mortem photographs. We use graphics to show you the injuries.'

'But . . .'

I look over at the remaining panel – not many left. I must make decisions. I have, before now, had to assess some odd demands: a footstool for when 'my feet swell like an elephant's'; a cold bath 'for my haemorrhoids'; taxis to and from Epping 'because the Underground is dirty'; and 'appropriate facilities for Neville' (Neville, it turned out, was a chihuahua). What's a little blood phobia when measured against this?

'Take seat number twelve, Mr Rosenblum. This is a case with only limited blood.'

One by one the twelve affirm or swear on their holy book to bring in 'true verdicts according to the evidence', though Mr Forbes does it through clenched teeth and Mr Rosenblum is very pale. You can tell a lot from the swearing-in. By the time the process is complete I know I have a good mix of genders, ages, ethnic and social backgrounds, intelligence and common sense. A jury.

3

At a nod from me, Miss Wright gets to her feet and prepares to open her case. 'Members of the jury, the Crown alleges these three young men' – she pauses, looks meaningfully at the dock – 'are guilty of the murder of Daniel Devon. On the first of September last year, Daniel, then but fifteen years old, went as he did every Saturday to work at the chicken shop in his local high street. Shortly afterwards one of these defendants drove the other two to a road near that high street. He parked and the two got out. They found Daniel outside the chicken shop and chased him into a secluded alleyway where he was stabbed three times. The fatal wound penetrated his heart. The Crown says Shadrach was the driver, Meshach the stabber and Abednego his willing accomplice. It is the Crown's case that the three acted in concert, with a common purpose, and that each was responsible for Daniel's death.'

The usher hands out an A3 graphic containing maps and plans, stills from CCTV footage, photographs, telephone schedules, cell site analysis, and images of a knife showing where fingerprints and DNA were recovered from it. The jury has in its hands much of the evidence on which the Crown relies. If Miss Wright opens well, it will soon be in their heads, and by the end of the case in their hearts.

With scrupulous care she takes them through the story. They look at the picture of Daniel and suddenly he is no longer just 'the deceased'. He is a real boy. They draw a collective breath. Mr Forbes shakes his head as if in disbelief that this child has been wiped out of being. Does Mr Forbes have a fifteen-year-old son of his own? No one has told them that Daniel's family are in the courtroom but now the woman sitting next to Mr Rosenblum looks over at the mother, the grandmother, as if she knows. She's a large black lady, in her late forties. Her face is full of compassion. I make a note to remind them, at the first opportunity, to keep open minds until all the evidence is complete.

Sobered, the jury follows Miss Wright's opening as she takes them through the scene photographs. All is well until we get to page twenty-two. We are in the alley now. We spend some time where the knife was found. It's a hunting knife, the sort used to eviscerate animals. The blade is long and broad. Its holes reduce suction for easier removal from the body. The tip is sharp, one edge partially serrated. Recently I have seen many of them. They have become the weapon of choice for many youngsters. I turn the page just ahead of Miss Wright. Page twenty-three shows the scene further down the alley. There is a large pool of blood where Daniel lay dying. Too late I remember Mr Rosenblum. Miss Wright has already asked the jury to turn the page, and before I can do anything to stop it, they do. There is an ominous thud, and Miss Wright stops. We all stop. Mr Rosenblum is lying back, prone, in his chair, his head against the wall, his face the colour of overworked pastry. Before I can either encourage or prevent it, the woman next to him leans over and with a practised ease slaps his cheeks, twice on each side. They are sharp, clean slaps. Mr Rosenblum opens his eyes. 'Who are you?' he asks juror number eleven. 'Violet,' she says. He smiles faintly and shuts his eyes again.

I send the jury off for a break, entrusting David Rosenblum to the care of Violet, who, it turns out, is a nurse and well used to human frailties. I'm glad to have Violet on my jury, but it seems I have made a mistake with Mr Rosenblum. We can't have a juror who faints every time he has to look at page twenty-three. Junior counsel, with unforgivable Schadenfreude, discovers that page thirty-seven is just as bad. Mr Rosenblum has to go. And since I can't embark on the trial with only eleven jurors, we have to re-ballot and start all over again. And it is all my fault. I call the jury back and explain the situation to them.

'But I'm fine now,' says Mr Rosenblum. 'I've seen the worst. I'm over it.'

I hesitate. 'You haven't seen page thirty-seven,' I say.

David Rosenblum looks at Violet. Together they open exhibit one at page thirty-seven. He goes very pale then gives a thin smile. 'I'll be fine,' he says. 'Really, I want to do it.' The other jurors all nod as if they want him to do it too. Even Mr Forbes. Especially Mr Forbes. This is a jury. This, despite everything, is why the jury system is among the best in the world.

So Miss Wright is ready to call her evidence. She has a witness – a cab driver – who was near the scene but none who saw what happened in the alley. Her case is almost entirely circumstantial. That is to say, although there was no eye-witness to the stabbing, other pieces of evidence taken together create an irrefutable inference of guilt – or so Miss Wright would have the jury believe. Circumstantial evidence can be very powerful. Unlike an eye-witness, it won't be mistaken or misremember; it won't get caught out in cross-examination or fail to properly convey what it wishes to say. It is what it is, and Miss Wright has a bagful of it.

She calls the taxi driver first. He stands in the witness-box, a bemused expression on his face, as if he can hardly believe where he is or why he is here. His voice shakes as he swears to tell the truth, the whole truth and nothing but the truth. I smile encouragement, point out the little seat behind him, the water jug and glass, the microphone, the jury who must hear his every word. He nods, perches on the seat, reaches to pull the microphone closer and knocks over the water jug. He leaps from the seat and sends the glass flying. I reassure him that everyone knocks over the water. I say it in a tone that suggests we are permanently awash, that all my witnesses are damp ones.

Miss Wright asks him to give his full name. He does. It's long with origins in many languages. He shrugs. 'Call me Joe,' he says. 'Everyone does.' Under Miss Wright's skilful questioning Joe tells the jury he had dropped off a fare in the high street and decided to get something to eat. He parked and walked back up the road. He passed a little alley and, glancing down it, saw something on the ground. Joe stops, remembering what he saw, reliving that moment when he realized the bundle on the ground was crawling slowly towards him. The jurors lean forward, the defendants look down. Joe's silence paints a picture clearer than words, but words are needed.

'Tell us,' says Miss Wright gently.

The usher hands him a glass of water. He takes a sip. His hand is shaking. He describes how he went into the alley and saw the blood – I glance at David Rosenblum but Violet has a firm grip on his arm and he seems as caught up in the story as everyone else. Joe takes us closer to the dying boy, and closer. He describes how he knelt and took the limp hand. There is a smothered sob from the back of the court where Daniel's mother and grandmother sit. I see – though the jury cannot – the tears running silently down their cheeks, unwiped, because their hands are clasped in each other's.

Miss Wright allows the moment to develop then wrests it back into her grasp. 'You used your mobile phone to dial 999?' Joe nods.

'Let's listen to the call, shall we?' She presses a button on the recording device.

'Emergency, which service do you require?' says a voice, and then we hear Joe – there is no doubt it is him – but it's a different Joe from the one before us. This is a Joe who can barely catch his breath as he begs for assistance, tries to follow instructions, and when he can't find a pulse, can't properly perform CPR, calls wildly for someone, anyone, to help him. In front of us all now, Joe hangs his head.

'Joe,' says Miss Wright, 'it couldn't have made any difference. The medical evidence shows that Daniel was already beyond help.' Her words are a gift to Joe, a small, humane act that will do her no harm in the eyes of the jury. Joe smiles sadly and, when defence counsel indicate they have no questions for him, stumbles out of the witness-box to be led away by the lady from witness support.

Joe saw nothing that could prove the guilt of any defendant. There was no challenge to his evidence. His statement could have been read to the jury or been reduced to a couple of agreed facts. Technically there was no need to call Joe at all, but any good prosecutor would have done what Miss Wright did, for his appearance in court has brought the dead to life.

Now Miss Wright can open her bag of circumstantial evidence. Here's what she has in it:

- evidence of telephone usage and cell site analysis
- closed circuit television footage
- automatic number plate recognition (ANPR) recordings
- evidence of DNA

She begins with the DNA. A police officer produces the knife found in the alley. It's wired into a flat box and covered with clear plastic. It mustn't be touched without surgical gloves because the chemicals used to test it can be carcinogenic. The sealed box is handed round the jurors. They stare at it with fascinated disgust. This is the blade that travelled into the dark, warm heart of a boy and slit the thin-spun life. He is gone, and here it is, in their hands. The knife has its effect. It is given an exhibit number and put on the ledge of the witness-box for Miss Wright's next witness, the first of the forensic scientific experts.

His field is identification by DNA analysis, and he is well used to the courtroom, well used to explaining to laymen the incredible science of his job. He tells the jury how deoxyribonucleic acid, or DNA, is the hereditary material in nearly every cell in the human body, and everybody's is different – at least the chances of identical DNA occurring in two unrelated people is rare to vanishing point (which experts have decided is the chance of one in one billion). Since half your DNA is inherited from each of your biological parents, the odds are different for blood relations, but it is possible to distinguish the DNA of even identical twins. Mr Forbes makes a careful note on the pad in front of him. Meshach shakes his head. He knows very well what's coming.

The scientist explains how he produced a full profile of the DNA from Daniel's blood and from that of each defendant; and how he produced a profile of the DNA from the blood that was on the knife. The result did not match any of the defendants' profiles, but it gave a full match for Daniel. The blood, he says, in the cautious way of scientists, could have come from Daniel. The blood, thinks everyone in court, could hardly have come from anyone else. But the knife has revealed a further secret. The swabs from the knife handle yielded more DNA. There was no blood there and the DNA was likely to have come from the hand that held the knife – from sweat perhaps, or flakes of skin. The scientist managed to extract from these swabs enough DNA to produce a partial profile which matches part of Meshach's profile.

'Of course,' warns the scientist, 'a partial profile yields much greater odds of a random match than the one in one billion for a full profile.'

Mr Forbes, fairly, makes a note of this and Miss Wright frowns, as if she might be concerned. But Miss Wright is a wily old bird. 'So what is the chance of the DNA having come from anyone other than and unrelated to Meshach?' she asks.

'Oh, much greater,' says the scientist. 'Perhaps as great as one in sixty-six thousand.'

Mr Forbes makes a further note, and Meshach, who had looked up hopefully, looks down again.

Meshach's barrister, Mr Barrington, rises to cross-examine. Barrington of the Bar. It has a good ring about it. So does he. Beyond casting his junior Miss Whittall-Blythe before me, he has played little part in events so far. He has raised no objections and no difficulties. Of the three defendants, his case is the hardest to argue. Now he leans forward on his lectern and pulls his gown about him. He pauses just long enough to get the jury's attention.

'Let us suppose,' he says, 'it is my client's DNA on the knife handle.'

There is a gasp from the dock. Meshach is not prepared to suppose any such thing, Meshach is prepared to argue the odds, even when they are 66,000:1. But Mr Barrington is no fool. He knows Miss Wright still has the telephone cell site evidence to come, which will show that seven minutes before Daniel made his fatal run, Meshach's mobile phone was using a mast positioned within 150 yards of the alley. Mr Barrington doesn't know what multiplier this must add to 66,000 but he knows these are odds with which he can't cope. However, he has another thought.

'Supposing,' he says to the expert witness, 'that Meshach was unwise enough to have made a murderous friend. Supposing that some time in the previous twenty-four hours – all unknowing that this friend had in his possession a knife – he shared with this friend not a plan to stab, but a plate of chips.'

The scientist looks taken aback. 'Chips?' he says.

'Or chops,' says Mr Barrington. 'The nature of the meal matters not.'

'I found neither chips nor chops nor any other food substance on the handle,' says the scientist doubtfully.

Mr Barrington stops him with a lifted hand. 'Suppose that having shared a meal together, on parting there is a manly handshake between them.' Mr Forbes makes a point of laying down his pen, and even Mr Barrington recognizes the improbability of his suggestion. 'Or rather,' he says, 'let us imagine them exchanging at least a hand clasp, a shoulder bump. Are you imagining that, Sir?'

The scientist nods manfully.

'Is it possible, in those circumstances, that my client's DNA would end up on the hand of his murderous companion?'

The scientist agrees it is possible.

'And if the companion then pulls out his knife, is it possible that my client's DNA will be transferred from the murderous hand to the knife itself?'

'Always supposing the knifeman didn't wash his hands before he pulled out the knife. In my experience of fast food, after you have eaten—'

'We are not interested in your sanitary habits,' says Mr Barrington sharply, 'only in your expertise. The process I have described is so well known it has a name, does it not? It's called secondary transfer.'

It is. Point made, Mr Barrington sits down. Meshach is smiling. Abednego, perhaps wondering who is to be fingered as the murderous companion, isn't. Shadrach only bites his thumb. Mr Larch and Mr Paul have no questions for this witness, but Miss Wright still has the right to re-examine.

'The proposition advanced by My Learned Friend,' she says, 'is that someone else held the knife handle with a hand contaminated with Meshach's DNA. Did you find any other DNA on the handle that might have emanated from this mysterious person?'

'I did not,' says the witness.

I am about to thank the witness for his attendance and dismiss him from the witness-box, but Mr Barrington is on his feet again. 'My Lady, may I ask a further question?'

'The time for your cross-examination has passed, Mr Barrington.'

'It's entirely my fault, My Lady. I overlooked a matter – it may be important.'

No point in sighing or quibbling. It's quicker to let him do it. 'You have my leave to ask a further question. Miss Wright will then be allowed to re-examine on it if she wishes.'

'The fingerprints,' he says.

The witness looks blank. 'There were none, I believe; at least none were recovered.'

'But if my client's hand held the knife firmly enough to stab, his fingerprints should be there, should they not?'

The witness hesitates. 'There are circumstances when no prints would be left.'

'For example?'

'For example, if he wore gloves . . .'

Mr Barrington adopts a forensic frown. 'But if he wore gloves he could hardly have left his DNA.'

'I was going to say, or if his hands were cold.'

The defence has scored a point and – the day Daniel died having been a warm one – Miss Wright doesn't care to re-examine.

The next morning brings the pathologist. He holds up Daniel's T-shirt – no longer new, no longer white – to show us the three rents in the chest area. We are given another bundle of graphics showing the knife on its wicked journey. Mr Rosenblum is fine, but Daniel's grandmother isn't. This is always a difficult situation. In homicides, the Crown often asks the judge if members of the bereaved family can sit in court. There are very good reasons for this, for who has such an interest as them in witnessing the doing of justice? Only, perhaps, those close to the defendants, and they are likely to be in the public gallery. At the Old Bailey the galleries are above and over-look each courtroom, and are reached by separate entrances from the main one. It would be inhumane and unwise to have the families of victims and defendants sitting up there together in the febrile atmosphere generated by a murder trial. But if the bereaved are to sit in the well of the court, their anger and grief must not be allowed to influence the jurors. And now Daniel's grandmother – poor dis-traught soul – cannot bear what is unfolding before her and, with a low moan, slips from her seat on to her knees and rocks herself back and forth. In a moment, her daughter and the family liaison officer are beside her, whispering to her, lifting her to her feet, helping her to the door. The jury gasps, stares. Violet presses a tissue to her mouth. As a nurse, she has, I guess, seen such grief many times. The rest sit, frozen. Such situations occur from time to time and must be dealt with. The key is neither to underplay nor overplay them.

'Might this be a good moment for our morning break?' Miss Wright asks helpfully. The defence think it would not. The last thing they want is for jurors to sit over a cup of tea reflecting on the dis-tress of an elderly woman whose heart is as broken as her grandson's. But something must be done.

'Ladies and gentlemen,' I say to the jury, 'you will understand and respect the terrible grief of losing a child. It's difficult not to be affected by the sight of it. But your task in this courtroom is not to share that grief. Your task is to do justice by deciding what happened and whether any of these defendants are criminally liable for it. That task requires cool heads and clear thinking. It's essential that you are not influenced by revulsion on the one hand, nor by sympathy on the other, for that way lies injustice, and that is not what we are about here.'

After a moment, twelve heads nod. The temperature is lowered. Now, after all, is a good moment for our morning break.

Over the next few days the rest of the prosecution case is presented.

There is CCTV footage from cameras in the high street. The blurred black-and-white images are good enough to pick out two figures following Daniel into the alley; good enough to see their general type and tone of clothing, their respective heights and builds. Good enough for this, but for no more. In general terms the figures match Meshach and Abednego and the clothing and trainers found in their homes. But the figures could equally match hundreds of youngsters in that quarter of London. The police, however, have been diligent. They have scoped CCTV in the surrounding area and found two similar youths coming towards the high street from an adjacent side-road. There is no sign of these figures walking into that side-road, but a small Peugeot drives into it from the far end. Two minutes earlier and a short distance away, ANPR equipment shows a very similar car. Its number plate, checked with DVLA, shows its registered keeper is Shadrach's mother. Telephone evidence demonstrates the phones of the three boys were accessing mobile phone masts that suggest they were close together in the period just before and after the killing. The net of circumstantial evidence is closing. At the end of the prosecution case Miss Wright looks . . . not smug. Counsel for the Crown doesn't aim for smug. But she looks as if she is having a good day at the office.

4

Miss Wright's case is clear. Shadrach drove the other two to a road near the high street and waited while they chased Daniel into the alley where Meshach held the knife that killed him, then they ran back to the car and all three made their escape. It is a very complete case. It is circumstantial evidence at its most powerful.

Next day it's the turn of the defence. No defendant has to give evidence but each must have the opportunity. Shadrach is first on the indictment. Mr Larch rises to his feet and using time-honoured words says, 'I call my client.' It's a curious expression when you think about it but Shadrach doesn't seem to be thinking about it. He seems to be thinking about his thumb.

'Shadrach . . .' I wouldn't normally call an eighteen-year-old by his first name, but we have fallen into the habit of calling the younger defendants by theirs, and parity is important. 'Shadrach, would you come to the witness-box, please.'

Shadrach, as he has been throughout the trial, is anxious to please. He gets up and, escorted by a dock officer, makes his way across the courtroom. He doesn't attempt to read the oath but dutifully repeats it after the usher. He sits in the little seat provided and looks about him. Mr Larch asks him to listen carefully to the questions and to answer them truthfully. Shadrach nods, solemn with the moment. Slowly the barrister takes his client through the limited life history he has. Brought up by his mother, he has no recollection of ever seeing his father. He says he wasn't very good at school and left as soon as he could to work, packing shelves in a local supermarket. He helps his mum. His mum has two jobs. Between 5 and 7 a.m. she cleans offices. Between 10 a.m. and 3 p.m. she works in a shop. She has a little car. A Peugeot.

'Is that the Peugeot which went to the high street the day Daniel died?' asks Mr Larch.

Shadrach frowns. 'I think so. I'm not sure.'

'Surely you know?'

Shadrach shakes his head.

'But weren't you driving it?'

Shadrach looks surprised. 'You know I wasn't.'

Mr Larch smiles encouragingly. 'I know, Shadrach, but the ladies and gentlemen of the jury don't. You tell them how your mum's Peugeot went there that day when you didn't.'

Shadrach gives the matter some thought. 'Meshach came,' he says.

'Came where?'

'To my house. Meshach came and said they wanted the car. I said no, my mum wouldn't like it. But he said they would have it back before she was home.'

'So . . .'

'So I gave him the key. He took the car. He brought it back later.'

'You didn't go with him?'

Shadrach shakes his head.

'You didn't drive?'

'I can't drive. My mum tried to teach me but . . .' He shrugs.

Silence, as we take in what Shadrach has just said. He can't drive. Meshach and Abednego are whispering, eyes wide. The jury look at each other. Miss Wright turns to the senior investigating police officer in the prosecution team. He blinks helplessly.

'Did Meshach and Abednego know you can't drive?'

Shadrach flushes red. 'I don't tell people,' he says. 'They think I'm stupid. I never even told you, till you got it out of me.'

'Yesterday,' says Mr Larch.

Shadrach nods.

A number of things happen at once. Miss Wright says something to her officer, who leaves the courtroom. I guess she is sending him to see if the DVLA has a record of Shadrach ever having driven a motor vehicle. The answer will be no and she knows it, but still she must check. At the same time Mr Barrington, worried about the effect of this on Meshach's case, is busying himself with his computer. I make another guess – that he is doing the same thing I am and looking on the Digital Case System to see if, among Meshach's many previous court appearances, there is any hint he can drive. I don't know who gets there first, but within a minute both Mr Barrington and I are confronted with the fact that last year Meshach was convicted of taking and driving away a car without the owner's consent. I allow myself to look at Mr Barrington. His lips are silently forming a word I take to be 'shit'.

Cross-examination of Shadrach by other defence counsel is a half-hearted affair. It's hard to get up a head of steam with a witness who takes so long to understand, to formulate his answer, to give it. It's dispiriting when the answers come with total lack of guile. Mr Paul and Mr Barrington decide to leave it to Miss Wright. She does what she can. She asks Shadrach many things, including how come his phone was using the same mobile telephone masts and cells as the phones of his co-defendants.

'My phone was in the car,' he says. 'I don't use it much. It's mostly for my mum to call me.'

We check. The use of Shadrach's mobile at the relevant time is all for incoming calls forwarded. None are answered. None are made on the phone. Still Miss Wright keeps at it.

'Why would you lend them the car?' she demands. 'You knew your mother would never permit it. How could you explain if she got home before the boys brought it back? What did you think they wanted it for? Did you ask them that? Didn't you . . . why didn't you . . . what . . . how . . .?' She keeps at it a good while, and by the time she sits down she has amply demonstrated the unlikelihood of Shadrach's account. At least she has demonstrated that no sensible person would behave as he claims he did. Her problem is that Shadrach is giving a very good impression of not being a sensible person.

The following day it's Meshach's turn. He is only sixteen years old and small for his age. He has a cheeky grin, which he flashed about readily enough at the start of the trial, but he seems to be losing the heart to produce it. He crosses the courtroom to the witness-box accompanied by a dock officer twice his size. He climbs the steps and turns to the jury. He looks very young but, unlike some young witnesses, Meshach is up for this. I see suddenly, in the way he looks across at Abednego, that

Meshach is the leader. He is probably a murderer. He is probably about to be undone. But he intends to go down fighting.

He is too young to take the full oath, which involves saying 'I swear by Almighty God . . .' Instead, as a witness under the age of eighteen, he must promise by Almighty God to tell the truth, the whole truth and nothing but the truth. He reads out the words confidently enough but the promise is pointless. If he was the stabber, he isn't about to admit it to this jury, not for Almighty God nor for anyone else. When I tell him he can sit if he wishes, he declines. Perhaps it's an unconscious desire to be physically as well as mentally 'on his toes'. Stubborn denial is all that is left to him, and so he stubbornly denies. Yes, he can drive (no point in denying it – he remembers his previous conviction) but he has never driven the Peugeot and Shadrach is lying. He did not go into the alley that day though he may have visited the barber's in the high street with his friend Abednego, which would explain their phones cell-siting in the area. If the CCTV images of two figures going into and out of the alley match him and Abednego, it's coincidence. If his DNA is on the handle of the knife, it must be as a result of secondary transfer, which, he accepts, means he must know the killer but does not make him, Meshach, a killer. He says it with a degree of righteous indignation. After all, he points out, the Peugeot was there so Shadrach must have been, and . . . now he comes to think about it, he recalls bumping into Shadrach earlier in the day when they high-fived.

Meshach has a quick mind and an engaging smile. They have probably helped him out of many scrapes in his young life but now he is up against the ropes and Miss Wright, with disdainful insouciance, lands blow after blow. Mr Larch, whose care is Shadrach, smiles softly to himself. Mr Barrington looks resigned. He is, perhaps, thinking that at least things can get no worse for young Meshach. He is wrong. His client finishes his evidence just after 3 p.m. and Jeremiah Paul rises to his feet. His face is grave.

'My Lady, may I ask that Abednego's case begins tomorrow morning?'

I raise a querying eyebrow. 'We have some time this afternoon.'

'I wish to consider certain matters with my client.'

I accede to the request. Abednego has some difficult decisions to make and it's Mr Paul's job to explain them to him. So far, Abednego has marched to Meshach's drum – 'we weren't there, it wasn't us, it's all a mistake, a coincidence, the wickedness of others'. And, of course, however bad it looks for both of them after Meshach's evidence, their story may be nothing but the truth. Abednego's lawyers must take care not to put inappropriate pressure on such a young defendant. On the other hand, Meshach has come across as a desperate, lying child and Abednego's legal team has a duty to point out the difficulties he too faces. His choices are these: he can get into the witness-box and give the same account he has given up to now; or he can decline to give evidence at all; or . . . or there is one other card that Jeremiah Paul can play. With Meshach's DNA on the knife handle and no one else's, the highest the Crown can put matters against Abednego is that he assisted and encouraged Meshach in the stabbing. But even if he was in the alley, what is there to say he knew Meshach had a knife, or that he had any idea what Meshach might do with it, let alone that he wanted it to happen? If he sticks with the original story, the jury may conclude he was in it with Meshach, beginning to end, top to bottom. But what if his original story is untrue? What if that story was one the two boys came up with, believing it would give them the best shot at being acquitted? What if it is now clear that that story is unlikely to work? And what if Abednego was there, but, in truth, played no part in the stabbing?

A defence lawyer is not allowed to suggest versions of events to his client; but he can encourage his client to tell the truth . . . and what if the truth is that Abednego thought they were only going to talk to Daniel, or at worst give him a little dusting-up? Then the jury might only convict him of manslaughter, or even acquit him altogether.

Of course, I don't know what Jeremiah Paul said to Abednego in the cells beneath the Old Bailey that afternoon, nor what thoughts went through the boy's head as it lay on his prison-issue pillowcase that night. But I do know what happens when he climbs into the witness-box next morning.

Mr Paul says, 'Abednego, up to now have you told the truth about what happened that day?'

Abednego turns away from his friend in the dock, looks square in the jury's face and says, 'No.'

'Are you willing to tell the truth now?'

Abednego nods. He is ready to talk. Mr Paul makes an assessment, decides the risk is worth taking, and instead of leading his client step by step, question by question, through his evidence, launches him free with three words: 'Go on, then.'

And Abednego does. He takes a deep breath and begins. The account he gives us goes back a long way. He explains how, once upon a time, Daniel and Meshach had been friends but there had been a falling-out. Abednego didn't know why, but Meshach said Daniel had disrespected him. It had turned into a beef, and then into a bad beef. Meshach said Daniel had to be taught a lesson. They knew Daniel worked in the chicken shop on Saturdays. 'Meshach asked me to go with him,' says Abednego. 'I thought it would just be words. Meshach chased Daniel into the alley. I followed.' Abednego stops. The courtroom is very silent. In the dock, Meshach sits staring, the pain of betrayal written clear on his face. 'I didn't know he had a knife. It was inside his tracksuit bottoms, strapped to his thigh. He pulled it out and—'

Abednego stops again as from the dock Meshach screams 'I wasn't there!' Abednego for the first time turns to his friend. 'Of course you were,' he says.

Miss Wright cross-examines. 'You didn't know anything bad was going to happen?'

'No, I didn't.'

'But you arranged to go by car.'

He nods.

'That meant you would not be seen on the way there?'

'It was Meshach's idea.'

'And that you could get away quickly.'

'I suppose.'

'And why did you suppose it was important to get in and out quickly, important not to be seen?'

'I . . . I didn't think about it.'

'Shadrach drove you . . .'

'Shadrach wasn't there. It's like he said. Meshach got the car from him.'

Miss Wright sighs. Shadrach is slipping from her grasp. But she isn't letting go of Abednego without a struggle. She cross-examines for an hour. At the end of it, Abednego is still saying he had no idea what was going to happen, but he has had to concede he knew Meshach was very angry and that he knew there was going to be a confrontation.

'And you knew Meshach had something strapped to his thigh. You must have done. You must have realized it as he sat in the car, as he got out of the car.'

Abednego considers this. We all do. It had been a very big knife strapped to a very small leg. 'I thought he had something inside his jogging bottoms, but not a knife.'

'What did you think it was?'

A pause, then, 'A knuckleduster?' Abednego says hopefully.

5

The barristers make their speeches. Miss Wright ties together all the evidence until it resembles a Gordian knot. Mr Larch on behalf of

Shadrach says Miss Wright might be correct about the other two, but she is wrong about his client, who had nothing to do with the killing. Mr Paul must, of course, accept Abednego was in the alley but insists his lad had no idea what was going to happen when he went there. Mr Barrington maintains Meshach wasn't in the alley at all, but if Abednego was, Abednego must be the stabber. It's a tough case to argue in the light of the CCTV and the DNA evidence, but he makes great play of the absence of fingerprints. All three underline the gravity of the jurors' decision, the effect on young lives, how once done it cannot be undone, how they must not convict if there is any doubt. That last, at least, is in accordance with the law.

When the speeches are over, it's my turn. We have been in court for fourteen working days and are almost at the end of the third week. It will take me a day to sum up, leaving the jury a full week to consider the cases of the youngsters whose futures are in their hands. I don't think they will need that long but, after all, no judge can know how long it will take a jury to reach its decision.

My summing-up falls into two parts: (i) directions of law, and (ii) a summary of the evidence. Drafting directions of law is an art. Almost the first direction I give any jury is that concerning the burden-and-standard-of-proof. This is the foundation of all our criminal trials, and what a thing it is. We are so proud of it. We run it up the flagpole and wave it about. When you get under the fancy lawyers' language it means this: a defendant may only be convicted if the prosecution makes the jury sure of guilt. It sounds fine, and it is. The State, with all its power and resources, prosecutes the individual; and though the defendant may get legal aid for a solicitor and barristers and appropriate experts, still it is the State's 'game'; so the law tries to redress the balance by putting the burden of proof on the State, and making it a heavy one.

But here's the surprise. Because of the burden-and-standard-of-proof, no one tried by a jury is ever found 'innocent'. I can say that with certainty because in England and Wales (unlike Scotland) there is no such verdict.* A verdict of not guilty only means the prosecution has not made the jury sure of guilt. Even if the jury concludes the defendant is very probably guilty, they must return a verdict of 'not guilty' – because 'very probably' is not 'sure'. It sounds odd, but the alternative is even odder. Imagine a world where a defendant was convicted on the basis that he or she just might be guilty. Of course, this is no more than a choice our legal system has made. There have been plenty of places and times where a different test has been applied. But here, at this time, this is the way we do it.

The next direction of law I will give are the 'Steps to Verdict' – a written route map laying out step by step the questions the jury must answer in the order in which they must be tackled. If I do it properly, each answer will drive them forward to the next question. And when all the answers are given, they will have their verdict. The law can be very complex. A book could be written on the statutes and authorities involved in the case of Shadrach, Meshach and Abednego. I must reduce it to something comprehensible to non-lawyers. In simple terms, to find a defendant guilty of murder the jury must first be sure he was either the killer or a party to the killing. If they can't be sure of this, he cannot be guilty of anything. If they are sure of this, they must then consider if he intended that either death or at least really serious injury would be caused. If they are sure of this, he is guilty of murder. If they are not sure of this but are sure he intended some lesser injury, he is not guilty of murder but guilty of manslaughter.[†]

---

* In both jurisdictions, a jury's verdict of 'guilty' means the jury was sure of guilt. In Scotland the conclusion 'we are sure he is innocent' receives a verdict of 'not guilty'. The conclusion 'we are not sure he is guilty' receives the verdict 'not proven'. Whilst in England and Wales, a verdict of 'not guilty' covers everything short of certainty of guilt.
† See Appendix A, pp. 282–3.

After this, I give other legal directions. Judges may have to direct jurors on what defendants have or haven't said in police interviews and in defence statements, on their 'good' or 'bad' character, on identification evidence, on hearsay evidence, on expert evidence, on circumstantial evidence . . . there is a whole book of complex law which must be used where appropriate. I pick out the bits that apply in this case and give them to the jury in writing. They are long and sometimes difficult. I translate the law into the plainest language to which I can lay my tongue. Mr Forbes nods as if he gets it all. Mr Rosenblum shakes his head as if the shaking will put what I have said in manageable order. Violet stares at me as if I have lost my senses. Then I summarize the main parts of the evidence, setting out all the pieces chronologically and in their context. It's the first time the jury have heard this done because each of the barristers has concentrated on the material favourable to his or her case. Sometimes this complete picture can be a revelation.

Finally, I tell them three last things: their first task should be to choose one of their number to be foreman, to chair their discussions and to return their verdicts in court; there is no pressure of time; and whatever they have heard about majority verdicts, they must forget it because unless and until I direct them otherwise, they must reach unanimous verdicts. And then I'm done. Now it's over to them. In the dock, Meshach and Abednego look grim. Shadrach consoles himself with his thumb.

6

For three days, the jury work in their room. On the fourth day they send me a note: 'We have verdicts.' I read the note again and suspect the hand of Mr Forbes. He's sure, I think, to be foreman. But when the court reassembles, it isn't Mr Forbes who takes the foreman's seat. It's Mr Rosenblum.

There is no moment like the moment before a jury returns its verdict in a murder case. You never get used to it. The air crackles with tension. Members of the press push in. The public gallery is full. Daniel's mother and grandmother are in their usual seats, eyes closed, lips moving a little as if in prayer.

I nod to Angelique. She gets to her feet, says, 'Would the defendants please stand.'

Shadrach and Abednego do. Meshach hesitates. When a dock officer offers him a helping hand, Meshach shoves it away. The boy is taut as a bowstring. If he is found guilty, there might be trouble. The last thing I want is violence in the dock during the taking of verdicts. It will mean more difficulty for Meshach, and a torture of delay for the other defendants, for the jury, for Daniel's family and everyone else. I signal to Angelique to come close and whisper, 'Take Meshach's verdict first.'

She understands. She turns to the jury. 'Would the foreman please stand.' Mr Rosenblum rises. 'Mr Foreman, answer my first question either yes or no. Mr Foreman, have you reached verdicts in respect of each defendant upon which you are all agreed?'

'Yes,' says David Rosenblum.

'In respect of the second defendant, Meshach, do you find him guilty or not guilty of murder?'

A moment's pause. Indrawn breaths all around the courtroom. Meshach staring at the jury, as if by power of will he can change what he knows is about to happen.

'Guilty,' says David Rosenblum.

'You find him guilty of murder, and that is the verdict of you all?'
'It is.'

Meshach opens his mouth to object, lifts a fist to reinforce his objection, and – at an exchange of looks between me and the dock officers – before he realizes what is happening is taken through the green baize door, down to the cells below, and to all the cells in which he will live his life for a very, very long time to come.

Angelique continues seamlessly. 'In respect of the third defendant, Abednego, do you find him guilty or not guilty of murder?'

'Not guilty.'

In the dock, Abednego sags as if his legs won't hold him. The officer at his side holds him up. But Angelique isn't finished yet.

'Mr Foreman, do you find the defendant Abednego guilty or not guilty of manslaughter?'

'Guilty.'

'And that is the verdict of you all?'

Of course it is. But still the ritual must be gone through.

We move on to Shadrach.

'Guilty or not guilty of murder?'

'Not guilty,' says Mr Rosenblum.

'Guilty or not guilty of manslaughter?'

A pause, during which I wonder if Mr Rosenblum has ever been an actor. Violet is staring up at the public gallery, which, as in almost all the Old Bailey courts, is opposite the jury-box. Her eyes scan the rows and settle on a woman who leans forward, looking from the jury to the last boy in the dock. Has Violet found Shadrach's mother? Surely his mother must be there, though no one has mentioned her before. Violet nods, she smiles. And I know everything, for Shadrach, will be all right.

The verdict is delivered. Shadrach stares. 'You have been acquitted,' I say to him. 'You will be taken downstairs and when the paperwork is completed, you will be free to go.'

He looks up at his mother then back to me. He takes his thumb from his mouth and raises it in a universal gesture that all is well, for him at least.

What else remains? The sending of two boys into custody for many years . . . exactly how many is my call. I must try to balance their lives against the life that has been lost and the harm that this has done to the whole of our society. Lawyers speak of punishment and rehabilitation, laymen of justice and vengeance. Whatever words you use, it takes a lot of thought to get it right. I adjourn the sentencing to the following week and in the days that follow, work hard on it.

It will be the beginning of a very long end for Meshach. He is sixteen years old and likely to be locked up at the very least the length of that life over again. But before I can make a final decision about the sentence, both prosecution and defence will have a chance to put before me all the material they want me to take into account. Still, the law is clear and uncompromising. For murder, the only sentence is life imprisonment. It goes by different names for different age groups* but whatever you call it, it's mandatory. No ifs, no buts. No date for release. I will set a minimum term of years which Meshach must serve before he can even ask the Parole Board to consider his case. In fixing that term, for anyone aged eighteen or over convicted of murder, the law requires me to begin with fifteen years, but if he or she takes a knife to the scene and uses it to kill, the term rises to twenty-five years, an increase of two thirds. For those under eighteen, I must begin with twelve years, and then factor in the knife. An increase of two thirds would bring me to twenty years. But there are many other features I must take into account, to increase or decrease the final figure.†

Abednego is in a very different position. Manslaughter can carry life imprisonment, but it is not mandatory and is rarely imposed. Instead a specific term of years is set, of which a defendant serves

* For those under eighteen life imprisonment is called detention at Her Majesty's pleasure, for those aged eighteen to twenty it is called custody for life, and for those aged twenty-one and over it is life imprisonment.
† If you are interested in my final sentencing remarks in Meshach's case, see Appendix B, pp. 285–6.

either a half or two thirds. For the sort of manslaughter committed by Abednego, an adult might be sentenced to twelve years' imprisonment. For someone of Abednego's age, I might sentence him to eight years of which he would serve a half.* So these are the bald facts: Abednego will be released when he is nineteen; Meshach will be lucky if he is released in his early thirties; Daniel is dead for ever. And Shadrach? Shadrach is free to make what he will of the life that has been given back to him.

7

I said earlier that by locking up more and more youngsters for longer and longer, we may be stoking up trouble for ourselves when they eventually try to reintegrate into a society whose norms they have not experienced for perhaps decades. Everyone agrees the far better course is to prevent knife crime happening in the first place. Parliament has tried to do this by legislating for ever-longer deterrent sentences . . . but they don't deter these boys. Perhaps the time has come to stop trying to deter and to ask why young people are prepared to face swingeing sentences, because we certainly haven't understood the reasons thus far. Those I hear advanced in the courtroom include:

- fear of being attacked by others who are armed
- the wish to hurt those who don't show what is perceived as proper respect

* If you are interested in my final sentencing remarks in Abednego's case, see Appendix B, pp. 286–7.

- the desire to impress
- the desire to belong to and be accepted by a group of others –
  the street gang

The first is self-generating. If you carry a knife because others are carrying knives, everyone ends up carrying knives. The second and third might have to do with immaturity. The last might come from a sense of not really being accepted by the society that makes the law, or a sense of being owed something society isn't giving them. Society might reply, 'But they have a choice. They could choose to belong: to study, qualify, get a job, a home, a family.' Of course, Society will accept, it's more difficult if you grow up on a drug-ridden inner-city estate than if you're brought up in a leafy suburb. It's more difficult if your mum is trying to hold down three jobs to provide for you and your siblings than if your aspirational parents provide a childhood with opportunities at every turn. But difficult isn't impossible. It's just that against this background, doubling the minimum term for a murder wasn't ever likely to make any difference, and it hasn't.

Despite the many committed groups working against it, knife crime continues to grow. The fight against it is often led by families who have lost a child to a blade through the heart, the femoral artery, the jugular vein. They work tirelessly with kids to try and stop the carrying of knives, but all their monumental efforts are not so far stemming the tide. It's not easy to see what is the best way forward. I have no more insight into this than anyone else, but it's obvious that by the time youngsters appear before me, they are almost lost. By the time they are drawn into gangs, they are on a road to nowhere but that loss; by the time they even think of carrying a knife, they are heading straight for that road to nowhere. But it's not how they started out. When I deal with very young children – those of seven or eight – they see the way clearly. They are without prejudice and generally kind. They understand that it is wrong for people to hurt them, and they are amenable to the concept that in turn they shouldn't hurt others. But by the age of twelve, many have lost that clarity. We need to work out why. We need to think harder about our own responsibility as well as theirs. We need to hesitate a little longer before we cast blame. We need to understand what is operating on their minds. And they need to understand something too: they need to understand what only Shane and all the Shanes can tell them about the raw pain of death and how when death has been done it can never, ever be undone. If our next generation grasps as fundamental that carrying knives is wrong, that wrong is bad, and that bad makes everyone unhappy, perhaps, just perhaps, when they are older and reach for their trainers and baseball caps, they won't also reach for a knife.

TRIAL TWO:

Amid the Alien Corn

MRS MANDERS CLIMBED the stairs slowly, careful to make
no noise. If you had asked her why, she might have said she
didn't want to disturb the baby. She and Ruth had been
sitting together when they heard little Zara give a cry. Not
much, but her daughter had gone up to check. That was ten
minutes ago. Now Mrs Manders was going up to check on
Ruth. Not that she would have put it that way. Never. Not
even to herself.

Her daughter's bedroom was at the top of the stairs.
The nursery, leading off it, was very small. Perhaps it had
been designed as a dressing room – it was that sort of
house, big and bright with a big, bright garden. Very Surrey.
Very nice. Everything about the Manderses life should have
been very nice. But still Mrs Manders climbed the stairs
silently.

The door to Ruth's room was open, but the door to the
nursery was closed. When Mrs Manders eased it open she
saw that the pretty curtains printed with teddy bears were
drawn. But it was mid-afternoon and the window south-
facing so, surely, that was understandable. As Mrs Manders'
eyes adjusted to the dimness, she saw Ruth bending over the
cot. She smiled. It was good to see Ruth behaving tenderly
towards the child at last. She shouldn't have worried about
Ruth, for here she was, close to her baby, holding out the pink
rabbit that Zara loved, and Zara's legs were kicking under the
light blanket.

How long did it take Mrs Manders to realize the rabbit was over the child's face? That the little legs were kicking too feebly, like a wound-up toy almost spent?

1

It's a monday in late September and Ruth's trial is in my list of cases for the day. London is grey and damp. In the Pyrenees it's hot and cloudless. I know this because I have checked – a small act of self-mortification which has done me no good. Neither has thinking about the pretty little hotel room with its view of the mountains and the comfortable bed with its pristine sheets in which I haven't slept. The holiday on which I should have been has gone the way of so many judges' holidays because the jury in my last trial is still in retirement. Counsel and I thought it was a straightforward case, but the jury are thinking otherwise. They don't seem able to agree upon their verdict. They've been at it for days.

'Look on the bright side,' says the list officer, who decides what cases appear in which of our courtrooms. 'Now you can do the baby case.'

'Your bright side,' I say. 'Not mine.'

So here I am. Monday morning. One jury out, another to be sworn in the case of Ruth Manders. Regina v. Manders is a case with only one defendant, few witnesses and no dead body, so there is only one barrister for each side. For the prosecution I have Mr Bell, a Solid-and-Experienced sort of chap. For the defence I have Mr Maddox, a Bright-Young-Man.

'Gentlemen,' I say.

They stand.

'Are we ready for a jury panel?'

'I am,' says Mr Maddox. He is really a very Bright-Young-Man.

'What are the issues in this case, Mr Maddox?'

'My client didn't do it.' Pressed for a little more detail, he says, 'It never happened. Her mother did not see my client trying to kill the child. She is lying.' He pauses, reflects. 'Lying or mistaken. I do not commit myself at this stage.'

'No matters of law on which you need me to give a ruling? No evidence the prosecution says is admissible and the defence says isn't?'

'No.'

'No applications for adjournments, no missing documents?'

'No.'

'No psychiatric issues?' In this sort of case I would expect the defence to have obtained a psychiatric report on their client. After all, women rarely try to kill their babies unless something is amiss.

But, 'No,' he says. 'She just didn't do it.'

I look at him narrowly, but the BYM seems to think he knows what he's about, and I don't. I can't know what has passed between him and his client. He might have explored the psychiatric question and found there to be nothing in it, or found there was something in it not to her advantage, or she may have refused to see a psychiatrist at all. Counsel must be trusted with these matters, and this one isn't going to ask the jury to consider Ruth's mental health or state of mind. Everything is to be staked on the simple proposition that she didn't do it.

In the dock, Ruth is a forlorn little figure. Not yet twenty years old and, standing between two burly officers, she looks younger. She is frail, her hair light and thin, her skin pale to whiteness. I can't tell if this is terror or prison pallor. She has already spent five months in custody. It won't have been easy for her. If there's one thing your average prisoner hates it's a mother who harms her child, and her fellow inmates will have made her life hard. Of course attempted murder is a common enough charge here at the Old Bailey, but women defendants are unusual, and cases of mothers trying to kill their babies mercifully rare.

Defendants like Ruth are rarer still. Most defendants end up in court because of the circumstances of their lives – poverty, addiction, bad company, tragic events. It doesn't excuse but it at least explains. Ruth has no such explanation. She has been brought up in an affluent household, been to good schools, had every advantage. There is nothing obvious that could have led her to try to kill her baby. If she did. That, of course, will be for the jury to decide. Her eyes are red-rimmed, but there are no tears. She just looks blank. She should be distressed or angry or frightened, but she seems only bone-weary. She doesn't look like any murderer I have seen before, but murderers come in all shapes and sizes.

'Am I to understand the only issue in the case will be if the witness is right when she says she saw her daughter try to smother baby Zara?'

Both barristers nod. There is almost no other evidence. If Mrs Manders hadn't dialled 999, her daughter wouldn't be in the dock. One person's word against another. It is very often so in domestic cases. Behind closed doors, who knows what goes on but those who are there?

'It's a very straightforward matter,' says the BYM.

Really? Only time will tell. But then a police officer is tugging at Mr Bell's gown, whispering in his ear, and now Mr Bell is no longer nodding. He is telling Mr Maddox something and Mr Maddox is looking pleased with life so I'm guessing Mr Bell isn't. I'm right. Time has told, and it didn't take long.

'My Lady, it seems my main witness, the defendant's mother, is refusing to come to court to give evidence. I must apply for a witness summons.'

A summons ordering a witness to court should be issued if that witness can give relevant evidence, and refuses to do so. Mrs

Manders can certainly give relevant evidence. I grant the summons.
It's handed to the officer, who goes off to serve it on her.

Mr Bell's application has caused a weight to fall over me; a scru-
ple, but enough to tip the balance. I just know this is a day in which
everything will go badly. Right again. Barely has Ruth been taken
back to the cells when I get a note from the jury in retirement. They
are quite unable to agree on any verdict at all. After I have discharged them and made arrangements for a retrial, Ruth's case is
called back into my court.

'Can we swear in a jury now, Mr Bell?'

Am I surprised when Mr Bell shakes his head? I am not. He
calls his officer into the witness-box. Ruth's mother had read the
summons, understood its import, given him a cup of tea and
told him she would not give evidence against her daughter. The
officer produces a second statement from her. Like all witness
statements, it begins with a declaration that its contents are
true and that the maker knows she can be prosecuted if she has
deliberately stated in it anything which she knows to be false or
does not believe to be true. Mrs Manders has signed this, then
written that baby Zara is fine and flourishing; that since the
birth, her daughter has seemed mentally unwell and needs help
not punishment; that she will not be witness against her. A not
unreasonable position for a mother to take. Three straightforward sentences. There is a fourth. 'I did not lie in my first
statement, but I am not willing to repeat its contents in court.' It's
the question every experienced officer would ask of a recalci-
trant witness – was what you said in your first statement true? If
the answer is yes, Mr Bell's duty is clear, and he does it. He applies
for a witness arrest warrant and the case is adjourned for Mrs
Manders to be brought before me.

2

It has been a long, unproductive day, and it isn't over yet. Not by a long chalk. The failure of my jury to reach a verdict will probably mean all the expense and grief of a retrial in the future. Still, if jurors form different views about the evidence, and each is true to their oath, it's bound to happen from time to time. There's no point in worrying about it now. But there's every point in worrying about Ruth. All I have seen and heard about her – including her mother's opinion – suggests that I should have a psychiatric report, but a bright young barrister has decided otherwise. It doesn't mean Mr Maddox is wrong. His hands may be tied. He must take his instructions from his client. She is saying her mother is not truthful, her mother could not have seen her trying to smother the baby because it never happened. If she insists that she has no mental health problems, he can't force her to see a psychiatrist. I can do more – at least I can order that a psychiatrist goes to see her, but I can't force Ruth to speak or to explain or to be assessed. And, being unable to do anything more constructive, I go down to tea.

The judges' tea is an important part of our day, the only time we can sit down all together without others present. We gather around the long dining table which has been cleared of the lunch we ate earlier with the City's guests and set with pots of tea and plates of biscuits. It's our opportunity to discuss the problems the day has brought each of us. In my case the problem is Ruth. But by the time I get to the table, a serious situation has arisen. There is only one chocolate biscuit left and H's eye is on it. There are plenty of Vienna Swirls and Coconut Thingies but only one Fat-And-Chompy-Chocolate-All-The-Way-Through-Biscuit and H's eye is on it. I see from the crumbs on his waistcoat he has already had an Iced Gem, but now his hand is reaching for the chocolate biscuit, and so is mine.

'How bad a day have you had?' he asks.

'Pretty ghastly.'

'How bad on the Fat-And-Chompy scale?'

'I've discharged a hung jury.'

His eyes narrow. 'You lucky beggar. That means you don't have to sentence. I've had a conviction on arson.'

Arson is tricky to sentence. I resign myself to not getting the chocolate biscuit.

I look round the table. 'Can I run something past you?' Dutifully, they stop talking about their nightmare barristers, sick jurors and lost documents and turn to me. 'It's attempted infanticide,' I say. 'At least, I'm wondering if it might be.' It's only as the words pass my lips that I realize this was where my brain had been taking me . . . to an offence that carries a less serious sentence. I can see it now. I hadn't before because infanticide is so rare a charge. A lesser charge. Many judges, even those at the Old Bailey, will go through a whole judicial career without coming across one. I have their attention. 'At the moment the defendant is charged with attempted murder of her baby but I really think that an attempted infanticide might be added to the indictment if—'

'Attempted infanticide?' It is S who has spoken. He is a dear, dry man, and an excellent lawyer. He reaches for his spectacles. He thinks better with his spectacles on. He reaches for his laptop. He goes nowhere without it. 'I don't know . . . I seem to recall . . . let me check.'

S has a phenomenal memory for trivia. Not that attempted infanticide is trivial. Not for Ruth. Not for baby Zara and Mrs Manders. The computer, like a faithful dog, brightens into life. S enters the electronic library where a modern judge can wander among more books than Alexander dreamed of. We wait. H hesitates, breaks the chocolate biscuit in two and hands me half. Attempted infanticide is trickier than arson. While S presses buttons, he says, 'Tell us about the case.'

I marshal the facts.

'The baby was four months old and the defendant's mother says her daughter had seemed mentally unwell since the birth.'

'What does the psychiatric report say?' asks H.

'No report.'

'But . . .'

'Quite.'

There's a silence while the computer hums through millions of items. It presents us with a small handful. Apart from the Infanticide Act 1938,* there's nothing significant beyond one case, a report by the Criminal Law Revision Committee now over thirty years old and a Law Commission consultation paper in 2006. S pushes his spectacles back up his nose and reads aloud from the Act. I have no idea why statutes are written with so many 'wilfuls' and 'to wits' and 'by reasons of' but the meaning is clear. In 1938, post-natal depression was just beginning to be understood by legislators. The Infanticide Act allows what would otherwise be murder to be dealt with more leniently if the offence was due to the balance of the mother's mind being disturbed by reason of giving birth or lactation. It's a merciful Act. In reality almost no one convicted of infanticide goes to prison. Almost everyone convicted of attempted murder does. For a long time.

'Well, there it is,' I say, 'a perfectly good offence of infanticide. Except that there is no basis for asking the jury to consider it because there is no medical evidence to suggest it because Mr Maddox hasn't got a psychiatric report.'

'And except, of course, that the baby didn't die,' says S.

* See Appendix C, p. 289.

'So what?' retorts H. 'There's a charge of attempted murder. Why can't the jury consider an alternative of attempted infanticide?'

S is still deep in the computer. 'Ah, here it is. I thought I remembered ... you know there is debate as to whether the offence of attempted infanticide really exists?'

I did not know. Neither, it seems, did the others. S reads us a long passage from the report. Then he reads us a contradictory passage from the consultation paper.

'Surely there's a case on it?' My voice is ... what? Desperate?

'Well,' says S, pressing another button. 'There's Regina versus K.A. Smith.'

Of course. There's good old K.A. How could we have forgotten K.A.? The answer in my case is because I have never heard of K.A. It turns out that that is the answer in everyone's case. After all, each year in the UK over 100,000 cases go to the Crown Court. Though each is of interest to the judge who deals with it, it's the 4,000 or so that go up to the CACD* that create the 'authorities' which we in the lower Crown Court must follow. It takes a lot of research to dig up a case like K.A. Smith. Or it takes S. S tells us that in 1983 a judge in the Crown Court accepted K.A.'s plea of guilty to attempted infanticide. That may have made K.A. lucky, but it didn't make the decision good law. Only specific approval in the CACD can do that.

I think of Ruth, shut up in the prison van on its way back to Her Majesty's Prison Bronzefield. I think of her mother, racking heart and conscience. Ruth is no more to K.A. Smith than Hecuba to *Hamlet*'s play-actor, but if she were, wouldn't K.A. weep for her?

'Anyway,' says H, 'it doesn't matter because without a psychiatric report, however suspicious of post-natal depression a judge may be, there's nothing to act upon.'

And there, finally, he's right.

---

* Court of Appeal (Criminal Division).

3

I spend hours that night researching the law but get no further. I wonder if I should press the BYM again about getting a report but I must be careful not to encroach on what is his business and not mine. If a defendant has pleaded guilty or been convicted by a jury, and I have to sentence, I can ask for a psychiatric report to help inform the process; but Ruth is not to be sentenced – not yet. She is to face trial, and the nature of her defence is a matter for her and her lawyers. So overnight nothing changes and the next day I am back where I was. I join my usher and clerk outside the door that leads from the judges' corridor into the courtroom. Bill and Angelique are my eyes and ears to what is happening on the other side of that closed door.

'You're not going to like it,' says Angelique.

'You're really not,' says Bill. He brings the door knocker down with a sharp rap, a pause, two quick raps – the time-honoured way of knocking in a judge. He pushes open the door and steps in. He moves to one side to allow me to pass and go to my seat. 'Court rise,' he calls out. And then, as is done every time a court like mine embarks upon its day's work, 'All manner of persons who have anything to do before My Lords and My Ladies the Queens Justices, draw near and give your attendance. God save the Queen.'

This morning Ruth looks grey, Mr Maddox white and Mr Bell red.

'Are we ready for a jury now, Mr Bell?'

'My Lady, the witness has been arrested and brought to court but she is not' – he hesitates delicately – 'not cooperative.'

My sigh is picked up by the microphones and echoes through the courtroom.

'She's here on an arrest warrant. Should I have her taken to the cells?' he asks me.

'I don't think that's necessary, Mr Bell.' I really don't want her locked up in a cell. This is a loving mother caught between an adamantine rock and the hardest of places. She loves her child. She loves her grandchild. 'Have her brought into court.'

Mrs Manders isn't at all like her daughter. She is taller, bigger-boned, capable-looking. She stares at me with steely grey eyes. I have her placed in the witness-box. Well, I don't want her in the dock with her daughter, do I?

'Mrs Manders, I am sorry that you have been arrested but you have material evidence to give and the law requires you to give it.'

Her voice is as steady as her eyes. 'I'm sorry too, Judge, but if I give evidence, my daughter will go to prison.'

The BYM is on his feet. 'Only if the jury believe you,' he says.

This is inappropriate and I would remonstrate with him, but his words have an effect quite different from what he intended. Ruth's mother looks astonished. Clearly it has never crossed her mind she won't be believed. Her face speaks her thought. She articulates it.

'Do you really think I would lie about a thing like this?'

The BYM takes his seat without being told and stays there.

Ruth's mother looks straight at me. 'I don't like seeing my daughter in prison, even on remand,' she says. 'It's making her worse not better. I will not do anything to make her life more miserable than it already is.'

I take a deep breath. What I say next, and the way I say it, will alter Ruth's life, and her mother's and her child's. Whether it alters things for the better or worse is out of my hands; out of my understanding, for I don't know what is better or worse. I don't know if Ruth really did try to kill her baby, and if she did whether she will try again given the chance. If she did, I don't know if Ruth's mother can protect baby Zara from her. I don't know whether Ruth, if she is convicted upon her mother's evidence, will be allowed to keep any other baby she may ever have. Most of all I don't know what has made Ruth the person she is. What I do know is my job. It is to ensure the law takes its course fairly and impartially.

I invite Ruth's mother to sit down and try to find a tone of voice that neither threatens nor is over-friendly.

'Mrs Manders, if you refuse to give evidence, you may be in contempt of court. That is a serious matter. If proved, it carries a substantial term of imprisonment. You need to speak to a lawyer who can advise you. I can arrange that.' And I can. There is in the building a Bar Mess, full of lawyers, and when a judge needs help in a situation like this one of them will step forward to take up the brief.

'I've already taken legal advice,' she says.

Of course she has. This competent woman. This mother facing the court. I wonder, where is Ruth's father? Shouldn't there be a father supporting the mother who is supporting the daughter? Perhaps he's at home with baby Zara. Perhaps he's the one who arranged legal advice. Perhaps – good grief – he's the lawyer.

I can only repeat myself. 'Mrs Manders, you've been arrested for refusing to obey a court summons. If you persist in your refusal to give evidence you may be in contempt of court for which you may go to prison. I'm going to consider this matter, and while I do, you will be taken to the witness suite. Please do not think that means I won't ultimately have you taken to the cells.'

The witness suite is a place of calm for those in turmoil and terror. It will do no harm to have Mrs Manders sit there reflecting for a while. Still, I take the precaution of ensuring the arresting officer watches over her.

When she has gone, I turn to Mr Bell. He gives me a small, tight smile that might be a grimace.

'Well, Mr Bell?'

'I suppose,' he says, 'we're ready for trial.'

'But you have no witness,' says the BYM, addressing Mr Bell rather than me. 'You can't.'

'I certainly can,' says Mr Bell.

And he's right. In fact, he has few other options. The BYM frowns, trying to work out what Mr Bell is up to. The prosecutor takes pity on the lad. 'Archbold chapter eight, paragraphs 197 to 204,' he whispers loud enough to be heard throughout the courtroom. I have had the Bench copy of Archbold open in front of me from the moment I set eyes on Mrs Manders.

The BYM opens the heavy red practitioners' textbook wherein lie the mysteries of criminal practice – but not necessarily their solutions. He reads. He knows it, of course, as he must know most of the law that applies in my court; but this is an area rarely used, and there is so much to remember, and who can think of everything . . . so says the expression on his face as he takes in what he reads. Finally he looks up and says, 'Denman's Act.' Mr Bell – and, regrettably, I too – nod. Mr Bell is warning us that he is considering taking the extraordinary step of applying to cross-examine his own witness.

Here is how the law works: when one side (prosecution or defence) calls a witness, they must get evidence from that witness by 'examining in chief' in a series of 'non-leading' questions; that is, questions that do not contain the answer the advocate hopes to get. Then the opposing advocate cross-examines, asking questions as 'leading' as he or she wishes. So the examiner-in-chief might ask 'What is your name?' whereas the cross-examiner might say 'Your name is John Robert Smythe, isn't it?' And if the witness denies it, the cross-examiner might follow up with, 'Come, come, Mr John Robert Smythe, that is certainly you. It's the very name in which you were convicted of perjury twelve years ago, is it not?'

But what if the examiner-in-chief finds his witness turns 'hostile' and deliberately gives a different account from what they put in their witness statement, or refuses to say anything at all? What then? Until 1865, an examiner-in-chief like Mr Bell was stuck. But then along came Denman's Act.* This allows someone like Mr Bell to apply to someone like me to cross-examine someone like Mrs Manders – to challenge her with her earlier witness statement and ask why she has changed her account. In such a way, the truth may out. Or at least the jury may have a clearer picture of what is going on in the witness's mind.

The BYM has averted his eyes from Archbold as if the page offends him.

'May I make submissions to persuade Your Ladyship not to allow Mr Bell's application?'

'Of course you may,' I assure him, 'when Mr Bell makes it. But he can't make it until Mrs Manders becomes a witness and refuses in front of the jury to give her evidence. So we will swear in a jury and see what Mrs Manders does when the moment comes.'

4

And so the familiar process begins. A panel of potential jurors is brought to the courtroom. From them, a jury is selected and sworn. The case is opened. Mr Bell plays it down, knowing he may not get very far with this one. Even so a number of the jurors look narrowly at Ruth as they hear the allegations unfold. Will Mr Bell give a hint of Mrs Manders' reluctance to attest? Will he suggest how difficult it is for a loving mother to give evidence against her child? The BYM sits on the edge of his seat but Mr Bell only opens with the facts as the Crown says they are, and then calls his witness, his fingers (I suspect) firmly crossed.

* Criminal Procedure Act 1865 s3.

So the moment comes when Mrs Manders follows Bill across the well of the court. The jury watches silently. I put my hand on Archbold. I am waiting for her to be sworn, to be asked what she saw, and then we will see what happens. She climbs the steps to the witness-box with the air of Sydney Carton mounting the scaffold. Bill asks on what holy book she would like to take the oath. She shakes her head. He offers her the affirmation. She shakes her head again.

'What would you like to swear on?' asks Bill.

'Nothing,' she says. There is a tear, bright in the corner of her eye, but she won't accept any holy book and she won't take the printed affirmation or oath. In the silence that follows I look at Mr Bell, who looks at the BYM, who looks down. I ask Bill to take the jury out. When they are gone, I turn to Mrs Manders. It is now that it dawns on me that she – or at least the person from whom she has taken legal advice – is one step ahead of us all. To be treated as a hostile witness, you must first be a witness. To be a witness, technically you must be sworn before the jury.

'Mrs Manders, are you refusing to be sworn?'

'I believe I am,' she says. As well as the tear there's a glimmer of apology in her eyes.

'But why?' As if I don't know.

'I believe that once I am a sworn witness, if I refuse to give evidence the prosecutor can apply to . . .' She has forgotten the word, but she has the principle. 'But he can't do it if I'm not a sworn witness.'

Oh, Mrs Manders, I fear you are correct. She really has taken legal advice.

'I'm sorry to cause so much trouble,' she says. 'I'm only trying to do what's right.'

I have no doubt of it. She doesn't think it right to put the child she believes is sick into prison for years. This is her decision and she's sticking with it. This is her judgement and she is putting it above the court, above the law. She is putting it above the rules by which everyone else is expected to live and by which she has lived all her life. She is putting it above her own liberty, for she knows I can send her to prison for this.

'You've given this a lot of thought.'

'Of course I have.' And then, as if she recognizes it needs some explanation, 'I can look after them both.'

'Your daughter and your granddaughter?'

'Ruth and Zara.' She says it as if I have deliberately stripped them of their names, deliberately taken away their humanity; as if that is why she must act, to protect them against a dehumanizing system. There's something about her I can't help admiring, but her judgement is wrong. At least, I think it's wrong. And that's my judgement. She's wrong because she can't protect them both. Even if there is a husband and money and all the things she thinks she can rely on, the system is tough to beat. It will slot into place with unforgiving certainty. Step one: contempt of court proceedings leading to a period in prison for her. I won't want to and I'll keep it as short as I can, but the authority of the court has been challenged and if the court doesn't deal with it, the same thing will happen in other cases up and down the country as the word spreads. Step two: without her mother's evidence, a verdict of not guilty will be recorded and Ruth will be released. She will go home, but if I put Mrs Manders in prison, her mother won't be there to care for her. And even if she is, step three will almost certainly follow: Social Services will begin care proceedings. An acquittal in the Crown Court only means the prosecution was unable to put evidence before a jury to satisfy it of guilt. In this case, where the witness's motive for withdrawing her evidence is clear, it will carry little weight. The baby must be kept safe.

I can't say these things to Ruth's mother. I can't take her hand and say listen to me. But I know someone who can. I know a whole bunch of someones who can. They are sitting up in the Bar Mess or in the Bar Library or in the Robing Room.

'I'm putting legal aid in place,' I say firmly. 'I want you to speak to a barrister. I can't force you to give evidence.' This is a statement of the obvious. No one can open a witness's mouth and wrest the words out. 'But I want to be sure you understand exactly what you are doing and its consequences for you and your daughter and your granddaughter.'

She hesitates.

'Please,' I say.

'Well?' says H at lunchtime.

The judges' lunch isn't for talking about cases. It works like this. The City of London owns the building, which functions not only as the site of eighteen courtrooms, but the 'home' of the City's two Sheriffs who host the judges' lunch every day. The Sheriffs also invite other guests. The judges are the floor-show. So lunch isn't for the law. It's for sitting with the Sheriff and Alderman and such of the great-and-the-good as have accepted their invitation. Today I'm next to an astrophysicist, and what with dark matter and baked fish, there's no time to exchange more with H than a shake of the head. Two o'clock and I'm back in court. So is Mrs Manders. She is standing beside a sensible-looking woman barrister who has undertaken the task of speaking to her.

'My client wishes to apologize to the court for her earlier attitude,' says the barrister.

I nod. I don't want an apology. I want to know if Mrs Manders will give evidence.

'She has fully reflected upon all the consequences that might flow from her various actions,' says the barrister.

I daresay. But will she give evidence?

The barrister hesitates. 'May I respectfully suggest you call the jury back into court.' I note the shrug beneath her black gown. I read it. It says: I really don't know if she will bring herself to give evidence, or if she does, whether she will bring herself to say what she saw; but at least she understands the potential consequences of her choices. She understands that if she gives evidence her daughter may go to prison, and that if she doesn't her granddaughter may be taken away by Social Services. She understands that if her daughter really didn't do it, she is suffering wrongly; and that if her daughter really did do it, her granddaughter may suffer a deal worse. However much Mrs Manders has thought about her decision not to give evidence, this is the first time she has been brought to see these things. She looks shaken.

I thank the barrister and send for my jury. Ten minutes later they are back in their seats and Ruth's mother is in the witness-box. The jurors stare at her, lean forward in their seats. Will she take the oath this time, or won't she? The BYM shifts his glance between the witness and the floor. The prosecutor rises. You could cut the tension with a knife. Only Ruth sits, apparently unmoved, staring at nothing.

Bill offers Mrs Manders a selection of oaths and the affirmation. She takes the latter. She holds the card in her hand, staring at it. She bites her lip. We hold a collective breath while she thinks, weighs up, makes her decision. She looks at me. I think she is going to say no but, 'I do solemnly, sincerely and truly declare and affirm . . .' She speaks the words. Mr Maddox closes his eyes. Mr Bell sighs with relief. He still has a job to do. He still must get the evidence out of her mouth. But now at least she is a sworn witness. Now at least if she refuses to give her account, he can apply to cross-examine her on her witness statement.

5

He begins, unorthodoxly, with the words, 'All I want from you is the truth.'

Her answer, equally unorthodox, is, 'It's not easy.'

He nods. 'Let's start with something that is easy.'

By slow stages he draws from her the account of the pregnancy. She tells us they – she and her husband – had known of no boyfriend and Ruth had never said who was the baby's father . . . they are reconciled to not knowing . . . they have enough love to give Zara all she needs . . . they have supported Ruth throughout . . . there have been no recriminations, no expressions of disappointment, though of course they are disappointed . . . she was such a bright girl and they had – have – such hopes for her. I glance at Ruth. There is nothing bright or hopeful about her now. Mr Bell doesn't stop Mrs Manders when she tells the jury, earnestly, how Ruth changed after the baby's birth; how she became quiet and withdrawn and seemed to take no pleasure in things.

'You suspected she was ill?' asks Mr Bell.

'I see it now.'

'You suspected it at the time?'

'I must have.'

'But not enough to seek medical help.'

A silence. 'No,' she says at last.

The BYM is on his feet. 'My Lady, Mr Bell is cross-examining his own witness and he has made no application to do so and I—'

Mr Bell interrupts. 'My Lady, I apologize to My Learned Friend and to the court. I should not have said, "But not enough to seek medical help." I should have said, "Did you seek medical help?" I believe the answer must have been the same.'

The BYM resumes his seat, red-faced. Cleverness and enthusiasm are no substitute for experience.

After that, Mr Bell takes his witness to photographs of the Manderses home. There are twenty of them neatly docketed in tab three of the jury bundle. They show a leafy suburb, a detached house with large rooms, good furniture, a piano . . .

'Who plays?' asks Mr Bell.

Mrs Manders sighs. 'We bought it for Ruth. She used to play a lot, but she hasn't touched the instrument since the baby was born. She hasn't seemed to have the heart for it.'

Some of the jury look across at Ruth. Perhaps they are seeing, for the first time, a sad child rather than a murderous woman. Even Mr Bell makes mistakes.

The photographer takes us up the staircase to the first floor and into Ruth's bedroom. It is decorated in shades of cream and beige. The baby's room adjoins it, a proper little nursery in pink and white with a teddy bear and a mobile, a tiny white cardigan on a tiny hanger. All too perfect.

'And it was here that you entered that Sunday afternoon and saw what caused you to make a 999 call?'

She nods. 'What I believed I saw, yes.'

'What did you see?' He corrects himself. 'What did you believe you saw?'

She closes her eyes then opens them again quickly, as if in the darkness the scene that has reconstructed itself is too painful to contemplate. 'I thought my daughter was leaning over my granddaughter's cot. She was holding Zara's toy rabbit. I thought at first she was only adjusting the blanket, but then I thought she was . . .' Ruth's mother puts a hand in front of her mouth and the words stop.

A less skilful advocate than Mr Bell would force her to say what she had thought but instead he lets the image that had presented itself to his witness that Sunday afternoon inflate in the air of the courtroom. The jury takes a collective breath.

'I think now that I might have been mistaken.'

'Really?' says Mr Bell. He sees she is about to retract the content of her statement. He sees he may need to make an application to me to cross-examine her on it. He sees he may need to argue the law. His hand reaches out for Archbold, hovers over it, draws back as he catches at a different wind and sets off on a different tack. 'I think,' he says, 'the pictures in tab three were taken by the police photographer some time after Ruth's arrest?'

Mrs Manders recovers herself. 'They were taken next morning.'

'But we have images taken closer to the time.'

'No. Those were the first.'

'You have forgotten the video recording from the arresting officer.'

She stares at him. She hasn't forgotten. She didn't know. Everyone else in the courtroom knows – we had heard it in Mr Bell's opening. Only Ruth's mother didn't know the officer had been wearing a body camera. And now she does. And there's more to come.

'We also have your 999 call.'

Mrs Manders picks up her water glass. I think, for one wild moment, she might throw it at him but she only takes a small sip of water and puts it back down.

'Let's begin with the emergency call,' says Mr Bell. 'We'll play it and you can explain to the jury what was happening.'

He hands to the usher transcripts for the jury and the witness. Mrs Manders stares at the document as if it's a viper. There is a little seat in the witness-box. I have told her she can use it whenever she wishes. Now, for the first time, she sinks into it. At the side of the courtroom, an officer moves to a machine, presses a button, turns a knob. There is crackling, a beeping, the sound of a phone ringing in another place at another time, and then, 'Emergency, which services do you want?'

We all hear a sharp in-drawing of breath then the voice of Ruth's mother, cold with shock. 'Ambulance,' she said. 'Quickly. Please. And the police.'

Mr Bell nods to the officer, who presses another button and the tape stops. He turns back to his witness.

'You called for an ambulance because Zara needed medical assistance?'

She looks at the barrister as if she has grown to hate him. 'Obviously,' she says.

'What was the problem?'

'She seemed to have difficulty breathing. She was gasping or choking . . . you can hear her on the 999 call.'

We could. We had.

'But she was fine within a very short time. It was just at that moment I thought . . .'

'You thought she couldn't breathe.' He pauses, allowing each juror to formulate in their minds the next question before asking it for them. 'And why did you ask for the police?'

She knows there is no going back but she can't see a way forward, so she is silent.

'Was it because of something you had seen?'

A pause. A nod.

'In the nursery?'

She nods again.

'But, apart from you, there had been no one in the nursery but Zara and Ruth.'

She looks up and sighs. Mr Bell waits for the sigh to reach the furthest corners of the courtroom before asking if there was a telephone in the nursery. Such an innocent question. Such a clever one.

No, she says, no telephone in the nursery. She had to go to the downstairs hall.

'And, since we can hear Zara coughing during the phone call, should we understand you took the baby with you?'

'Yes.'

'So, you did not leave the baby in the nursery with your daughter?'

The BYM rises to his feet. 'My Learned Friend is not allowed to cross-examine his own witness.'

'He's not,' I say mildly.

'No. Well . . .'

Mr Bell waits for his opponent to sink back into his seat before he says, 'Mrs Manders, won't you tell us what you saw when you opened the nursery door?' He says it quite gently. She is, after all, a reasonable woman.

She looks at him for a long moment and knows it is all up with her, with Ruth. She has come further than she meant to and, having come this far, there is nowhere to go now but to the end. She bends her head and does what she must. Briefly and without emotion she describes how she stood in the doorway and saw her daughter bending over the cot, saw the coverlet pulled back and the baby's little legs kicking out feebly and realized her daughter had the child's stuffed rabbit in her hands; how, in the split second that passed, she thought the little toy was over the baby's face and how she pushed Ruth away and snatched up the baby; how the baby seemed not able to breathe and was blue about the lips. And so . . . and so . . .

And so it is done. Mr Bell has only, now, to play the footage recorded on the camera worn by the police officer who arrived minutes after the call was made and a little before the London Ambulance Service. The recording has captured both images and sound. It shows Mrs Manders, not carefully dressed and made-up as she is now but in a house coat, breathless, clutching the baby to her. It shows a golden Labrador following her, whining anxiously. The officer wearing the bodycam asks if there is anyone else in the house, and when Ruth's mother tells him, he makes his way upstairs.

We see his boots, hear his heavy tread, his voice calling out, the silence that follows. When he walks into the nursery, we see Ruth sitting on the edge of a chair beside the empty cot. Her hands are folded neatly in her lap. The jury stare at the little screens in front of them, stare at the grainy image of Ruth as she stares at the bedroom wall.

When Mr Bell sits down, Mr Maddox rises. He makes all the points he can. The witness is more than willing to help him. She readily agrees that she didn't see everything clearly, that it was only an impression she had, that perhaps she was mistaken. He doesn't put to her what he had threatened to – that she invented the complaint against her daughter. He isn't a fool. We have all seen Mrs Manders and no one could think this woman deliberately fabricated something to get her child into trouble. But she may be mistaken – anyone may be mistaken. He pushes her as far as he dares. She even, hesitatingly, agrees that perhaps it was her snatching up the baby that shocked the child into breathlessness. She is more than happy to say she overreacted because in fact the baby was fine – no injuries were found on her and no after-effects suffered. Slowly, the points which the prosecution have built up are pulled apart. But there is nothing any defence counsel can do to take away the effect of the 999 call – the fear and shock in Mrs Manders' voice as it drifted disembodied across the courtroom.

After Mrs Manders has left the witness-box, Mr Bell calls the paramedic who attended. Yes, he confirms, the baby had clearly suffered some sort of episode. There was an obvious blueness about the lips. The child was limp and pale. But – in response to questions from the BYM – there was no injury about the face to suggest anything had been put over her mouth and nose, there was no mark on the neck to suggest strangulation. Within a short time the child had seemed perfectly normal and later tests in hospital found nothing amiss. An expert is then called to say the symptoms which had been observed were consistent with deliberately inflicted suffocation, but when cross-examined he accepts they are equally consistent with an accidental suffocation, a child who in sleep got her own little face pressed into a soft toy or a pillow. And there really isn't any more to the prosecution case. This is all Mr Bell has and he has got it before the jury.

6

The BYM has given his client a chance of acquittal. Now he must decide whether or not to call her to give evidence. To put her in the witness-box is to expose her to cross-examination. To keep her silent in the dock risks the jury inferring she has no answer to the charge. He gets to his feet and, after the slightest of hesitations, calls her forward. At the sound of her name, Ruth follows the dock officer across the courtroom. She has to hold the rail to get up the steps into the witness-box. She affirms in a small voice. When I point out the little seat behind her, she sits as if her legs won't support her. She is paler than ever and looks much younger than her years. I see what she cannot – that behind and above her the door of the public gallery opens and her mother slips in, and down to the front row, as close to her daughter as she can get.

The BYM takes Ruth through a happy childhood, a happy adolescence. She enjoyed school, but then lost interest in it and left before she took her A levels. The piano gets full play. Especially Chopin. Especially the Nocturnes. Night music. She spreads her delicate hands – long fingers curiously strong about the knuckles – on the ledge before her. Am I the only one who has a sudden image of these hands holding a stuffed toy firmly to a baby's face? Don't think of it. Concentrate on keeping a clear note of the evidence. That's the job.

The happy years give way to a happy pregnancy and birth. She can't think what her mother means by illness. She has never been ill, except for appendicitis when she was ten. There is nothing mentally wrong with her. Perhaps her mother is a little – she hesitates, delicately seeking the right word – unbalanced, she says at last. I glance up to the public gallery where Mrs Manders sinks her head into her hands. On Ruth's white face there are two hectic spots of red as she explains it is all a terrible mistake. Her mother has an overwrought imagination. The truth, as Ruth would have us believe it, was that when she looked into the nursery, she saw the baby gasping in her sleep. Alarmed, she rushed to the cot. The baby's mouth was pressed to her toy rabbit. Zara loved the rabbit and liked to have it in the cot beside her, but somehow . . . Ruth was only removing it when her mother came in. Her mother had jumped to the wrong conclusion. She would never hurt her baby and never did.

The BYM, satisfied, sits down, and Mr Bell rises to his feet. For a long second he says nothing. I understand. She has been a good witness. An excellent witness. Surely you would not hesitate to believe her; at least you would not be so sure of guilt as to convict her. But then there were the grainy grey images on the bodycam footage that showed her staring at the wall. There was the flatness of her walking down the stairs and out of her home without a backward glance even at the baby she would have us believe she loved so much. Of course images such as these can be deceptive, but still . . . There is something amiss with her story. Mr Bell knows it, but he doesn't know what it is. He doesn't know where to look for it. He begins casting around like an old bloodhound seeking the scent. He explores gently, carefully, first one avenue then another. He asks about her feelings towards the baby, difficulties her mother has spoken of – none of these things, she explains in her small clear voice, are true. Her mother fusses too much. She reconsiders the word she has used and amends it to 'worries'. Mr Bell moves on to other things.

Only once does he break through her quiet certainty and that is when he asks about the baby's father. The BYM has gone nowhere near this subject, but father there must have been. Now, when she is pressed, Ruth reddens and her eyes brighten, but I can't tell if it is with tears or anger. I see her fists tighten on the ledge in front of her but she regains her self-control and says, 'It was the briefest of relationships. It was a mistake. I barely knew him. He was never part of my life. I really would prefer not to talk about him, if you don't mind.' And what can Mr Bell do but respect this plea for privacy; for what has a past relationship which ended before Zara was born to do with this trial? One after another the openings he creates close upon him. The morning passes and he gets nowhere. I can see he is nearing the end of his options. 'Win some, lose some' says the droop of his shoulders.

'It's almost one o'clock, Mr Bell,' I say. 'Would you like to find a convenient moment to pause for lunch?'

He nods. He will finish exploring the matter he is asking about. He will consider over a cheese sandwich and a strong coffee what else he can do. He may have a question or two this afternoon. Then he will be done. It is two minutes to one o'clock. He has been questioning Ruth about her reactions when she arrived at the police station. He has already put to her how she was taken before the custody officer and booked in and had wept. But weeping is hardly a sign of murderous intent. Wouldn't we all weep if we were wrongly accused of trying to kill our children? He is looking for anything to throw light now on what she was thinking in the immediate aftermath of her arrest. He has spread before him the custody records and is scanning them over and over for inspiration. Anything, says the frown on his forehead. Anything. And then he sees it. I don't know what it is, but I know it's something. I see him focus and stare at the paper in front of him. I see the frisson of response from the BYM. He knows too. Mr Bell turns back to the witness.

'One last matter before we break for lunch,' he says. 'You must have been alarmed when you saw Zara's condition.'

Ruth inclines her head in a gesture that says 'naturally'.

'You too must have thought of seeking medical help.'

'Of course.'

'But you didn't dial 999.'

'I needed to stay with my baby. I couldn't go to the phone.'

Mr Bell pauses, adopts the look of surprise that it takes counsel years to perfect, and says, 'But you had a phone in your pocket.'

'No,' she says.

Mr Bell looks down at the custody record. On it will be listed all the items she had in her possession when she got to the police station. She knows, as I do, that in that list must be a mobile phone. She bites her lip.

'I forget,' she says. 'If I did have my phone with me, I didn't think about it.'

'You didn't think about it? Your baby was unable to breathe and you didn't think about dialling 999 on the phone in your pocket?'

She is red again. The glint is back in her eyes. 'I remember now,' she says crossly. 'The battery was flat.' Disprove that if you can, says her look.

And so the morning ends.

At two o'clock Mr Bell sends a message to say he isn't ready. I assemble the court to find out why. The jury are kept out, but Ruth is there in the dock. She is chewing a nail on one of the fingers of her long, pale hands. The blank look has gone. She is clearly distressed. Mr Bell gets to his feet.

'My Lady, I apologize, but I'm afraid I must apply for some time.'

'What is causing the delay, Mr Bell?'

'Your Ladyship will recall that just before the adjournment I was asking the defendant about her mobile phone. When we rose, I sent for it. It has taken a little while to charge. Happily, it was not PIN-locked.'

Unhappily, says the expression on Ruth Manders' face.

'In the very little time we have had I can say there is material of interest on it. I fear I must ask for the rest of the afternoon to consider its contents and comply with any duties of disclosure that then arise.'

'I see.' I don't, but no doubt in due course I will.

Ruth raises her hand as if she is a child seeking permission to speak. 'Can I talk to my barrister?' she asks.

'I'm afraid not,' I tell her.

'But there are things on the phone . . . I can explain . . .'

'I'm afraid the rule is strict. While you are in the middle of giving evidence you may not speak to any member of your legal team without my leave.'

Her face creases in distress. 'Can I have your leave?'

'Not at the moment. First I must decide if Mr Bell can complete his enquiries.'

She doesn't argue but she does something else. For the first time she looks up to the public gallery where her mother is sitting.

I ask the BYM if he has anything to say. He hasn't. He doesn't like this development but for the moment there's nothing he can do. I look again at Ruth. Her tension is palpable.

'You may have your adjournment, Mr Bell.'

The jury are sent away till the following midday. This will give the Crown time to examine the phone overnight. It can take a while to get into the secrets of a mobile phone, but this one isn't locked, and the texts and voicemails at least will be readily accessible. What they will find, if anything, only Ruth knows.

7

Next morning Mr Bell arrives with a neat file of A4 paper which he passes up to me. 'We have downloaded and printed out the text messages from Miss Manders' phone,' he says. His voice is hoarse, his eyes red with exhaustion. He must have worked all night. I suppose his officers and computer technicians did as well. They have found something, but he doesn't look triumphant, only tired and a little sad. Not nearly as sad, though, as the BYM, who also has a copy of the file in his hands. I take my file and open it. There are perhaps a couple of hundred messages. I look at Ruth. The blank look is back. Up in the public gallery her mother's seat is empty.

'They have been printed in the order they have been recovered,' says Mr Bell. 'To find the earliest ones, you have to begin at the end.'

It was ever thus. The first messages are innocuous enough. A boy has texted Ruth 'You are really special' and she has replied 'Thank you'.

'Is this relevant to the case, Mr Bell?'

'Read on,' he says grimly.

I do. I read the exchanges. He to her: 'When I watch you play the Chopin I am moved beyond words.' She replies: 'That means a lot to me. I admire you so much. You are inspirational.' He to her: 'You are beautiful like the music.' She to him: 'You have helped me so much. I feel that you have made me.'

Before I get to the end of the first page, I know these words are all wrong. The relationship is wrong. This is no exchange between a boy and girl. This is an infatuated teenager and . . . and what? Someone much older; someone who knows how to press the buttons, to manipulate, to mould. I steel myself and read on. It's obvious from the context of the messages that he and she are seeing each other every day . . . there is mention of passing each other, exchanging glances, wanting to speak but being unable to. Where could she have been on a daily basis? I look at the dates which Mr Bell has caused to be attached to each entry. These early messages are from two years ago. She was only seventeen. She was still at school . . . and then, like a key turning in a padlock, the door is opened and what was hidden is clear to the view. Everything falls into place. The piano that was her joy, no longer played. The baby's father about whom nothing must be said. The leaving of school. The onset of her change of demeanour. The anger behind her blankness. The music teacher. This case isn't about Ruth and Zara. It's about Ruth and a man who is a dark shadow in my courtroom – abusive, insidious, unseen. I look again at the texts with their awful familiarity – the Chopin is a novel touch, but the lisping praise, the promise of love, the wicked words designed to trick a child into believing she is a woman, all this I have seen a hundred times. I am trying the wrong case. I have the wrong person in the dock.

It takes me a long moment to regain control, to remind myself that of whatever crime Ruth may be the victim, the question for this jury isn't why but whether she tried to kill her baby. If she did, the actions of an abusive teacher may be the motive for her offence and may mitigate it, but they cannot provide a defence to it.

There is something awful about sitting in court reading all this. Whatever Ruth has or hasn't done, she shouldn't have to sit in front of strangers while they absorb how she was abused and abased. It's as if we are stripping her all over again. It is too hard.

'Mr Bell, I think I should rise to look at this new material.'

Mr Bell nods. 'That would be best, My Lady.'

In my room, armed with a cup of strong coffee, I read it all.

The affair had begun before Christmas of the year she was in the lower sixth and developed over two terms. By Easter, the exchanges were overtly sexual. By summer she was pregnant. The thought of a baby thrilled and frightened her in equal measure. He was instantly, cruelly, sobered. He fell out of passion as if he had been tipped out of a hammock. His messages changed as if they were written by another man. She must have an abortion, he said. But why, she replied, when we could live together with our child? He told her he could not leave his wife, his children, his job . . . he would lose everything. It's clear he had no intention of doing this, however beautifully she played nocturnes. Leave school, he told her. You can pick up your education later, he said. Her responses were heart-breaking. I read through her infatuation, her bewilderment, her fear, her despair, her bitterness, and finally her hatred. She would not have an abortion. She was too much a child herself to understand why not. And in the end, it was too late. The pregnancy became obvious to her parents. She told him that if he wouldn't support her, they would. Good, he said. Just that. Good. As if anything in this was good.

And then, he asked if her parents knew who the father was. No, she texted back, but she will tell them unless . . . God, he said. Don't do this to me, Ruth. Don't do this to my wife and my children. They are innocent, he said. So is our baby, she replied. The more she texted him, the less he replied. In the end he was barely responding at all. Not even when the little girl was born. But she never stopped messaging him. Night after night. Finally he did answer. 'What do you want of me? I'll give you money. I'll give you anything if you will just leave me alone.' This came from him at 2.32 in the morning . . . was he lying in bed with his wife while he sent it? Later that day Ruth did or didn't press Zara's little pink rabbit over Zara's little blue lips.

I think of her that last night, lying in her bed in the cream-and-beige bedroom with the baby in the adjoining nursery. I think of her clutching the phone, reading over and over his last message. And I read over and over her reply: 'I'll make you sorry. You watch what I do.' I try to think myself into her head as she lay there. Could she hear Zara snuffling contentedly in baby sleep? Did she think of the child with love, or as a bargaining tool, or only as a daily reminder of how she had been treated; a reminder that would always be there unless . . .

I have to accept it. This isn't the effect of giving birth or lactation. This is an abused child, hurt and frightened, trying to hurt and frighten in return. How could I have been so foolishly presumptuous as to conjure up an attempted infanticide? I had allowed myself to imagine something of which there had never been a scintilla of evidence. And now I am going to have to confront things about which there is only too much evidence. An abusive teacher, and the question of what is going to happen to this trial.

When I finish reading the file, I reassemble the court. 'Mr Bell, Mr Maddox, the evidential landscape has changed and now a number of alternative scenarios arise. One is that this material is ignored and the trial proceeds as before. I assume that is unrealistic?'

'I'm afraid it is, My Lady,' says Mr Bell.

I turn to the BYM.

'I am in a difficult position, My Lady. I haven't been able to take instructions. While my client is still in the middle of giving evidence—'

'Mr Maddox, no one would expect you to commit yourself until you have had the opportunity to speak to Miss Manders. In the circumstances I'm sure Mr Bell won't object?'

Mr Bell doesn't and I give leave to the BYM – no longer so bright, no longer so young – to talk to his client though she is still giving evidence.

'Mr Bell, while Mr Maddox takes instructions from his client I'd be grateful if you would take instructions from yours.'

'From the CPS?'

'Yes. Of course I wouldn't dream of putting any pressure on you or them. But the Crown might wish to consider if a motive other than actually killing Zara now arises?'

'Does Your Ladyship mean there may be a crime with an intent less . . . less heinous than murder?'

'I mean is there a realistic possibility that if Miss Manders put the toy over Zara's mouth, she was trying to frighten the baby's father, to hurt him rather than the child. I only ask you to consider. I only say that in achieving justice you will want to look at all possible alternatives.'

Mr Bell's face gives nothing away. 'I will reflect, My Lady.'

8

Next morning Bill looks into my room and says, 'They're not ready for you.'

'What are they up to, Bill?'

'You tell me.' He sounds querulous. 'Mr Bell had a conference with the CPS and Mr Maddox had a conference with the defendant. Then Mr Bell and Mr Maddox had a conference with each other. Then a police officer was brought in. Then the girl's mother. My corridor is like Piccadilly Circus in the rush hour.'

'Poor Bill. Still, this is an odd one and we must let it take its course.'

'I like a trial to be a trial,' says Bill morosely. 'I don't like all this starting and stopping. I like to hear the evidence come from the witnesses and the speeches from the barristers and the verdicts from the jury. That's what I like.'

'Me too, Bill. But sometimes it doesn't work like that. Tell counsel to let me know when they're ready.'

'And what am I supposed to tell the jury?'

'Tell them they have plenty of time for a coffee.'

'They'll have caffeine poisoning before this case is done.'

Finally I am called back into court where Ruth, the barristers and some harassed-looking police officers are waiting. Ruth's mother is back in her seat in the public gallery.

'My Lady,' says Mr Bell, 'the Crown has been considering the material recently uncovered on the defendant's mobile phone.'

'We have all been considering it, Mr Bell.'

'On one view we believe the texts are capable of supporting the Crown's case on attempted murder. They provide a motive for the killing that was absent before. On another view we can see that the texts are capable of a different interpretation . . . that the defendant was trying to draw attention to her plight or to exert pressure on the baby's father, rather than to actually kill the child.' He pauses.

Is the Crown going to drop the allegation of attempted murder? Would I have done so in the days when I was at the Bar? Probably not. But I would have been sufficiently concerned to give the jury an alternative lesser offence to consider as well as the attempted murder. What alternative would I have been thinking of? Without a psychiatric report, and with those texts, it wouldn't have been attempted infanticide, even if there is such an offence . . .

'My Lady, we maintain the case of attempted murder,' he says, 'but we have concluded that we should in fairness add an alternative lesser charge – that of child cruelty.' He hands up a new indictment. The count of attempted murder is now neatly headed 'Count One'. Beneath it is set out 'Count Two: child cruelty'.

'You are making an application to amend the indictment by the addition of a second and alternative charge?'

'I am, My Lady.'

'Mr Maddox?'

Mr Maddox says 'Ummm . . .', which I interpret as 'If this new count isn't added, the jury can only acquit her entirely or convict

her entirely of attempted murder.' He follows this with 'Errrr . . .',
which I take to mean 'But if the new count is added there's a halfway
house, which is preferable to conviction of attempted murder'; and
finally, 'Oofff.' This is clearly 'What are the odds one way or the
other?'

With this, I cannot help poor Mr Maddox. He must resolve it
himself.

'I have no objection to the new Count Two,' he says at last. 'But I
do object to the Crown producing these texts.'

'How can you?' says Mr Bell. 'They are clearly relevant and probative. To keep them from the jury would be to deprive them of
material going directly to an issue they must decide, namely whether
or not Ruth Manders tried to kill her baby.'

'I accept they are relevant,' says Mr Maddox, 'but they have come
too late. It's not fair. I have conducted my whole case on the basis
that no such texts existed.'

'So have I,' said Mr Bell. 'And whose fault is that? Who knew
about them all the time? Who kept their existence a secret from us
both?' He doesn't turn to look at the dock. He doesn't need to.

I consider the submissions. Mr Bell is right – the texts are relevant to the case. They should be before the jury and would have
been, had he discovered them earlier. Mr Maddox is right – it is
very late to be adding into the mix such potent evidence. He might
have conducted his case differently had he known about it. Whose
fault is that? Ruth could have told him about the phone, but it's the
Crown's job to find the relevant material. It was in their possession
and examining it would have been a simple and obvious thing to do.
There's no point in trying to apportion blame. Or rather, the better
point is to work out something that will give both sides a fair trial. I
know what it is. I know neither of them will like it.

'Gentlemen, I am satisfied the material in the texts is so relevant
and probative that it cannot be shut out.'

Mr Bell smiles. The BYM frowns.

'However, I am equally satisfied it is too late for it to be adduced before this jury.'

The BYM smiles. Mr Bell frowns.

'So I propose to discharge this jury from bringing in a verdict, and to order a retrial.'

Both men frown.

'At the retrial, the Crown may adduce evidence of the texts and the defence will have plenty of time to prepare for that.'

9

The jury discharged, there is one administrative matter left to deal with. We have a new Count Two and Ruth must be asked what her plea is to it. The process is called arraignment. Angelique gets to her feet.

'Ruth Manders,' she says, 'you are indicted on Count Two with cruelty to a person under sixteen contrary to section 1(1) of the Children and Young Persons Act 1933 in that being a person who had attained the age of sixteen years and having responsibility for Zara, a child under that age, you wilfully ill-treated the said child in a manner likely to cause unnecessary suffering to the said child or injury to its health. Ruth Manders, how do you plead, guilty or not guilty?'

'Guilty,' says Ruth. Just like that. Angelique stares at her. So do I. So do the barristers and everyone else in the courtroom. We are all, suddenly, very silent. The only sound comes from the public gallery where Ruth's mother has clapped a hand over her mouth.

I lean forward. 'Did you say "guilty", Miss Manders?'

'Yes.'

'Did you mean to say that?'

'Yes. It's all out now. There's no reason to lie any more. I did it, and it was a terrible thing to do. I was just so angry and so . . . I never meant to kill Zara. I would never have really hurt her. But it was cruel, wasn't it? It was . . . what your clerk said . . . child cruelty.'

The BYM is on his feet begging for a moment with his client, to find out what . . . to make sure that . . . to check she understands . . . Of course I will give him all the time he wants, but I don't think it will make any difference. Ruth, at long last, is past the lies. And when – if – her plea is confirmed, Mr Bell will need more time to speak to the CPS lawyer to see if this plea will suffice or whether the Crown still wants a trial on attempted murder.

Yet again I rise. During this case I have spent more time out of the courtroom than in it. Matters have taken the strangest twists and turns. Sometimes that's how it goes. But we are, after all, within sight of the end. I don't think Ruth will change her mind now. I don't think the CPS will press for a trial on attempted murder. To do so they would have to conclude there was a more-than-even chance a jury would reject what she said to me. Mr Bell heard the candour with which she spoke and how it contrasted with every word she had uttered before.

And if I'm right about both these things? Then what remains? At some point I will have to sentence Ruth for child cruelty. I might just as well have a look at the Guideline now, while I'm waiting for them to sort themselves out.

The Sentencing Council's Definitive Guidelines require the judge to assess in each case the culpability of the defendant, the harm done, the aggravating and the mitigating features.* To assess Ruth's culpability, I will need to consider her mental state; and to do that I

* See Appendix D, pp. 290–2.

will at long last have to get a psychiatric report. I'm confident now that Ruth will cooperate. It is possible that her culpability is high, involving deliberate disregard for the welfare of the victim. But even if it is, the harm she has caused – there being little or no measurable physical, psychological, developmental or emotional injury to Zara – is low. The Guideline tells me that for such an offence I should start with twelve months' imprisonment, then adjust it up or down within the range, according to the aggravating and mitigating features of the case. The range falls between a high-level community order and a sentence of up to thirty months. This is a different ball-park from sentences for attempted murder. She is automatically entitled to release when she has served half of any prison sentence I might impose. She has already served five months – the equivalent of a ten-month sentence. But when she is released, what then? I need a pre-sentence report to see what suggestions the probation services will make about where Ruth might live and what access she should have to Zara both in the short and long term. Social Services and perhaps the family courts will want some say in this – after all and before all, Zara must be kept safe. But the baby has a loving grandmother, and Ruth has a loving mother. There may be no happy ending for Ruth, but we can all give it our best shot. After all, more than Ruth's future depends on this.

1 0

And lastly, there is what many right-minded people might think should have come first . . . the music teacher. Like so many offences, underlying that in Regina v. Manders there is another. Ruth Manders is both victim and perpetrator.

'Someone has to do something about it,' says H over tea. 'I mean about him. The teacher. He has committed serious crimes.'*

'The prosecutor is handing all the material over to a specialist unit for investigation. The music master is about to get his comeuppance. He won't get away with it.'

But of course he has been getting away with it, probably for years. The chances of Ruth being his first victim are slim. There will have been other girls. Maybe his way in to them had been Bach or the Blues rather than Chopin, but one way or another he will have worked himself into the hearts, into the bodies, of others before Ruth. One 'favourite' every few years would seem about average for such offenders.

And it's not just teachers. The crime of which Ruth Manders was a victim goes on all about us, unseen and undetected. When a murder is committed, it is rare that it doesn't come to light, and quickly. The same is true for burglary, criminal damage, kidnap and the vast majority of offending. Though we may not always bring the wrongdoer to justice, at least we know the crime has happened. But too often, with the sort of abuse that Ruth suffered, no one knows. It goes on not only in institutions and organizations but in our homes; and not just those homes where overcrowding can mean small children share beds with older siblings and parents, but in affluent households where separate bedrooms and studies allow the privacy for such things to flourish. It breeds in porn-laden computers and grows and spreads among those with similar interests. The development of the internet and social media provides a platform for abusers to meet each other and to access their victims. It is an insidious and wicked crime not least because it can make a child feel like a collaborator. It can turn a victim into an abuser. And it leaves a permanent scar on so many others.

* See Appendix E, p. 293.

Most Crown Court judges have tried defendants who were teachers or sports coaches or scout masters or priests or babysitters or workers in children's homes. Wherever we place trust, abusers will come, determined to betray that trust. Children of any age, in any situation, can become victims. A huge number of the cases that come before the courts do so only many years, sometimes decades, after the events themselves. Why does it take so long for these offences to come to light? Why are sexual abusers of children so notoriously difficult to bring to justice? There are some obvious and some, perhaps, less obvious reasons.

Firstly, many children just don't complain. They don't tell us what is happening to them. Or at least not in ways we comprehend. Sometimes that is because they are not sure if what has been done to them is wrong. Sometimes it's because they are too frightened. Sometimes they are too hurt, too embarrassed, or they think that by taking the harm upon themselves they are protecting another child, perhaps a younger sibling, from it. Adolescents often blame themselves for their predicament or they are tricked into believing they have consented. It is the abuser's stock-in-trade to make a child feel special, to feel different, to feel apart. And nothing makes a child more vulnerable than feeling they stand alone.

Even when children do complain, they are too often ignored or disbelieved. The teacher who abuses will have spent years building up a picture of himself as someone with status in society, someone doing good, someone clean-living and deserving of respect. The longer their offending has gone on, the more they believe they are untouchable.

The problem is also partly the responsibility of the criminal justice system itself. The adversarial court case is very difficult for a child or young person to cope with. These days we do what we can to alleviate the stress and the unfairness to a child witness by putting into place 'special measures' – for example, a screen, a video link, pre-recorded evidence – but still a trial can be brutal for the witness who all too easily can appear doubtful, unsure of detail, unable to find the words needed to describe to strangers what they have been through. It can be hard for jurors to be sure they can rely on the word of the child. Few cases will be as easy to prove as that involving Ruth, whose baby's DNA will tell its own story. Usually it is the word of the child against the adult. Often the child has presented as troubled, difficult, a liar or a fantasist – not least because abusers so often target troubled children. It is hard for jurors to give all of this due weight when measuring it against the very high standard of proof that the law requires for a conviction.

Police investigations are really the key to presenting in court evidence capable of securing convictions against the guilty. Often the way to get justice for one child is by getting justice for many others. It may be difficult for jurors judging the word of one defendant against one witness, but when a long train of witnesses – many of whom will not even know each other – all attest to the same abusive behaviour by the same defendant, juries seldom find it difficult to convict. To put together many witnesses – tracing victims from decades before who may have moved abroad, taken different names, tried to put the past behind them – takes patient hard work by dedicated police units with expertise in this field. But when it has been done, convictions usually follow.

And convictions by juries are needed because sexual offenders seldom plead guilty, or at least they seldom plead guilty to anything like the full wrong they have done. Rather than accept their guilt, they may prefer to be convicted by a jury because then they can say 'the jury got it wrong' and they can go on telling the same lie they have been telling for years: 'I did nothing wrong.'

There are no easy answers to why sexual abuse is not stopped where its commission must be clear to at least some of those who know the perpetrator. Perhaps it goes unchecked because to credit it is to acknowledge what we cannot bear to accept. Perhaps it goes unseen because we cannot believe what our eyes are showing us. If so, we all need to open our eyes. Because in many cases the guilty could not go on hurting children week after month after year unless we, the innocent all around, let them. Which makes the innocent not so innocent after all.

TRIAL THREE:

In the Vale of Tears

JUDE SAT IN the wreck of the car, trying to work out what
had happened. Across his lap lay Lamb. A moment before,
Lamb had been laughing, but he wasn't laughing now. Jude's
hand was caught in the twisted steering wheel. He extricated
it with difficulty and touched Lamb's cheek. Warm. But
Lamb's neck was at an impossible angle. Something long and
thin that should have been outside the car had somehow got
inside. Jude stared at it. It was a sort of pole, with a rectangle
of metal on which were numbers in little squares. He
frowned. He was sure he had seen something like this often
before, but he couldn't focus properly. The numbers seemed
both familiar and random.

'It's a bus stop, thicko,' said Lamb with a smile.

And it was. At least it was part of a bus stop, though Lamb
did not say what it was doing inside the car; could not say,
because it was clear to Jude – even in his fogged state – that
Lamb could not speak. Not with his neck at that angle.

Jude concentrated on the pole. It had come through the
windscreen. He didn't suppose the pole had got up and
walked into the road, so he must have left the road and driven
into the bus stop. He looked at the face in his lap. Lamb was
shining like an angel. At first Jude thought only that that was
entirely appropriate. Then he realized Lamb was covered in a
thousand tiny fragments of broken glass. He turned his
attention back to the pole. Its tip was buried in the back of
the passenger seat. Lamb had been sitting there. Lucky Lamb

wasn't wearing a seat belt, he thought, or he'd have been skewered by the pole. Though perhaps not so lucky, he now thought, looking again at Lamb's head twisted almost backwards in his lap.

In the car it was very silent but beyond the silence, somewhere else, were screams and sirens. He decided to stay inside the car. Just for a while. Just him and Lamb.

After a moment he leaned close to his friend. 'I'm sorry,' he whispered.

'No,' said Lamb. 'It was my fucking fault.'

Which again struck him as curious because Lamb shouldn't have spoken. Because Lamb was dead.

1

IN MY ROOM AT the Old Bailey, I turn on the computer and tap the icon that lets me into the Digital Case System. Every case in every Crown Court in the country is now at my fingertips as long as my fingertips hit the right keys. (Is this why it's called Digital?) The DCS allows every case to be uploaded and has endless sections for every conceivable thing you might want to upload. A place for everything. A miracle of the new paperless world of my work. At least it would be, if only people uploaded things where they should. I call up the case of Regina v. Jude Derwent. I'm looking for the recorded interview between the defendant and investigating officers. I look in Exhibits. I look in Transcripts. I look in all the places where it might reasonably be, before finding it in a place it shouldn't be at all. I tap and click my way into a system that allows me to play back the interview. I close my eyes and it is no longer seven o'clock on a summer's morning at the Old Bailey. It's a cold, wet winter's afternoon, and darkness has already fallen outside the police station.

'This interview is being recorded. The time is 5 p.m. The day is the eleventh of December and we are in Interview Room A at Darkwell Custody Centre. I am DS Mallory attached to the Serious Crime Command. With me is . . .'

'DC Coburn, also from Serious Crime Command.'

'We are interviewing . . . state your full name, Jude.'

Jude Derwent does. It's the first time I have heard him speak. His voice is thick with tears. After all, he is only twenty years old, and it's less than two days since he killed his best friend. Once Jude's solicitor has also identified himself, DS Mallory turns to business.

'Jude, I must remind you that while you are in police custody you have a right to speak privately with your solicitor whenever you wish, and we can pause the interview if you want to do that. Now I'm going to caution you. You do not have to say anything but it may harm your defence if you do not mention when questioned something which you later rely on in court; anything you do say may be given in evidence. Shall I break that down for you?'

Without waiting for an answer, DS Mallory does so, briskly, efficiently. He has done it a hundred times before. There is the sound of paper rustling as he consults his notes.

'OK, Jude, you have been arrested on a charge of causing death by dangerous driving. Do you understand? I see you're nodding, but the recording can't pick up a nod. You need to answer.'

'Yes.'

'Yes, you understand why you've been arrested?'

A sniff. A pause. I imagine Jude wiping away the tears that are flowing down his cheeks.

'Of course I know why I've been arrested. I crashed the car and killed Lamb.'

DS Mallory isn't used to getting a confession before he has even asked a question. He sounds put out as he says, 'We'll get to that shortly. First, I want to know what you and Lambert – Lamb – were doing in Corbutt Road yesterday afternoon. Why were you there, Jude?'

'We went for a drive.' The voice is suddenly wary.

'A drive. OK. But why there? Why in Corbutt Road?'

Perhaps Jude always finds it difficult to lie. Perhaps it's just the circumstances. He pauses, no doubt thinking furiously. Finally he says, 'Why not there?'

'Corbutt Road is the home turf of a gang called the G-men.'

'I don't know what you're talking about.'

'I think you do.'

'I don't. Why should I? I'm not a member of the . . . what did you call it, the G-men.'

'I know you're not, Jude. That's why I'm wondering what you were doing on their territory.'

'It's a free country. Me and Lamb could go there if we wanted to.'

'You could. You did. But we want to know if you went there deliberately to confront the G-men.'

'Of course not. Why would we do that?'

'Perhaps because you are – were – members of a rival gang. A gang like Heat 451. Perhaps because a guy from Heat got stabbed last week. Perhaps because he was stabbed by one of the G-men and Heat wanted revenge.' There is a long silence before DS Mallory says, 'None of that mean anything to you, Jude? Did you know the guy who got stabbed?'

A sigh, or something like a sigh, then, 'My head hurts. I got banged up bad in the accident.'

'Not as bad as Lambert. Lambert is dead.'

These last words are spoken by DC Coburn. It's the first thing he's said since his name. He's pushing his suspect. This might be a clever tactic – it might get Jude to talk – but it turns out not to be clever at all. It pushes Jude too far. A sob escapes him, and the solicitor intervenes.

'I think that's enough, I'd like my client to see a doctor.'

DS Mallory takes over again. 'He's seen a doctor. He's seen two. He's had X-rays. He's had medical treatment. He's been declared fit for interview.'

'His head hurts.'

In the pause that follows, racking sobs can be heard. At last DS Mallory says, 'Interview terminated.'

To discover what happened next at Darkwell, I have to go on a voyage of exploration. Deep in the DCS, I finally uncover Statement 175 made by the custody sergeant. A doctor had been called, who pre-scribed something for Jude's pain – probably aspirin under another name – and next day he was interviewed again. I need to find the next recording. I look in the places where it has no business to be and find it quickly. I feel smug. I could get good at this. But after all that, there is nothing of interest on it. Jude took his solicitor's advice and answered 'no comment' to all the questions he was asked.

2

Even after I have turned off the computer, it's hard to leave the police station behind. Of course, the weeping boy is no longer there. He was taken to the Magistrates' Court, remanded in custody in a Young Offender Institution and is now down in the cells of the Old Bailey, waiting to be brought up before me for a Plea and Trial Preparation Hearing where he will enter his plea – guilty or not guilty – and I will make orders for the trial or sentence that will follow. Such hearings are short and require only the presence of the defendant, counsel for the prosecution and defence, and myself. There will be no evidence, no witnesses, no jury; nothing that should raise the level of emotion. But I can't help wondering how Jude will cope when he's asked in open court if he accepts responsibility for killing his best friend.

This morning Esme is my usher. She is round and comfortable and motherly. She worries over her judges. Part of this worrying involves her standing me by the window and inspecting me. She finds an errant dog hair on my gown and, tutting, removes it. Dog hairs are a hazard of my job. As well as the courts, the Old Bailey houses the two City of London Sheriffs whose job it is to support and advise the Lord Mayor of London. There are new Sheriffs every twelve months. During their year living in the Old Bailey they often bring a dog or two with them. The dog of the moment is a hairy one. Esme turns me about and tuts again. While she does this, she says, 'That poor man.'

'What poor man is that, Esme?'

'The little lamb's dad.'

We have dogs but no lambs that I know of. Though it's an idea.

'The father of the dead boy,' she adds, still studying my gown.

'Lambert's father? He's come for the PTPH?'

'The family liaison officer says he's been everywhere the defendant goes – the hospital, the police station, the Magistrates' Court. He even went to the Young Offender Institution.'

'Is he all right?'

She shrugs. 'It depends what you mean by all right.'

Of course he's not all right. His son is dead. All bereaved parents have the keenest, the closest, interest in the trial process. They want to understand – to walk the last hours and minutes of their child's life with them, to feel what they felt. They think they want justice – sometimes they do – but mostly they want vengeance. Their child has suffered. They are suffering. Understandably, they want those responsible to suffer too. But the law is not made for the sharp blade of revenge. It is a dull-edged tool designed for nothing but the careful application of itself.

Today's hearing should be largely administrative and managerial, but as soon as I go into the courtroom I am aware of the atmosphere. The air is shimmering with anguish. Jude Derwent is in the dock, head bent, shoulders hunched, standing very still, as if he is trying to erase himself from the scene. Perhaps he is succeeding because it's hard to focus on him. My attention is pulled to the side of the court where a man in short shirtsleeves sits. He is a head taller than the family liaison officer beside him, and twice as broad. There is a sheen of sweat across his forehead. A barely suppressed fury comes from him like heat haze. His eyes are fixed on Jude, his mouth open as if ready to shout, but the officer lays a warning hand on him and the man closes his lips to keep the words inside.

The prosecutor gets to her feet. 'I represent the Crown, My Lady. The defendant is represented by Mr Burt. We are ready for arraignment.'

'Very well, Miss Caldwell.' I nod to my clerk, who asks Jude to stand, and I see him properly for the first time. He is tall and gawky like a half-formed thing. He is wearing a sweatshirt. The sleeves barely reach his wrists. His hair falls over his eyes, which he closes as if he can't bear to look straight at the world. Lamb's father half rises. The liaison officer whispers something and he sinks back into his seat, but he can't stay silent, not in the face of the affront that is Jude. He turns to the officer and says loud enough for everyone to hear,

'I took that little bastard in. I fed him and gave him a bed. I made him welcome and he . . . he . . .'

Esme goes over to him and puts an arm round his shoulder. She is so small and he so big she can barely reach across his back. She says something to him. He subsides. I pretend I'm unaware of any of it. Of all the anguish that passes through my courtroom, there is nothing like that of a parent who has lost a child.

'Arraign the defendant, please,' I say to my clerk. Arraignment is a formal process. Formal words. A formal question put. A formal answer required.

'Jude Derwent, you are indicted on a count of causing death by dangerous driving contrary to section 1 of the Road Traffic Act 1988. The particulars of the offence are that you, on the tenth of December 20—, drove a mechanically propelled vehicle dangerously on a road and thereby caused the death of Lambert Dixon. Jude Derwent, how do you plead, guilty or not guilty?'

What is it like to be Jude, right now? Standing there, accused of killing your best friend, under the eyes of his father, under the eyes of everyone. No doubt he feels his own terrible grief, but will he bring himself to publicly accept responsibility for Lamb's death? I don't know. Perhaps he doesn't either. Perhaps no one knows what they will say until the moment comes when they must speak.

At first, he says nothing. His barrister turns, tries to meet his eye, nods encouragingly.

'Jude Derwent,' repeats my clerk, 'do you plead guilty or not guilty?' Jude looks down. 'Guilty,' he says.

'Bastard.' Mr Dixon spits the word across the court. What would he have said if Jude had pleaded not guilty?

I look at the liaison officer and shake my head. Esme speaks again to Mr Dixon. I let it go a second time. I won't be able to do it a third. Both counsel rise to their feet.

'My Lady,' says Miss Caldwell, 'there is an issue between the Crown and the defence that needs to be resolved.'

This distracts me from Mr Dixon. 'An issue? But the defendant has accepted his guilt of the offence.'

'Yes, My Lady, but it is the Crown's case that the defendant went to Corbutt Road because it is the home territory of a gang called' – she looks down, turns a page – 'the G-men. The prosecution says that, among a number of features which aggravate this offence, Derwent deliberately set out to taunt members of that gang; and we say this is because the G-men are rivals to his own gang.' She goes on to explain that the defence disputes this, but her words are lost in the noise that now comes from the side of the court where Mr Dixon is whispering fiercely.

'A gang member!' He is outraged. Not only has he harboured and helped a boy who has killed his own son, but the viper in his nest belonged to some gang! His disgust is only too plain. He can't contain himself, and suddenly the liaison officer can't contain him either. Neither can Esme. He is on his feet. 'You little thug. You little . . . a gang? You kept that from us all, didn't you! You kept that from Lamb!'

Jude bites his lip and looks away.

'Please, Mr Dixon,' I say. Two police officers step forward. I indicate for them to wait a moment. 'Mr Dixon . . .'

But Lamb's father is beyond himself. 'You deceived Lamb and you killed him. Christ. And to think I let it happen. I should have seen you for what you are!' He steps forward and the officers take hold of him. He throws off their arms and storms out of the courtroom.

I wait for the dust to settle.

'Miss Caldwell, I understand a father's grief, and I won't treat Mr Dixon's conduct as a contempt of court on this occasion, but I am afraid he is not to come back into the courtroom until he has calmed down and can control himself.'

Miss Caldwell nods. Mr Burt decides his better course is to act as if nothing has happened, which in the circumstances is eminently sensible. He hands up a document headed 'Basis of Plea'. I read it.

IN THE CENTRAL CRIMINAL COURT
BETWEEN:

Regina

-v-

Jude Derwent

BASIS OF PLEA

1. The defendant accepts he was driving the motor vehicle at the time the accident occurred. He accepts he was going too fast and lost control of the car but asserts that would not have happened merely because of his speed. He asserts it happened because a group of youths in the road threw bricks at his car and struck at it with sticks. It was this, combined with his excessive speed, which caused him to lose control of the car.

2. He does not accept the Crown's contention that he deliberately taunted and inflamed the youths who behaved in this manner. But he does accept his speed was dangerous in the circumstances, and that this was in part responsible for the accident and the death that followed. However he prays in aid that the responsibility did not lie entirely with him. He is deeply remorseful and bereft at the death of his friend.

The 'Basis of Plea' is supposed to represent Jude's position, but the language is pure lawyer. It's a dialect of Mr Burt not Derwent. I'm willing to bet Jude Derwent has never 'prayed in aid' anything in his young life, and never will.

'Miss Caldwell and I have been discussing,' says Mr Burt, 'whether a Newton Hearing is necessary. She thinks it is. I hope to persuade Your Ladyship it is not.'

Newton Hearings. In the Crown Court they are common enough, though I suppose you could go through a dozen Clapham omnibuses before you found anyone who knows about them. The Newton in question was one John Robert* and in 1982 he was charged with anal rape of his wife and appeared first at the Old Bailey, then in the Court of Appeal (Criminal Division). The words used by the CACD have come down on tablets of law reports which bind me now. The judgement amounts to this: where a defendant pleads guilty but there are differing factual bases put forward by prosecution and defence for the offence, and where these would lead to different sentences, I am not allowed simply to accept the prosecution's version; either I must accept the defendant's or hear evidence to decide which version is right.

So the first task is to decide if the competing versions of the facts would lead to different sentences. Miss Caldwell says they would.

* Regina v. Newton (John Robert) (1983) 77 Cr. App. R. 13. For the thankfully unusual facts, see Appendix F, p. 294.

She invites me to look at the Sentencing Council's Guideline on Causing Death by Dangerous Driving. While I am finding the right page, Mr Dixon returns, chastened but still upset. He glares at Jude as if he'd like to use the Guideline upon him as Mr Newton used his penis upon his wife. It makes no difference to Jude, who is sunk deep in his own despair.

'The statutory maximum sentence,' says Miss Caldwell crisply, 'is fourteen years.'

Not enough, says Mr Dixon's face. Not even in the right ballpark.

'The Guideline provides three categories of seriousness, depending on whether the danger to which the defendant has exposed others is "great" or "substantial" or only "significant". If he has created great danger . . .'

He has, says Mr Dixon's face. He did. He killed my boy.

'. . . the starting point for sentence is one of eight years.'

Mr Dixon registers frank disbelief – only eight years! I try not to think how he will react when he learns that eight years would be reduced by a third for the defendant's early guilty plea, and of the resulting five years four months he would serve only half. I drag my attention back to Miss Caldwell.

'The middle category has a starting point of five years, and the lowest category, of three years.'

I think that Mr Dixon might have an apoplexy. 'Miss Caldwell, the starting point isn't the finishing point. Each category also provides a range within which a sentence would normally fall.'

She is quick to pick up on this. 'That is the very thing upon which the Crown relies. In our submission, if Derwent's driving was part of an ongoing gang dispute, played out on the public streets, putting innocent pedestrians and other road users at risk, the starting point should move up to the top of the most serious range. That is to say, close to fourteen years.'

Mr Dixon nods energetically.

'On the other hand,' she continues, 'if Your Ladyship sentences on the defendant's basis, the case will fall into the lowest category, the bottom end of which is as little as two years. Once that is reduced by a third for his guilty plea, and the time he has already spent in custody, he will be free almost immediately. Accordingly, we submit, the basis on which you sentence will make a vast difference, and there must be a Newton Hearing to decide it.'

Mr Burt tries, in hope rather than expectation, to convince me of the opposite, and that I should just accept the defence contention.

Of course there must be a Newton Hearing. But the consequences for Jude if I don't accept his account are draconian.

'Mr Burt,' I say, 'you are aware that if there is such a hearing and I find against your client, he is at risk of losing the credit for his plea of guilty.' Seeing the expression on his face I add, 'I don't make the law, Mr Burt. I only apply it. The one third discount is meant to reflect a defendant's taking full responsibility for what he did – to save witnesses giving evidence, to save the court's time and public money, and above all to demonstrate his remorse. If he disputes the Crown's case in a Newton Hearing, I may accept his account. But if I don't accept it, he loses all or part of the discount.'

'Double whammy,' says Mr Burt. Unlawyerly though the language is, it accurately sums up the position.

If Jude wins this argument and I sentence him on the basis there was dangerous driving but no gang rivalry involved, he wins big. His sentence falls to the lowest level and he gets a third off. He will probably be released immediately. If he loses, he really loses. He gets sentenced at the highest level and does not get his third off. There's a middle ground: he could accept the Crown's assertion that this incident had a 'gang background'. That way, although he would be sentenced at the higher level, he would still get his third off. Mr Burt could advise him to do this, but the only person who knows what really happened is Jude. Only he can decide what to do.

'Miss Caldwell, Mr Burt, can we deal with the matter today?'

Miss Caldwell frowns. 'I don't think so, My Lady. Now the defence has explained its position, I must disclose to them some material in the Crown's possession.'

The hairs on the back of my neck rise. Why has the Crown with-held material? If it helped the defence, she had a duty to disclose it previously. If it helped the prosecution, why did she keep it back? Something is going on. Miss Caldwell is leaning towards Mr Burt, whispering. Mr Burt's eyes are widening. His lips form a single syl-lable. While he is struggling to digest whatever she has told him, she says, 'My Lady, I believe we can be ready by next Monday.'

'Mr Burt?'

Mr Burt nods, apparently beyond words.

3

The rest of my week is occupied with another case, but on Friday a thick file of papers appears in my room. It bears the title 'Prosecution Mater-ial relevant to the sentencing of Jude Derwent'. The first page reads:

Tab 1: Crown's opening note

Tab 2: Defendant's Basis of Plea

Tab 3: The Crown's position on gangs

Tab 4: Crown's evidence in support of its position
       Stop and search records
       Police National Computer checks
       Intelligence

Tab 5: Sentencing Council's Guideline on Causing Death by
       Dangerous Driving

Tab 6: Case law and authorities
Tab 7: Impact statements
   Paul Dixon (father)
   Melanie Dixon (sister, aged ten)
   Sally Dixon (sister, aged eight)

I push the file into my bag and take it home to work on over the weekend. I have already seen tab two. Tabs five and six are familiar from other cases. The rest must be read, studied, digested. But not tonight.

It's Sunday morning when I settle down with the file. The weak sun seeps across my desk. There's a tree outside the window. Shadows dance over the papers, taking on the shape of two boys. Neither Jude nor Lambert can see this sun. And if Mr Dixon can, he's surely closing his eyes against it. To a bereaved parent, the taking of any pleasure seems like a betrayal of grief and love. Get on with it, I tell myself. Start with the impact statements. These will be the hardest, the most painful to read. Get the worst out of the way first. So I turn to tab seven.

VICTIM PERSONAL STATEMENTS

Criminal Procedure Rules, r 27.2; Criminal Justice Act 1967, s.9; Magistrates' Courts Act 1980, s.5B. Statement of Paul Dixon. Age: Over 18.

This statement consisting of one page signed by me is true to the best of my knowledge and belief and I make it knowing that, if it is tendered in evidence, I shall be liable to prosecution if I have wilfully stated in it anything which I know to be false, or do not believe to be true.

I have been asked by the Police if I could write a short statement about the impact the death of my son Lambert has had on my family and me. I can say it has broken us. Lambert was everything to me and his sisters. After the death of his mother seven years ago I thought we would never smile again, but Lambert made our lives worthwhile. He was always laughing and lit up the house. He was kind and thoughtful. He was bright and though he wasn't academic I knew he had a great future ahead of him. I could not have been prouder of him. Now he is gone I can't see a way forward. Neither can the girls. I cannot put into words the emptiness that surrounds us all. I am so angry that my Lamb's life has been taken from him by the wickedness of his so-called best friend. I am disgusted to learn Jude is a gang member. I am sickened to think I made him welcome in my home. I don't know how I am going to go on without my boy. I don't know how my girls will manage without their brother.

Paul Dixon (father)

After this there's a statement from Melanie. She says: 'I dream of Lamb and everything is OK again. I wake up and it isn't.' There is one from Sally who confides she is very naughty at school and is worried her brother has been taken away because of this. I have a sudden image of two little girls waking, morning after morning, flushed from sleep, their cheeks wet with tears. Don't think of it, I tell myself. But I must, because Mr Dixon and Melanie and Sally must figure in my calculations as I try to find the right sentence for Jude.

Still, the first task is to find the facts upon which that sentence will be passed. Gang offence or only a road traffic accident? Starting point eight years or three years? Finishing point a long time in prison or a possible suspended sentence? I must decide what really happened. For the moment I skip tab three – this is the Crown's interpretation of the facts; I'll read the source material first, otherwise I might form a slanted view. So I turn to tab four.

I know the sort of thing I'm likely to find there – a history of low-level offending, appearances in youth courts, failures to respond to court orders … and there it all is. In the past year he has been stopped by police on seven occasions in the company of known members of a gang known as Heat 451, warned about possession of cannabis, suspected of being part of an affray (though there was insufficient evidence to prosecute), a caution for riding a stolen moped. Nothing to shock me here except for one extraordinary thing that supersedes all else. I double-check, as if I might have mis-read it. Now I know why Mr Burt was startled into silence. Never see anything through anyone else's eyes. Especially never see a dead boy through the eyes of his grieving father. The person referred to in all these documents isn't Jude. It's Lamb. Little Lamb, his father's angel, the loving brother, the supportive son who lit up a room when he walked into it, had another side to him about which his father did not know.

I hunt through the papers, looking for any mention of Jude in these reports. There are references to a youth being with Lamb on occasions, but there is no identification of Jude. So how does the Crown put its case against the defendant? I turn, finally, to tab three. It reads thus:

The Crown has no direct evidence that Jude Derwent is a gang member. However it has material to directly support the following:

- Lambert Dixon belonged to Heat 451 whose territory includes the area where he lived
- The rival G-men gang occupies an adjacent territory which includes Corbutt Road
- Lambert Dixon was a very close friend of Jude Derwent

- Neither Dixon nor Derwent had any known legitimate reason to go to Corbutt Road on the day in question
- Evidence from independent witnesses in Corbutt Road shows that:
  - A group of youths who frequented Corbutt Road were present at the time
  - Derwent's car travelled south to north and back in the road
  - Derwent drove at vastly excessive speeds, swerving across the carriageway towards the youths congregating on the kerb
- None of these youths has been prepared to make statements to the police but Intelligence suggests they are very likely to be members of the G-men gang.

The Crown submits the following inferences are available to the court:
- Given the close friendship between Dixon and Derwent, it is inconceivable Derwent was unaware of Dixon's gang affiliation
- Since the area of Corbutt Road is established G-men 'territory', it is inconceivable that a member of Heat 451 did not know this
- There being no other reason to account for Dixon and Derwent driving up and down Corbutt Road, it must have been related to the presence there of G-men
- Since Derwent deliberately endangered G-men, he must have been either acting in concert with or under direction of Dixon in full knowledge of the circumstances
- While it is accepted that the propositions in paragraph one above, taken individually, could not make the court sure Derwent deliberately drove so as to endanger the lives of members of G-men, it is submitted that taken together they create an

irrefutable inference that either Derwent was a member of
Heat 451 or acted in support of Dixon's affiliation to that gang

I sit for a long time thinking about the implications of the Crown's
case. It means Paul Dixon is going to hear that his beloved Lamb
was not what he thought. At best, Lamb was as deeply involved as
Jude, at worst he was the instigator of Jude's driving. It will all be
reported in the newspapers, online, in social media. Ultimately it
couldn't be kept from the two little girls. And I am powerless to stop
it. I'm not being asked to decide if Lamb was a gang member – he
clearly was. I'm only being asked to decide if Jude knew it, and
deliberately joined in with him. I read the papers again then put
them back in my bag. After that, I try very hard to put the whole
thing out of my mind. It will have to be faced tomorrow, but tomorrow is another day.

4

It comes, of course. Monday. Jude is in the dock. He offers me only
a view of the top of his head while Mr Dixon offers me his full
anguished face. Mr Burt and Miss Caldwell give each other sideways
looks. What are they up to now? I'm about to find out. Miss Caldwell
rises to her feet.

'I have an application to make, My Lady.'

'You have?'

'I ask that the court goes into Chambers?'

Astonishment isn't in the register of approved judicial expressions, so I try not to show it. Putting the courtroom into Chambers
means putting everyone – except me, counsel, defendant and

witness – out of it. It's a procedure adopted very exceptionally because justice must take place in public unless there is a very good reason otherwise.

'Only for a short time,' adds Miss Caldwell.

You have to trust counsel. At least, I do. At least, in the first instance. 'Very well. The court will sit in Chambers while I find out what the problem is. Clear the public gallery, please.'

In the public gallery are a couple of tourists, an earnest student, and some youngsters who might be friends of Jude or Lamb, or both. There is also a thin woman with greying hair who looks as if life has wrung her dry. One of my security staff ushers them all out. Down in the well of the court, the press leave and the liaison officer is trying to get Mr Dixon to go too.

'But I want to hear,' protests Paul Dixon loudly. 'I want to know what's going on. It's my boy that's dead.'

Esme tries to help but the man has planted his feet and looks as if he will lash out, or weep, or both.

'Mr Dixon . . .' I begin.

He ignores me, continues to argue with Esme and with the officer.

'Mr Dixon, listen to me for just a moment. I need to explain something to you.'

Reluctantly he turns.

'All I'm going to do is find out what the difficulty is. I will then make a decision about how to proceed. I will not conduct any hearing involving the defendant without reopening the court and explaining what I have decided and why.'

He blinks. He glares at Mr Burt. He shakes the officer's hand off his arm. He walks out. Once he and everyone else has gone, I turn back to Miss Caldwell, trying to keep the irritation out of my voice.

'All right, the court is now in Chambers. Would you care to explain why?'

'I know my application is an unusual one but there is a reason.'

'Surprise me.' I don't mean to say this. Certainly not in the tone in which it emerges.

Miss Caldwell kindly ignores the slip and goes on. 'The Crown would be very grateful if this Newton Hearing could take place in closed court. I appreciate the law requires there must be a good and pressing reason for it . . .'

The law requires a deal more than this, but I'm prepared to start there. 'So what is the good and pressing reason?'

She pauses, rearranging her thoughts in a shape she hopes will appeal to me. 'Your Ladyship will have read in the file how the Crown puts its case.'

'You say Lambert Dixon was a member of a gang called Heat 451 and that Jude Derwent must have known it, and together they were acting against members of a rival gang.'

'Your Ladyship has it in a nutshell.'

'I have. What I don't have is why that should make me put my court into Chambers.'

'Ah.' Her thoughts undergo another rearrangement. 'That Lambert Dixon was a member of Heat 451 will not be disputed by Mr Burt. Having seen the material served last week, he accepts it must be the case. But the defendant says he was unaware of it, and that it played no part in his course of driving.'

From the back of the court comes a voice, suddenly, shockingly loud. 'No.' Jude is on his feet. 'No,' he says again. There is an urgency about him. I have no idea what he is disagreeing with but whatever it is, now is not the time.

Mr Burt shoots to his feet. 'May I have a word with my client, My Lady?'

He goes to the back of the court. There is a hurried whispered exchange. The voice raised loudest, longest, is Mr Burt's. Jude subsides. Mr Burt returns to counsel's row. 'Mr Derwent wishes to apologize for interrupting the court, My Lady.'

'Is there a problem, Mr Burt?'

'No,' says Mr Burt firmly.

'Yes,' mouths Jude behind him.

All is not well with the defendant. But then, all is not well with Miss Caldwell either. I decide to sort her out first. My court is closed, and if it shouldn't be, I need to reopen it as soon as possible.

'Miss Caldwell, you were explaining the position of the prosecution, and why it should require the court to sit in Chambers.'

'Mr Paul Dixon . . .' She stops. She doesn't need to say that if he hears what is in that file, his image of himself as the father of a beloved son will be tainted for ever. She is desperate to keep him from learning the truth about his son. She is trying to avoid breaking his heart all over again. Even as she stumbles to put into lawyerly language this purely human problem, she realizes she cannot cast the application within the legal rules for closing the court.* The law is not a bereaved parent. The law isn't equipped to feel human emotions. Still, she tries.

When she has finished trying, I say: 'Miss Caldwell, I sympathize with your difficult position, but you are not thinking clearly. You invite me to sentence Jude Derwent on the basis laid out in your file of papers. You have some powerful evidence to support that contention. Even if I could hold the Newton Hearing in Chambers – or even if the defendant had accepted your case and there was no Newton Hearing – at the end of the day I must pass the sentence in open court. The law requires me to spell out the basis of the sentence. If I am persuaded the right basis is your basis, I must say so. I cannot avoid it. You cannot avoid it. None of us can or should attempt to prevent the press properly reporting the matter.'

She nods sadly.

Mr Burt is on his feet now. 'The solution,' he says, 'is obvious.

* See Appendix G, p. 295.

Miss Caldwell could accept the defence position that the course of driving was not motivated by anything. It was just bad driving.'

'Mr Burt, you know perfectly well that Miss Caldwell prosecutes in the name of the Queen. She acts on behalf of the public. She has a duty to pursue what the Crown believes to be the true position. She is trying to carry out that duty without hurting anyone more than necessary. I'm sure we all want that.'

'I do,' says the voice in the dock. Jude is on his feet again, this time ignoring the officer tugging at him. 'I mean I don't . . . I don't want to say Lamb was . . . you know. Not because it can hurt him or because it might hurt me. But because . . .' Jude Derwent isn't accustomed to using so many words. He runs out of them. He sits down, very white.

Mr Burt looks at me. I nod permission. He goes to the dock again. There is a second urgent whispered conversation. When he is back in his place, I turn to Miss Caldwell.

'Wouldn't it be better if the truth were explained to Mr Dixon beforehand, in private, so that he has time to absorb the fact that his son was a member of a gang?'

She is silent for a moment, during which Jude again tries to attract Mr Burt's attention, and Mr Burt determinedly refuses to look round. Finally, Miss Caldwell says, 'Could I have a little time?'

It's the least I can do. I look at the courtroom clock. 'You can have an hour. We will then sit in open court and you will call whatever evidence you rely upon in the Newton Hearing.'

5

Sixty minutes. Sixty seconds in each minute. A lot can happen in that time. Who is explaining the truth about his son to Mr Dixon? How will he take it? Will he still want to come into court? After his son's death, he has kept going by promising himself he will see Jude brought down. He has tracked Jude, believing only Jude is to blame. Now someone is going to tell him he must look at things very differently. But the human mind doesn't turn like a sailing yacht in the wind. It takes the time of an ocean liner to absorb new instruction, to slow down enough to act on it. I stare out of my window at the tree in the square below. When I've had enough of that, I stare at the clock on the wall instead. I wait. I stare out of my window at the almost visible clock of St Paul's. With the end of the hour comes Esme.

'Court's ready, My Lady.'

'Is Mr Dixon back?'

Esme nods grimly.

When I see Mr Dixon, I think Esme was right to be grim. The poor man is bolt upright in his chair, wound up so tight he can barely stand – as custom and courtesy require – when I enter. The liaison officer moves towards him. He leans away. His eyes are very bright in a very white face. The great size of him seems diminished.

Miss Caldwell rises to open the case. I'm not a jury. I won't be swayed by emotion or rhetoric. I need the facts and good advocacy. She knows it.

'My Lady, the Crown's case is this. Prior to the day of the incident, the defendant was staying at the home of his best friend, the now deceased Lambert Dixon. Shortly after midday on the tenth of December, Jude Derwent drove his Corsa motor car to Corbutt Road. Lambert was the front passenger. Reconstruction by a forensic scientist shows Lambert was not wearing a seat belt.'

'Kids don't,' hisses Mr Dixon loudly.

Mr Burt opens his mouth to object but decides against it. Let's see how it goes, he's thinking. So am I. Miss Caldwell continues with her opening.

'They drove from Lambert's home, which is in an area where a gang known as Heat 451 operates. It is sadly the Crown's case that Lambert Dixon was a member of that gang.'

A sound like a steam kettle escapes from Mr Dixon.

'We will invite the court to draw this inference from a variety of "intelligence" and other material, including the evidence of local officers who have on many occasions recorded him publicly associating with known members of the gang in circumstances where police attended, though no prosecutions followed.'

'Don't believe a word of it,' says Mr Dixon. I look at the liaison officer. A warning I won't let this go on. The officer whispers to Mr Dixon, who shakes his head but, for the moment, is silent.

Miss Caldwell picks up her thread. 'It's the Crown's case that, best friends and living together, Jude Derwent must at least have known of Lambert's affiliation. At worst he shared it. Evidence from roadside CCTV cameras and automatic number plate recognition devices show they drove directly to Corbutt Road, where a gang known as the G-men has its base and where its members often congregate. The G-men are rivals of Heat 451. G-men have been identified on local CCTV footage as being there that afternoon. The same footage clearly shows Derwent driving from south to north, the length of the road. The speed limit is 20 mph. An expert in road traffic accident analysis will say that Derwent's car reached speeds in excess of 60 mph, so fast that when it crossed speed humps, it left the ground. On this first pass, it sounded its horn. Youths from the G-men were seen to respond with obscene gestures. They threw bottles and even a brick after the car.

'At the end of the road, Derwent must have turned round because less than a minute later the vehicle returned. He could have left the area at the northern end of Corbutt Road or via any of the numerous side-streets. Instead he drove back towards the G-men. The Crown says this was a deliberate confrontation, in the knowledge that those on the street would be hostile; a deliberate engineering of circumstances where the danger created by his driving was increased. More bricks were thrown. His speed again reached over 60 mph. This time eye-witnesses speak of the car swerving as if aiming at the youths on the kerb. Eventually Derwent lost control of the car and left the carriageway altogether, smashing into a bus stop.

'It was by good fortune that a bus had recently passed through and picked up members of the public who had been waiting there. The shelter and a pole bearing bus timetables were demolished. The pole went through the windscreen. Lambert Dixon was thrown first into the windscreen and then across the steering wheel. He ended up lying over the defendant. Emergency services attended but Lambert had suffered unsurvivable injuries, among which was a broken neck.'

She stops, but the images created by her bald, calm description of carnage and terror do not. They fill the courtroom. It's a simple enough case. A combination of eye-witness, scientific and technical evidence. Very little is challenged by Mr Burt and most of the evidence is read. The only witnesses actually called into court are the two who say Jude seemed to deliberately drive towards the youths at the kerb. One of them is a young mother. The other is a man who had been on his phone to his wife at the time. Mr Burt cross-examines and efficiently demonstrates that a toddler and pizza-or-chicken-for-supper were absorbing so much of the witnesses' attention as to leave little for what was happening in the road; at least until the crash superseded everything else.

But he cannot challenge the CCTV and does not try to challenge the science. The nature of Jude's driving is clear. The speed, the startled pedestrians, the youths on the street gesturing after him as he drove away, ready for him with bricks and bottles when he drove back. Mr Burt's purpose is equally clear. He wants only to show there was no deliberate targeting of the rival gang and thus no basis for saying that Jude and Lambert went to Corbutt Road for the purpose of driving dangerously. It takes less than an hour to complete the Crown's case. Then it is the turn of the defence.

Mr Burt gets to his feet and says, 'I call Jude Derwent.'

Jude is led across the courtroom by the dock officer. He keeps his eyes averted from Mr Dixon, who, under instructions from the liaison officer, makes a supreme effort to stay seated, to stay silent. Am I imagining that I hear his teeth grinding as Jude passes? In the dock Jude had cut a pathetic figure but now he seems to walk with purpose. As if he has determined what must be done and intends to see it through. He climbs into the witness-box. He takes the oath. He places his hands on the ledge in front of him and waits. Mr Burt begins.

'Is your full name Jude Derwent?'

'Yes.'

'You have seen the CCTV footage of a black Corsa in Corbutt Road on the day in question?'

'Yes.'

'Is that your car?'

'My cousin's. I'm insured to drive it.'

Miss Caldwell indicates that she accepts this is so.

'Were you driving it that day?'

'Yes.'

'Do you accept, as the Crown alleges, that your driving was dangerous?'

'Yes, I do.'

'Do you accept, as the Crown alleges, that your dangerous driving led to the car crashing into a bus stop and Lambert Dixon being killed?'

'Yes, I do.'

'But do you accept, as the Crown alleges, this was a gang-motivated attack on youths belonging to a gang known as the G-men?'

This is the moment when Jude is supposed to say, 'No, Sir. Whatever else I did wrong, I didn't do that.' We all know this is the script, so when he doesn't say it, we wait; as if he is an actor who has forgotten his lines, and if we are only patient they will come back to him. And still he doesn't speak.

After what seems like a long while, Mr Burt tries again.

'Mr Derwent, you don't accept, as the Crown alleges, that this was a gang-motivated attack on the G-men, do you?'

This is a desperately leading and entirely improper way to frame a question of your own witness and I would intervene, except that there is no need because it is clear Jude has no intention of following where Mr Burt is trying to lead him. He is staring down at the glass of water in front of him. He takes a sip from it. Then he does something I have never, in over thirty years as a barrister and nearly fifteen as a judge, seen any defendant do. He turns away from his counsel; he turns away from his script; he says quietly, and quite deliberately, 'Yes, I do.'

Mr Burt looks as if his ears must have deceived him. 'No, you don't,' he says.

'Yes, I do,' says Jude again.

In a voice heavy with disbelief Mr Burt says, 'Are you accepting that you knew Lambert was part of a gang and that you helped him target a rival gang?'

'Yes,' says Jude. 'I accept it.'

'No you fucking don't,' says Paul Dixon loudly. 'You can't. Lamb didn't belong to any gang.'

For a moment I can't think what Jude Derwent is doing. Why are we having a Newton Hearing at all if he accepts the Crown's case? Why has he stepped into the witness-box to admit something that only underlines the depth of his guilt? I suppose the expression on my face must say this. The expressions on the faces of Miss Caldwell and Mr Burt certainly do. But Jude has lost all interest in us. He has turned to Mr Dixon.

'I'm sorry,' he says. 'I'm sorry for everything. I'm sorry for killing

Lamb. I'm sorry I drove like that. I'm sorry you had to find out about . . . about . . .'

'It's not true!' shouts Mr Dixon, less angry now than desperate. 'If Lamb belonged to a gang, I'd have known. He was my boy. I would have stopped it. He—'

'It's no good,' says Jude simply. He points to Miss Caldwell, to me. 'They know.' He points to Mr Burt. 'Even he knows, really. Lamb belonged to Heat. He had belonged for a long time. He asked me to . . . to do what I did, but we never meant anyone to be hurt. We were just . . .'

'Just what?' asks Mr Dixon. He is as white as Jude.

'We were . . .' The young face is set, the jaw solid as if carved out of a very old piece of wood. Mr Burt opens his mouth as if to speak, but then shrugs and sits down. He can't control Jude, and he knows it.

'Mr Derwent,' I say, 'Jude. What is it you are trying to say?'

The boy is barely coherent. 'He needs to understand but he won't listen.'

'Who? Mr Burt?'

Jude shakes his head impatiently, as if I am being very stupid. Perhaps I am. He says, 'I wrote a letter, but he sent it back unopened. I tried to phone, but he wouldn't speak to me. He won't believe the truth because it isn't what he wants to hear. But the truth isn't as bad as he thinks. Or maybe it is, but still he'll feel better if he understands.'

'Are you referring to Mr Dixon?' I clarify.

Jude nods.

There is no sanction for this – the use of the court for a conversation between a defendant and his victim's father – and I should stop it because it's not what a courtroom is for. Is it? But what is a courtroom for if not to serve the needs of the people who use it? Some courtrooms are about the interpretation of land rights, of shipping lanes, of contracts; but a Crown Court is about people and the needs of people. And here, in front of me, are two people in desperate need.

Still, I must tread carefully. I am going to have to sentence this young man. I think, 'The Court of Appeal is waiting up the road to review whatever I do.' I think, 'The Court of Appeal won't like this.' Finally, I think, 'Bugger the Court of Appeal.' It's Lamb's death. It's Jude's life. It's Mr Dixon's grief. I take a breath.

'What is it you want to say?'

Without the need to force his voice over all the others, Jude suddenly loses the ability to speak at all.

'Take a moment,' I say. 'Work out what you need to tell us.'

It's the basic rule for good advocacy. Work out exactly what you need to say, open your mouth, say it, close your mouth. Jude is silent for half a minute, organizing his thoughts. Then he turns his back on me and looks directly at the bereaved father.

'Mr Dixon, please don't think Lamb was all bad because he joined Heat. Of course he knew the gang used violence. He knew they dealt drugs. But that's not why he wanted to be part of them.'

This is something new – a street kid trying to explain to us what makes youngsters like him, or at least like his best mate, involve themselves in street gangs. Despite himself, Mr Dixon is listening. So are we all.

'I don't understand. Why did he do it?' Paul Dixon's voice is dry as dead leaves.

'He just wanted to be part of something . . .' Jude hesitates, checking he has the right words. He knows this chance won't come again. 'He wanted to belong. It's that, really. Belonging somewhere when you don't belong anywhere else.' He wipes a hand over his face. 'It began a long time ago,' he continues.

'How long?' Mr Dixon's voice has fallen to a whisper.

'Just after his mum died.'

'But he was only . . .' A calculation, a look of shock. 'Only twelve.'

Jude nods. 'It was really hard for him. He hated to see you so upset. He hated to hear his sisters crying. He just wanted to be somewhere else. He liked to laugh and to make people laugh, but he couldn't do that at home any more. When you're small, the gangs have a use for you. You can run drugs across the estate. You can hide where the police can't find you. You can outrun them and climb where they can't go. And even if you get caught, police don't prosecute little kids too much. So it's like . . .'

I see what it's like. I picture Lambert . . . and all the twelve-year-old Lamberts falling into the hands of gangs. This stops my thoughts in their tracks, but it doesn't stop Jude.

'When Lamb got too big to run the drugs, he began to hang about with the olders, but he didn't want to carry knives . . . he felt bad about it. I think he felt responsible for his sisters and for you, Mr Dixon.'

In Paul Dixon's throat a lump seems to lodge so that he can't swallow.

'And he didn't want to run county lines or hold dirty phones. Heat still liked him – he still made them laugh – but he was no use to them. He began to feel he didn't have a place with them either. It made him . . . well, sad. Then a guy got knifed. He was a good guy. Well, he was a good gang-man. The G-men did it, and Heat were all talk of revenge. They were planning an attack. They didn't even ask Lamb to go with them. He was kind of gutted. He felt useless, I think. Then he came up with this idea to revenge Heat all by himself. He needed my help but that was OK. We'd drive up and down their turf, and make them run, make them look stupid on their home turf. We weren't going to hit them with the car, just make them think we were.'

He looks with pity at what remains of Paul Dixon. Nothing reduces a man like being reduced in his own eyes.

'I just wanted you to know he really cared about you and his sisters. It was because of you he didn't do the really bad stuff. That's all I want to say.'

That's all he wants to say. It's a lot.

6

And so we come to the last scene of the last act of Jude's little drama. Mr Burt puts forward what mitigation he can – he pleads his client's youth, his lack of previous convictions, that Lambert willingly put himself in the position that killed him, that the G-men contributed to the accident by throwing things at the moving car. He stresses that Jude did not lie on his oath in the Newton Hearing – far from it – and so should still get his one third credit for pleading guilty. These are significant factors to reduce the sentence, he says. But Jude has done a good job of shafting himself. His driving falls at the most serious level of this offence, his admission of being knowingly involved in gang retaliation makes it much worse, and there's nothing Mr Burt can do about that.

And so the moment comes. The epilogue of the story. Traditionally defendants must stand when they are sentenced, but these days sentencing is a complicated business and can take a long time. The judge has first to set out the facts on which she or he will sentence, then must weigh the impact on the victims and the bereaved, the relevant law must be examined, and the Guidelines, after which the law must be applied to the facts, aggravating and mitigating features factored in, and the length of sentence finally calculated. It all takes time. It's a small and unnecessary cruelty to make a defendant stand while it is all gone through.

'You may remain seated,' I tell Jude, and he sinks down as though his legs won't hold him any longer.

After this, every word I speak must be carefully assessed because when I am done, each will be scanned by Mr Burt to see if he can raise an appeal; and if he can, every comma and colon will be scrutinized by the Court of Appeal. I look around the courtroom. Both barristers are looking down at the papers in front of them, but I can tell from the hunch of their shoulders – I sat like that myself often enough in the past – that their air of studied calmness is taking an effort. Jude is pale but resigned. Paul Dixon looks as if one more blow from life will end it for him; but he is no longer glaring at the defendant, nor at anyone else.

Now, the sentence. Adjust the microphone so everyone can hear clearly. Pace it so that everyone can follow and understand. Pause till everyone is silent and still. Take a breath. Begin.

'Jude Derwent, I have to sentence you for an offence of causing death by dangerous driving. In December last year when you were just twenty years old, you were staying at the home of your closest friend, nineteen-year-old Lambert Dixon. He was a member of a gang known as Heat 451. I accept you were not a member, but you knew he was, and that Heat 451 had rivals in the form of a gang known as the G-men.

'In the first week of December last year, a member of Heat 451 was stabbed by the G-men. Revenge was planned by Heat 451 but Lambert was not included in those plans. He was hurt by this and worried he was being excluded as in some way unworthy. He decided to take action himself – perhaps to impress other gang members. You facilitated what he decided to do. You and he drove to where you knew G-men were likely to be found. Your intention was to race through them in a way that would taunt and scare them in equal measure. You travelled north on Corbutt Road, drawing attention to yourself by your excessive speed and aggressive gestures to those you had come to face. Your speed reached levels in excess of 60 mph and was such that when you crossed raised traffic speed bumps, your car left the road. You were endangering the lives of every man, woman and child there.

'At the top of the road you turned and came back. This time you added to your dangerous manoeuvres by swerving across the carriageways to make the members of the G-men think you were trying to hit them. The danger you now caused to everyone in the area was even more acute. Eventually and unsurprisingly you lost control of the car and crashed into a bus stop. It was the merest good fortune that people were not queueing there. Had they been, you might have killed them too. As it happened the one person you did kill was your best friend. The terrible and tragic effect upon his family has been beyond measure, and no words of mine can explain the pain they have and will continue to suffer.

'Before I turn to the Guideline issued by the Sentencing Council which must dictate my approach,* I make clear that you will be disqualified from driving for a period which I will calculate to mean that for a period of six years after your release from custody you may not drive a motor vehicle. And even after that time, you must pass an extended test before you may drive again.

'As to how long that period in custody will be, I am satisfied from all the evidence I have heard, including your own admissions to me, that your course of driving was prolonged, and involved grossly excessive speed and swerving manoeuvres in the direction of pedestrians. This created an obvious very great danger to others which must have been clear to you. Accordingly I place your offence into the highest level of seriousness. For this, the Guideline provides a starting point of eight years.'

Mr Dixon looks up. He does not smile or grimace. He only listens very carefully.

'Next, I must decide if there are any features which aggravate your offence. In my judgement there is one very serious such feature, namely that it was part of an ongoing conflict arising out of gang rivalry. These courts will not countenance the use of public streets and the endangering of all on them for private and wholly

* See Appendix H, pp. 296–7.

illegal vendettas, and this aspect of the case increases the sentence from the starting point of eight years to one of ten.'

Jude nods briefly, as if he is saying 'That's right.'

'Now I must see what mitigation is available to you. I must look at both the offence and the offender. As to the offence, I find very little in mitigation. The fact that Lambert Dixon was a willing participant in your crime and may even have instigated it cannot help you. Your driving endangered many others besides him. As to the conduct of the G-men in throwing objects at your car, I note that it was you who provoked that conduct. I do not condone them. Far from it. What they did was itself illegal and might merit prosecution for a public order offence, but it cannot assist you. I turn then to what mitigation there is for you. The Guideline and authority make clear I must take into account in your favour your youth and your absence of previous convictions. Then there is your plea of guilty. You entered it at a preliminary hearing and you are entitled to the standard discount of one third on your sentence for an early acceptance of guilt.

'However, there is something else about your conduct beyond the mere entering of a plea of guilty which, in my judgement, goes well beyond mere acknowledgement of responsibility. I have seen and heard you speak of events. I have seen that you are genuinely grief-stricken at causing the death of your friend. And I have seen more. You knew it was inevitable that the public revelation that Lambert belonged to a gang would greatly increase the anguish felt by his father and sisters. I accept your going into the witness-box to explain what happened and why was a real attempt to ease the suffering of Lambert's family. You did this selflessly, knowing you were throwing away any chance of your own conduct being assessed at a lower level. In my judgement this was an act demonstrating genuine remorse. The Guideline allows me to treat this as additional mitigation beyond the simple plea of guilty. It rarely arises. But in your case, it does.

'Taking into account all these features, both aggravating and miti-gating, the sentence of the court will be one of five years in a Young Offender Institution. You are likely to be released at the halfway point, but you will be on licence and liable to recall to prison if you behave badly again. The time you have already served counts towards this sentence.'

Jude Derwent and Paul Dixon look at each other. Mr Dixon gives a brief nod. Jude returns it. It is something that they can meet each other's eyes and see each other, instead of only the shade of Lambert.

7

If you asked people to name a single thing that epitomizes why the forces of law and order are struggling in today's society, many would say 'gangs'. And they might be right. But to reflect on the damage that is done to us all by 'gangs', we need to know what we really mean by the word. For a single syllable it covers a lot. From Robin Hood's medieval Merry Men through the emergence in the 1870s of the women shoplifters of the Forty Elephants to the organized gangs of New York and Chicago, the idea of the gang has featured in our con-sciousness for centuries. Historically there have been many different sorts of gangs – and though it can stretch the patience to read about matters historical when we are concerned with matters present, still an understanding of the past is worth the effort because it really can help us understand what is happening today.

As far back as you can imagine and further, groups of people have hated other people for no better reason than for being 'other'. From the border raiders of Stuart Scotland to the football hooli-gans of modern times, group has hated group. The Capulets and

Montagues hated each other neither more nor less than the Sharks and the Jets. Then there are other sorts of gangs where people join together for the sole purpose of making trouble for others, usually on the streets. The past is full of them: the late sixteenth century's gentlemen of the Damned Crew, the eighteenth century's aristocratic Mohocks, the disaffected youths who formed the Scuttlers in nineteenth-century Manchester. Quite different from these were the gangs acting together for illegal profit, like the smugglers and the highwaymen. And those where the making of such profit grew into huge business empires, for example the Krays and the Richardsons in mid-twentieth-century London. Inevitably, where rival gangs occupied overlapping 'turfs' another sort of warfare broke out, as in the 1980s Glasgow Ice Cream Wars.* Currently there is a proliferation of local, not-so-local and foreign gangs engaged in gun smuggling, money laundering, people trafficking, extortion and above all the dealing in illicit drugs.

We've always had gangs in one or another of their many forms but, as a nation, we seem never to have felt more endangered by them than we do now. There is a lot of talking done about the evil of the current gang culture, and when most ordinary law-abiding people do it, they are likely to have in mind urban street gangs. That is because a whole series of different factors have come together in our current society. We have youngsters who want to belong to and identify with a tribe. We have the internet and social media proliferating the gang's image. We have young men wanting to fight with those who identify with a different tribe. We have the gang as a centre for the holding and passing on of firearms and other weapons for these fights. We have the gang as a centre of drug dealing and consequent money laundering. We have gang violence as it defends its territory, its drugs lines, its image. We have a perfect storm.

* Drugs, I'm afraid, not Knickerbocker Glorys.

If you are wondering why we can't resolve today's gang problem, it may be because we haven't yet unpicked and understood all the different strands that require resolution. It's a huge subject. But I want to concentrate for a moment on one aspect of it – on Lambert's story; because whatever the nature of the gang, it can only thrive if people want to join it. However picky the gang is about whom it accepts, if nobody wants to belong it will wither and eventually die. So the things that draw a boy like Lamb into the world of the gang deserve to be understood, if only to see how they can be avoided.

Having seen it from an angle that not so many people have, I offer some thoughts.

From where I sit on the Bench, it seems that two linked but distinct forces are at work in leading youngsters into a gang. One is what they are running away from. The other is what they are running towards.

It's in the nature of children growing into adolescence to seek some independence, a life which their parents can't see. But for some children – too many – it's much more than this. Lamb was running away from his home, the changes in it with which he couldn't deal – the absence of his mother, the grief of his father, the bewilderment of his little sisters. Other children don't want to walk through a front door which will lock them into abuse, either physical or sexual. Others cannot cope with the caring responsibilities that have fallen on them when a parent becomes physically or mentally ill. These are all children who want out of a situation which, ideally, they should never be in. These are all situations where society has failed to provide what it should, and knows it. The support structure for these children is there, somewhere, rusting and creaking, without the money to put it back in efficient working order. And we have apparently thought other calls upon our public money more important. So when those children walk out of the house and roam the streets and look for comfort and support where they can find it – whose fault is that?

Then there is the ever-growing band of children excluded from school, wandering about with no one to supervise them. If we close the school gate on them, where do we think they are going to go? If we don't provide structure to fill their days, how do we think they are going to fill them? Society is a contract between it and each of the people living in it. If we fail to fulfil our part of the contract, it's tough to blame the children for not fulfilling theirs.

And after school, if a teenager can't get a reasonably rewarding job, and if we leave them with nothing to fill their time but the prospect of delaying the problem for three years of further education which will fit them no better for unemployment than they were fitted before, and if all this leaves them in debt . . . what then?

All this is what youngsters run away from, but there is also what they are running towards . . . what the gang offers. The devil of it is how it attracts the very young. The barely teens. The children. The gang, first and foremost, offers a place to belong. It has, however loosely, a hierarchy with the strongest, the most ruthless, the most charismatic at or close to the top. It has a structure, the protection of the 'olders' extending over the 'youngers', rewards for those who serve well and loyally. And if those services involve the breaking of the law? Look at it from the point of view of the twelve-year-old. Out on the street it's excitement; it's running light and quick and noiseless down alleys, through gaps in broken railings, up drain-pipes and along the balconies of blocks of flats. It's going where police can't follow. It's the heady, dangerous power that comes with having a Zombie knife strapped to your thigh. It's the praise and financial rewards that come your way for a job well done – when no one else praises and rewards you. It's like living out a video game. Except that in a video game there are no consequences: when you die, you spring up again for another go at life; and you can buy additional armour or weapons to make yourself safe; and when you tire of it you can switch it off.

Of course, even twelve-year-olds must know life isn't a game, that bodies riddled with bullets or sliced with blades or smashed by a car die and are dead for ever. Even twelve-year-olds must know that drug addicts are reduced to a mockery of the person they should be, and that families get ripped apart. But knowing something and understanding it are two different things. Even as they get older and know it in their brains, they still don't always accept it. Or even if they do, they don't care because what they want is to belong in this other world.

Think gang. Think being part of something bigger than yourself, with a language and code of conduct of its own. Think these kids aren't breaking their laws – they are breaking ours. Then think of desperate parents moving homes to get their child out of the hands of one local gang, only to move them into the hands of another; and of hard-working people who run youth clubs, or try to in times of increasing financial restraints. Think that by the time I see a child gang member he will either be in the dock or on the mortuary table. Either way, it's too late. And when you have thought all this, when you have reflected on gangs and the way we deal with them, you might want to think again.

TRIAL FOUR:

The Offering

SUGHRA AND ATA stood in the dark hallway, eyes wide, breath stopped, listening. Behind the door of the front room a terrible row was going on. Baba was shouting, Ammi was weeping, and Kubra . . . Kubra both shouted and wept. Sughra could feel her little brother trembling.

'It's OK,' she whispered to him. But when she put her hand to Ata's cheek it was wet with tears so she took his hand and led him back upstairs. A minute later they heard the front door slam and Kubra's feet slap-slapping the pavement as she ran away from the house. Sughra scrambled to the window in time to see her older sister arrive at the corner of the road where a group of girls waited. Then they were gone and there was only the empty road and pools of orange light from the street lamps.

Ata, now he was four years old, was no longer allowed to creep into bed with Sughra, but he was shivering, so Sughra held him in her thin arms and crooned to him as Ammi did when he was sometimes frightened at night.

'Will Kubra come home?' he whispered.

'Of course she will. She's only gone out with her new friends.'

Ata was silent for a moment, then he said, 'Baba doesn't like Kubra's new friends.'

It was true. Baba didn't like Kubra's new friends, nor her new clothes, nor her new determination to be free of the things he cared about. Kubra was sixteen, almost grown up, and lately she had taken to shouting back at Baba in a way that Sughra, at nine, could not fathom. So she said nothing, only stroked Ata's soft hair, and when he was heavy in her arms she carried him carefully to his own room. She climbed back into her bed and prayed to fall asleep, prayed that when she woke Kubra would be safely in the bed on the other side of the room. But sleep was slow to come and hard to hold on to. Somewhere long into the night she lost her grip on it. The shouting had started again – so at least Kubra was home – and her father was very angry. Even with the quilt over her head, Sughra couldn't shut out the sound. She slipped out of bed and padded, warm feet on cold linoleum, to the top of the stairs. Baba's voice in the void below was loud and harsh. Kubra's was angry and thick with tears. Sughra put a foot on the top stair, heard the sound of a smothered scream, hesitated.

The first thing she saw when she woke next morning was Kubra's empty bed. She studied the smooth coverlet, sighed and closed her eyes. She waited for Ammi to call, waited for the smell of cooking and the shudder of the pipes as Kubra took her long morning shower. When none of these things happened, she got up and went downstairs. There was no one in the kitchen or in the television room so she opened the door to the front room.

Heavy curtains shut out the light. It was so dark that at first Sughra could see nothing. She looked at the far corner of the room where Baba's model of the Blue Mosque stood, over a metre high on its low table – she knew exactly where – and by staring very hard, thought she could make out the white dome which Baba had built with such care, the glint of gold and silver where he had pasted foil decorations. As her eyes adjusted, she felt her way to the window and pulled at the edge of the thick velvet. A little light crept in and on to the nearest chair. Her mother was sitting there, but it wasn't like her mother because this person was very still, and Ammi was a busy, busy woman who never sat still.

'Ammi?' asked Sughra. But Ammi didn't answer.

She pulled the curtain a little more. Now the light moved across the carpet and on to the sofa, on to a shadow there. It took Sughra a long moment to realize it wasn't one shadow, but two. It was Baba holding in his hands an open Koran, though Sughra was puzzled to think how he could have been reading in the dark. And leaning against him was Kubra.

Sughra thought, 'Kubra is too old to cuddle Baba like this,' but still she was pleased the argument of last night was over and that her father and her sister were close again. They were in fact very close. Kubra was leaning into his shoulder so that you could not tell where Baba ended and Kubra began. Her long dark hair fell over her face. Her head lolled as if she was asleep. Perhaps she was asleep, thought Sughra, because she must be tired . . . she hadn't gone to bed and was still wearing the tight jeans and the leather jacket and the pretty top she had worn the previous evening. Sughra shook her head at the memory of the row – but it was over now and they were together again, very quiet and peaceful.

'Ammi?' said Sughra. 'I'm hungry.'

Her mother looked at her now, but didn't jump up to put on the pan and fry the bread and set out the dates. Did not go briskly, in her usual way. Only sat. Her father looked up from the Koran. Sughra was not allowed to disturb Baba when he was reading the Koran, and she feared his anger, but he only blinked as though to rid himself of some sight he didn't want to see, placed a finger on the page and let his eyes settle on her.

'Get Ata,' he said. 'Put on your clothes and go to school.'

She could not read the tone of his voice. It wasn't warm

and it wasn't cold and it wasn't anything. 'We haven't had breakfast,' she said.

'Do as you are told. Go to school. Take Ata with you.'

'But Kubra is still asleep.' It was Kubra's job to take the little ones to school because there was a dangerous road and Kubra was a big girl, big enough to cross wide roads.

Baba turned to gaze at his elder daughter, where her head rested on his shoulder. 'No,' he said. 'You are my big girl now.'

Sughra frowned, not seeing how this could be, but she didn't care to argue with Baba. She got her clothes on, and most of Ata's. The little boy was hungry and fractious. He wanted his mother, and Ata was used to getting what he wanted for he was the gift from Allah.

'No,' said Sughra, who though she understood little about that morning, understood this at least: those in the front room were not to be disturbed. So she went to school, taking Ata across the dangerous road. She took him to his classroom then went to her own. She ignored her growling stomach and heavy heart and made no complaint. It was Ata who did that. In the nursery class he wept and stormed at the injustice of hunger and shoes on the wrong feet. Gentle hands set about putting him to rights until it became clear that something was wrong beyond the power of gentle hands to heal.

By mid-morning police were at the house to which Sughra and Ata would never return.

1

THE LIST OFFICER POKES his head round my door. He looks harassed. The hour before the courts sit is his time for being harassed. No matter how carefully he stitches together the court lists, holes open up. It is now that a juror phones to say her child has come out in spots, the cells announce a required defendant has been transferred to a prison in Cumbria, the CPS discovers a vital witness has disappeared, or even – rarely – a judge gets ill. Today the rare has come to pass, and the list officer is on the hunt for a stand-in.

'A bad back!'

'I'm afraid so, Judge. The poor man can't stand up. There's no way he can sit in a courtroom. And if he could, there's no way he can stand to leave it.'

Together we contemplate the picture of my fellow judge sitting on in the eternity of an empty courtroom.

'Thank you, Judge,' says the list officer. It seems I have agreed to do the case. 'It's a section 16 witness to a murder,' he says. 'The GRH was last week, the section 28 is today, the ABE is in the DCS.'

Do other professions do this? Do doctors and dentists? Or is it only lawyers who think their time so precious they can't afford to use whole words?

The list officer is packing a lot of information into one sentence. He is telling me that I am to hear a procedure set down in section 28 of the Youth Justice and Criminal Evidence Act 1999, with a witness who is under the age of eighteen and so (deep breath here – don't worry, it all becomes clear once we get into court) falls within section 16(1)(a) of that Act, a Ground Rules Hearing having taken place the previous week under paragraph 5.2 of Practice Direction 3AA, and that I will find the Achieving Best Evidence interview uploaded on to the Digital Case System. Truly, this is how lawyers talk. What all the jargon represents, however, is perfectly clear. It represents years of striving for a semblance of justice for those in our community most in need of it, and least likely to get it. Those garbled letters and numbers are the best chance for the very young, the fragile, the mentally ill and otherwise disadvantaged to access the courts and receive a fair hearing.

In the past – though not so very far in the past – a child victim might be deemed too immature to take part in the process at all. An adult victim with communication difficulties might be shut out from having a hearing. And those who were able to lay their woes before a court and ask for justice were expected to do so live, in the court-room. They had to climb into the witness-box, even if they were so young, so small, it was necessary to stand them on a pile of books to be seen. They had to find words to tell a room full of strangers what had happened to them, however demeaning and humiliating those things were. They had to do it under the eyes of dozens of people studying their every flush and flinch. They had to face cross-examination (sometimes very cross examination) by a lawyer for the defendant.

We boast of the 'equality of arms' in our system, lawyer on one side against lawyer on the other; but that isn't the truth of it all. Because often it is lawyer pitted against witness – the trained forensic mind against the mind of a child, against the adult with the mind of a child, against the mentally ill and frail – and this is very far from equality in any sense. Of course it was, and remains, the job of the barrister, with carefully prepared questions, to set about pulling apart the witness's story, making the witness look inconsistent, unreliable or plain untruthful. Sometimes this does no more than expose witnesses who are indeed inconsistent, unreliable or untruthful. But sometimes it makes a witness look that way when it is not the case at all.

For a long time this way of proceeding had its supporters, even in very high places – because, after all, that is the adversarial system which the world applauds. The obvious fact that it is no way to reach the truth counted for little. But bit by bit the unfairness was acknowledged; and step by step the law has tried to put its house in order. Nothing has displaced the fundamental principle that adversaries from each side face each other across the courtroom, but it is now recognized that if the barrister is to set himself and all his skills and experience against the witness, that witness must at least stand on a level battlefield. And so there came into being packages of 'special measures': Achieving Best Evidence interviews, Ground Rules Hearings, section 28, all things which recognize the challenges for some people in taking part in the proceedings – the law, packed tight into the acronyms and numbers which the list officer is wafting in my direction. In the course of the morning's hearing I will see each of these special measures fall into place, but first I have to find out what the case is about.

So I pack away the unread paperwork that had promised to fill my day, open up the Digital Case System and meet for the first time Akhi Ibrahim, his wife, Irhaa, and their children, Sughra, nine years old, Ata, aged four, and Kubra, who was sixteen when she died.

The story falls into a short compass. Police, alerted by a distressed child at school, arrived at the family home at 11.27 one May morning. They found the front door unlatched so, when no one answered their knock, they went in. The front room was in semi-darkness, the curtain pulled aside only in the bottom corner. Mr Ibrahim was sitting on the sofa, his Koran in his hands, his dead daughter leaning on his shoulder. His wife sat in a chair, rocking herself slowly back and forth. The parents looked up when the officers came in but neither spoke. Neither looked at the body of their child as she was lifted from the sofa to the floor where the officers, refusing to accept the obvious, attempted to give her CPR. Neither said anything when they were arrested, nor when they were led, unresisting, away. Neither seems to have said anything much since for no defence statements have been uploaded. Still, if the parents are silent, surely there must be other evidence to speak about what happened to their elder daughter.

I look for witness statements and reports and find them. Forensic officers had attended. The front room had been minutely examined and photographed. There was no blood-spatter. Everything was neat and clean. Only the low table with its tall model of the Blue Mosque was knocked askew. You could see from the pressure marks in the carpet that the table had originally been placed centrally in the angle between two walls but it had been pushed to one side, almost up against the left-hand wall. The pushing must have been rough because one tower of the mosque had partially collapsed – with how many hours of patient, careful work undone? The movement of the table had created a wider space on the right side, big enough to let through a man. Or a woman. And this, it seems, is what had happened because in the corner of the room behind the table the photographer found scuff marks on the skirting board and a long pink scarf.

Had Kubra retreated from her father's anger, into the corner? Had he pushed the table aside and gone after her and trapped her there, between the walls? Had he beaten her to death? Or had Irhaa taken the scarf from her own or Kubra's neck and strangled her child with it? A quick scan of the scientific reports tells me that some long dark hairs were caught up in the pink scarf. Roots from two of them had been subjected to DNA testing. The hairs were Kubra's. But this doesn't tell me whether they got there because she had been wearing the scarf or because someone strangled her with it . . . or both. Neither parent has given a hint of the answer. And if they won't speak, who can? Perhaps Kubra, or at least her dead body, can.

The pathologist has helped her tell the story. His report is long and full of the language of his art, but it amounts to this. Kubra was a well-nourished teenager. Neither natural disease nor alcohol nor drugs caused or contributed to her death. From her neck down, save for a little bruising to the upper right arm consistent with the grip of a hand, she was as perfect and undamaged as a sixteen-year-old should be. From the neck up, however, it was a different matter. It was a blessing that Kubra's long black hair hid her face from her little sister. But the pathologist has seen it, examined it minutely, dissected it, laid bare all that is there. This is what he found:

(i) A large, very fresh bruise above the left ear.

(ii) Upon dissection, bruising across the left forehead.

(iii) The face markedly congested and distorted with abnormal accumulations of blood.

(iv) The inside of the eyelids and the whites of the eyes showing small petechial haemorrhages.

(v) The same petechial haemorrhages present in the upper part of the airway.

(vi) The lips swollen, the linings torn and bruised, with more bruising to the tongue, deep under the floor of the muscle of the mouth.

(vii) Bruising on and deep under the chin, the jawline and neck.

(viii) The hyoid bone and thyroid cartilage fractured.

(ix) Bruising on each side of the upper neck and over the larynx consistent with manual compression, though the pathology doesn't exclude a broad soft ligature being used too.

The pathologist offers his opinion: 'The bruising on lips, chin and upper neck are consistent with severe pressure being applied over the mouth, forcing the lips against the teeth. Petechial haemorrhaging was caused when blood pressure rose as blood flowed in from the arteries but could not flow away via the veins. The extent of petechial haemorrhages and facial congestion indicate a significant period of neck compression, at least twenty seconds but probably longer. There are four mechanisms of death by compression of the neck: (a) compression of the veins in the neck; (b) the cutting-off of arterial supply preventing blood reaching the brain; (c) closure of the airway; (d) pressure over the receptors in the neck causing the heart to stop (vagal inhibition). The pathological evidence supports the first, a more gradual event, giving the necessary time to produce the copious haemorrhages. However, more than one of the four mechanisms could have been and probably was involved.'

Kubra has spoken as loudly as she can with her bruised and bloodied mouth, her broken voice box. Out of the darkness she is showing us how hands held her, crushed her lips, closed about her neck or tightened a scarf around it. But she hasn't shown us whose hands they were.

There are two prime candidates – the two people who, in all the world, should have protected her. Are both parents guilty of killing their child? Or is one a killer, the other only protecting him? And why am I saying 'him'? Because I can't imagine a mother who could do that to her child? Oh, I can imagine it right enough, but I mustn't. I mustn't imagine at all, for that is not the job of a judge. Still, the round bruise marks on the upper left arm – one on the outside, four on the inside – are small. The pathologist gives the dimensions of each. Barely bigger than my own rather small fingertips.

2

If there is no more evidence than this, any jury will be left with a real problem, and so will the trial judge. The act of strangulation, particularly if done with a scarf, could have been carried out by either parent. The blow to the head might suggest infliction by a man but that is by no means certain. The fingertip bruising on Kubra's arm, consistent with the hand of a woman, could have been an act to hold the child down or the opposite – a desperate attempt to pull her free from attack.

The prosecution may be able to satisfy a jury that the parents acted together, both intending to bring about the same end. If this is proved, whoever actually throttled the life out of Kubra, both parents are equally guilty of murdering her. But if the prosecution can't prove such a 'joint enterprise', it might lose its case against both. Even if a jury is sure one or other parent committed murder, if they cannot be sure which one, and cannot be sure both acted together, both must be acquitted. That is our law, because no defendant can be convicted unless the prosecution makes the jury sure the defendant is guilty. In a domestic setting, where there is unlikely to be any independent witness, too often parents of a dead child may choose not to answer questions at the police station, to give no evidence at trial, their very silence their protection, leaving the courts with a terrible and sometimes hopeless task. Will Kubra's case be one of these?

In 2004, Parliament tried to reduce this problem by creating a new law that made it an offence not only for a member of a household who has frequent contact with a child to cause the death of that child, but also where a member of the household fails to take reasonable steps to prevent the child coming to harm from someone else in the house. The offence is complex and technical* but its effect is that a parent who stands by and lets the other parent kill their child is as guilty as the killer. And the prosecution doesn't have to prove which parent played which part. However, the offence carries only a maximum of fourteen years' imprisonment, whereas both murder and manslaughter carry life imprisonment. And for

* See Appendix I, p. 298.

Kubra, here's the rub: the Act only provides for a child *under* the age of sixteen.

So although Kubra's body has told its tale, it's not enough. If she is to get justice, more is needed, and there were no possible witnesses in the house but Sughra and little Ata. I hunt through the police reports to find out what happened to them. After their parents' arrest they had gone to stay with their maternal grandmother, and three days later she brought them to the police to be interviewed about what – if anything – they knew of their sister's death.

I close my eyes and think about what these two small children have been through. I picture them at home before all this happened. Their father determined that his family should live in accordance with his deep and truly held beliefs. Their mother caring for them all, keeping them fed and the household clean. A big sister looked up to and loved. All gone in the passing of a night. All gone beyond recall. The obvious place for them was with a caring grandmother. But Nani is their mother's mother. How long was it before someone realized that the only two potential witnesses were now in the care of the mother of one of the only two potential killers? What discussions did that generate? Who had to weigh the risk of Nani unduly influencing the children, against the difficulty of finding somewhere else for them to go? And where else is there? Every relative, every friend in this close-knit community is likely to side with one parent or the other. There is, of course, the option of taking them into care . . . but how cruel to do such a thing to two bewildered and grieving children. On the one hand, they need whatever loving normality can be salvaged from this desperate situation. On the other, society needs justice to be done. How do you balance these things? Police and Social Services put their heads together and decided to first find out if either child had any evidence to give. Sughra and Ata must be carefully, sensitively interviewed and, if they saw or heard anything, their evidence must be captured in a permanent form, before memories are lost or influenced by anyone else. And this is exactly what the Achieving Best Evidence interview was designed to do.

The ABE interview is just one of that large number of 'special measures' meant to ensure the jury gets the best-quality evidence.* There is an impressive array of these measures, from the simplest screen – a curtain pulled around three sides of the witness-box to hide the witness from anyone but judge, jury and barrister – through to the most complex disguising of identity, including the witness's voice. One of the earliest measures to be brought into the courtroom was the ABE interview, in which the account of a vulnerable witness is video-recorded as soon as possible after events. The recording can then be played to the jury as the witness's evidence-in-chief. This is particularly effective for witnesses whose memories may be worst affected by the passage of time. Children, obviously – the younger, the more so. Rape victims whose demeanour shortly after events may be as powerful as their words. But in truth every witness would benefit from this because memory is mutable and changes with each remembering. Even nightmares can stain and obscure the clarity of events beyond recall.

Anyone who listens to eye-witnesses in a courtroom will stare open-mouthed at how patently truthful witnesses can give accounts that are plain wrong. CCTV of the same scene may show them wrong as to who was present, what those people looked like, what they wore, what they carried and what they did. Witnesses may forget because in the midst of a fast-moving and horrific event no proper memory was laid down, or because, with the passage of time, the proper memory has been eroded. It's why police officers are trained to make notes as soon as possible. It's why we have come to rely more and more on the indisputable – on CCTV, telephone

* See Appendix J, pp. 299–300.

UNLAWFUL KILLINGS

records and cell site maps, blood analysis, DNA and other forensic evidence. But none of this can help Kubra, and we are back to first principles. Did either Sughra or Ata witness anything that will help the jury find the truth in this case?

So, three days after their sister died, Nani and her grandchildren were collected by a police car and taken to a place specially set up for such interviews – suites of child-friendly rooms equipped with audio- and video-recording devices. In such a room Ata and Sughra sat, one by one, with a kindly lady officer. She would have asked them to tell her what they saw and heard, and then, by questioning, drawn from them more information than they knew they had. The room would also have been linked to another where a second officer watched and listened and, if necessary, inputted other ideas and questions.

I search through the DCS, click a link, select a file and find myself staring at Ata. He is a sturdy little boy, the beloved son long awaited by his parents, but he is not the same child he had been three days before this recording. He gazes around blankly. When asked to, he climbs into the armchair and sits there, his feet dangling a long way from the ground. The lady who interviews him asks him if he would like to hold a toy. She points to the corner of the room where there is a pile of teddies and stuffed animals worn bare by anxious little hands; but Ata only stares at her. She gets a teddy and puts it on the chair beside him, close enough to reach if he wants it, but he doesn't. His face is without expression – no tears, no smile. He puts his thumb in his mouth, then, as if remembering this is not allowed, takes it out again.

The nice lady officer asks if he goes to school; if he likes school; what he likes best at school. In her training this is the part of the interview headed 'Establishing Rapport', but she cannot establish anything with Ata. He only looks at her and, every now and again, gives a deep sigh. After some minutes of this one-sided conversation Ata closes his eyes. The nice lady is losing him. She gives up on

160

rapport and moves on to that part of the interview where she must see if the child understands the difference between truth and lies, fact and fantasy. If Ata does understand this, he gives no sign of it. His eyelids twitch and flicker as if in sleep. Perhaps it is self-defence, or an election to leave this place where he does not want to be. The nice lady pauses, says his name twice, gets no response, then speaks into her microphone to the officer in the adjoining room. She shakes her head. 'Ata,' she says, 'I don't think you want to talk to me today?'

Ata opens his eyes, slides out of the chair and walks to the door.

'Will you come and talk to me another day?'

He does not turn, does not answer, reaches up to the door handle and walks out.

'Ata has left the room,' says the nice lady so that the machinery can record her failure.

It happens. A child too traumatized to speak. This small boy is lost in an alien world. He went to bed one night in his own home, the beloved child of a mother and father with two big sisters. He woke next morning to find it all gone. All except Sughra. And so Ata walks out of the investigation, and Sughra walks into it.

3

The officer who has failed with Ata goes off to fetch his sister. The CCTV recording shows her bringing the little girl into the room. Sughra looks about her, takes in the big soft chairs, focuses for a moment on the cameras placed about the room, then turns to the pile of toys.

'Would you like to hold one while you talk to me?' asks the nice lady.

Sughra would. She chooses a blue elephant and allows herself to be settled into the same chair where Ata recently sat. As if she can sense this, she says, 'Did Ata talk to you?'

The lady officer hesitates. She must not affect this child's evidence by giving any hint of what another child has said. 'He was a bit tired today,' she says.

Sughra nods. 'I'm tired too,' she says. 'Ata keeps me awake when I want to sleep.'

But tired or not, Sughra sets herself to the task she has come to do. She has no patience with Establishing Rapport. She is affronted when asked to demonstrate that she understands the difference between truth and lies. She has no time for any of this. She has come to tell about the death of her sister and that is what she means to do.

'Kubra,' she says. 'I want to tell you about Kubra.'

The next part of the nice lady's training requires that free rein is given to the child to say what she has witnessed. Then to take her back through the story, unpicking every aspect of it, teasing out half-hidden memories and things the child might not have realized were important.

'Something happened to Kubra,' says the nice lady by way of encouragement.

Sughra nods.

'Can you tell me about it? Can you tell me what you saw and heard?'

Sughra nods again, more vigorously this time.

'Sughra, it's very important you only tell me what *you* saw and heard, not what anyone else has told you.'

For the slightest of moments Sughra hesitates and the officer stiffens. Has Nani primed the child? Has someone . . . but no, Sughra is only rearranging the blue elephant and she is ready to begin.

'Baba was angry,' she says, 'because Kubra put on different clothes.'

'When was this?'

'After supper,' says Sughra.

'Can you tell me about it?'

Sughra can. She is a solemn and careful witness. She describes the clothes which Kubra put on – tight trousers and a green jacket made of something like leather. 'And a pretty blouse that . . . ' – she demonstrates a low, scooped neckline – 'and boots with high, high heels.' The officer knows Sughra is right about all of this, for these are the clothes in which Kubra's body was dressed.

'Baba shouted at her.' Sughra stands, and the camera follows her as she puts her hands on her hips, her legs apart, and imitates her father's voice. ' "Where did you get these things, Kubra?" ' She sits again. 'But Kubra wouldn't tell him. Baba sent her to her room, but she ran past him and out of the door.'

Sughra stops. The nice lady nods encouragingly. Sughra takes a deep breath and looks down, but her voice, when it comes, is quite steady.

'Kubra didn't come back till late, late, but Baba and Ammi were waiting for her. They took her into the front room. Baba hit her. And she screamed at him bad things and he hit her again and he took Ammi's scarf and put it around Kubra's neck and Kubra . . .' She demonstrates again, clawing at her throat as if to pull away the choking scarf. 'And then her hands went still and she was dead.'

Sughra has come to the end of her story and stops. It is now that the interviewer must delve deep into the child's memories to see what else might be there. Patiently she takes Sughra through the scene when Kubra left the house.

'Do you know where Kubra went?' asks the lady.

Sughra shakes her head. 'Just out. With her friends.'

'How do you know she was with friends?'

'I looked out of the window. I saw her run to them on the corner of the street.'

'Do you know who they were?'

'Girls,' says Sughra, 'from her school.' She pauses, then says wistfully, 'They had pretty clothes too.'

The lady officer nods, makes a note, takes the child forward to when Kubra came home.

'Do you know what time that was?'

Sughra thinks, decides she doesn't, shakes her head. 'I was asleep,' she says.

'What woke you?'

Sughra thinks again. 'The front door opening? Or maybe Baba shouting? Yes, I think it was Baba shouting.'

'What did he shout?'

But Sughra has no answer. The officer decides to move on, into the front room, but Sughra's enthusiasm for detail is fading fast. She can't remember how Baba hit Kubra or how many times. She can't remember what Kubra shouted at Baba. Ammi was there somewhere, but Sughra can't remember exactly where or what Ammi was doing or saying. She can't remember how Kubra got from behind the Blue Mosque to the sofa. She might remember these things tomorrow, she says apologetically, but not today because she is tired now and would like to go back to Nani, please.

'Of course,' says the lady officer, 'but are you sure you have told me everything you can remember?'

She would have liked more. Still, the police now have, from Sughra, clear evidence of the actions of Baba. As for Ammi, her presence, her lack of objection to what was happening and her grip mark on Kubra's arm are enough for the Crown Prosecution Service to put her before a jury. Anyway, the choice of charges wasn't the responsibility of this officer. Her job was to complete the paperwork before going off duty – and this she has diligently done. She has labelled and sealed the recording, which will be exhibited as Sughra's evidence-in-chief. Ata has said nothing, but she completes the paperwork for him too. And that, so far as the nice lady is concerned, should be that. But it isn't. Because I can see as I scroll down the system that the next day Sughra made a further statement. This one is short and to the point. The following morning, Nani brought Sughra back to the interview suite. The same officer had been found and soon they were sitting back in the familiar room, the familiar blue elephant back in Sughra's arms. And so I open the third recording.

'Your grandma has brought you back,' says the nice lady.

'I made her,' says Sughra. She strokes the trunk of the blue elephant. 'I insisted,' she says, with special emphasis on the word that sounds too grown up in her mouth, 'because I remembered more.'

The lady officer is cautious. 'How did that happen?' she asks.

Sughra shrugs. 'I went to bed, and when I woke up, I remembered.'

'I see.' The officer is thinking that Sughra has been with her maternal grandma, who might have reason to urge the child to help her mother. 'Did anyone help you remember, or did you remember all by yourself?'

'I just remembered,' says Sughra.

The officer frowns, opens her mouth, closes it again. After all, it is her job to let the child speak. 'So tell me,' she says, 'what have you remembered?'

'This,' says Sughra, and she stretches out her arm, sweeping it sideways as if hitting something hard with the back of her hand. 'Whooom,' she says. 'That is how Baba hit Kubra.'

The lady officer stares. 'Where did he hit her?'

'Here,' says Sughra, putting her hand above her left ear, just where the pathologist found the area of fresh bruising on Kubra. 'And here too.' The child moves her hand to her forehead, where upon dissection a second area of bruising had been found.

The officer nods. There can be no doubt. For whatever reason, Sughra had found herself unable to speak before. But she cannot have invented this, can she? No, she can't. 'Have you remembered anything else?'

Sughra nods. 'I remember what Baba was shouting. He said, "It is forbidden. You are my child and I tell you it is forbidden."'

'Are you sure of this?'

'And I remember where Ammi was.'

The officer lets the unanswered question go, because this new thing is more important. 'Tell me about that,' she says. And Sughra does. She describes how behind the table with the model of the mosque she saw Ammi leaning over Kubra, who was on the floor.

'Are you sure?' The officer does a good job of keeping the quiver of excitement out of her voice. 'Are you sure Ammi was with Baba when Kubra was on the floor?'

Sughra is quite sure. She even remembers how Baba picked Kubra up in his arms and carried her round the coffee table to the sofa and placed her on it and sat beside her and how Ammi lay Kubra's heavy head against his shoulder.

The officer doesn't say 'Bingo' but as I listen I can see the word forming in her mind. 'And then . . .?'

Sughra pauses a moment to think. 'And I ran away.'

The officer has more questions, but Sughra has told what she came to tell. She is done.

4

So here is the child's evidence-in-chief uploaded on to the Digital Case System, ready to be played in court. Until quite recently Sughra would still have had to appear before the jury to be cross-examined. Another of the 'special measures' available to judges now allows her to do this via a video screen from a little room in the witness suite elsewhere in the court building, but still, she would have had to wait many months to be cross-examined. However, the law, at long last, has caught up with itself. That is to say, the law has come to accept that if evidence-in-chief needs to be taken quickly, so does cross-examination. And *that* is where section 28 comes in.

Section 28 of the Youth Justice and Criminal Evidence Act 1999 permits the formal cross-examination by defence barristers to be recorded in advance of the trial. It can't be done as early as the ABE interview – certainly not until both sides have had time to prepare – but it can be done before memory fades and corrupts. The questioning takes place with the barristers in a courtroom, overseen by a judge, and with the witness present over the video link. At trial the recording will be played to the jury immediately after the playing of the ABE interview. Although it is part of the 1999 Act, it hovered, unimplemented and useless, until after many years it was brought out, dusted off and is proving . . . well, what is it proving? Today I shall see. It's the first section 28 I have ever done.

It is twelve weeks since Sughra recorded her ABEs. Five days ago when He of the Bad Back was still able to walk into court and out again, he held a Ground Rules Hearing. This is the last link between ABE and section 28, designed to make the whole process work smoothly. It is a hearing between judge and barristers to review the 'ground rules' for the way the Bar will be allowed to question a witness like Sughra. The judge in this case had the help of a report from an 'intermediary' – an independent person able to facilitate communication so that the witness can understand and be understood. Some intermediaries are brilliant, some are . . . well . . . not. This one is fine. She has met Sughra and learned a lot about her from a variety of sources. She describes the child as a bright nine-year-old, sturdy for her age, able to communicate in and understand age-appropriate language in both English and Urdu. She assesses the child's attention span as being no more than forty minutes before a break of at least fifteen minutes is necessary. She says Sughra, unlike some children, will not be unnerved if we wear wigs and gowns, indeed will welcome it because Sughra, it seems, believes in the formality, the importance of this occasion. (Good for Sughra. That's more than some of my witnesses do.) The intermediary says questions should be asked in short sentences, in clear and unambiguous language suitable for a nine-year-old, with no multiple clauses, no tags at the end, no double negatives. She says events should be taken chronologically to avoid confusing the child. It is part of the intermediary's job to flag up potential difficulties, and she has: she says if the child is to accurately describe acts of aggression by a male figure, questions should not be asked in a tone of aggression, particularly not by a male figure.

My fellow judge had read this report and laid down a series of rules for the conduct of the hearing in accordance with its recommendations. To barristers, all this is now familiar territory. Most will have been through a careful programme of training before questioning a child or vulnerable witness.* Many with children of their own will understand how to speak to a young witness. You would expect them to make the effort to get it right because who, after all, wants to look like a bully in front of the jury? Who wants to make a child cry? This is what I am asking myself as I walk with my usher to the courtroom, as she raps on the door and makes the formal announcement to open the court, as I walk to my seat. And then I look down on the barristers below, and I have the answer to my questions . . . Bryson Haig.

There are six barristers, a leader and junior for the Crown, and a similar pairing for each of the two defendants. The six have risen and bowed to me as I stand before them, but Bryson Haig's bow is

* See Appendix K, p. 301.

cursory, and on his face is a superior and challenging sneer. To be fair to him, I doubt he is sneering at me in particular. Bryson Haig is a big and bullying man at permanent war with the world and this is the way he looks at everyone – except his client, upon whom he looks with a gentle and synthetic sympathy. He only defends, and the recipient of today's gentle look is Mrs Ibrahim. To his opponents he is Haig the Horror but to his clients he is Haig the Hero. And why not, for his clients know that to secure their acquittal he will pick a fight with every barrister, every judge, every witness. He will do whatever he is permitted to do, and some things he is not. He does not lose graciously. He does not play graciously. Graciousness is all very well on the playing fields of England, says the set of his shoulders, but this is war. He doesn't care who gets broken, who gets scarred, only that he secures his acquittal.

To give him his considerable due, he is paid to fight his corner. But from the judge's point of view, Bryson Haig needs a deal of watching, and the prospect of him cross-examining a nine-year-old is making me feel a little sick. Nausea, however, is nothing to the point. The point is to carry out this section 28 hearing and hand the case back in good order to its rightful judge. Still, it's going to be a tough morning for Sughra. I hope we have a blue elephant for her. Frankly I could do with one myself.

In the wash of emotion that Bryson Haig brings with him, I barely register that the other barristers in the case are men I know to be good at their job, and thoroughly nice men too. But I can't help wondering, where are the women? If ever there was a case in which a woman might have been instructed, it's this. Has no one thought how hard it is for a child who is to give evidence against her father – a figure (as the intermediary says) of male authority – to face other such figures, even across a television screen?

Occupied as I am with the barristers I have got and the ones I haven't, for a moment I fail to notice the defendants have been brought into the dock. When I see them, I lose interest in Mr Haig. Temporarily. I don't know what I was expecting but it wasn't this . . . this husband and wife. They look as if they have strayed into the wrong place, taken a wrong turning. They seem not to belong in my dock and manage to occupy surprisingly little space in it. Mr Ibrahim is not a small man, but he is made so by the slump of his shoulders and the downward gaze of his eyes. His wife walks in his shadow. Both obediently follow the indications of the dock officers, take their seats, then rise again when my clerk asks them to answer to their names. They are quiet and respectful. They fold their hands in their laps, he holding his Koran. It is as if they are effacing themselves from the proceedings. They do not look like killers, yet it is certain that one of them is, and possibly both are. I turn from the dock back to counsel's row. I fix an eye on Mr Haig.

'Gentlemen,' I say – for who am I to make judgements? – 'I understand today's hearing is for the child Sughra to be cross-examined, and that cross-examination is to be recorded for the jury at trial.'

They all nod. Even Mr Haig.

'The process will be carried out in the usual way over the video link to the remote witness room.' This is a fancy way to describe the little place tucked away in the far corner of the witness suite where Sughra will be waiting. 'The purpose of this arrangement is to spare her the ordeal of being in this large courtroom with many people, and of seeing her parents while she attests.'

Mr Haig squares his shoulders as if to say nobody will be spared anything in his cross-examination.

'However, we will all be able to see her' – I indicate the screens placed around the court – 'and to hear her. She will see only the face of the person speaking to her.'

All this is very familiar to the barristers but it needs to be explained so the defendants and any other interested person can understand.

'I intend to go now to introduce myself to her, and I would like leading counsel to come with me.' This is the usual procedure with a very young witness, and usually counsel are happy to do so, but Bryson Haig, it seems, is not. I am already closing down my laptop when I see he is on his feet. 'Mr Haig?'

'I would prefer not to come, My Lady.'

From his tone you might have thought I had invited him into a bordello rather than a witness room, that I wanted to introduce him to a lady of the night rather than a child of nine.

'Why ever not, Mr Haig?'

'I can see her perfectly well on the screen when the moment comes.'

I make a conscious effort to soften my voice before saying, 'Mr Haig, the exercise isn't meant for your benefit. It is meant to make the child feel more comfortable.'

No sooner have I said it than I know I shouldn't have. Bryson Haig has no intention of making this little girl feel more comfortable.

'I don't believe it will help her to see me,' he says.

I look at him, pink under the grey of his wig. His eyebrows bristle, the starch of his collar crackles. For the first time that day I agree with him.

And now prosecuting counsel is on his feet. 'My Lady, in accordance with the Code for Prosecutors, I have already met the witness . . . and if Mr Haig does not go at all, I feel it is, well, inappropriate for me to see her a second time.'

They are dropping like flies. Any moment now, counsel for the father will say he can't go either – and, yes, he's on his feet. I can make them go if I press the point, but do I really want them crowding into the small room where Sughra will be, with Mr Haig emanating hostility and the others embarrassment? I do not.

So the clerk and I go alone to a different floor, a different part of the building, to the witness suite. Here there is an extensive run of rooms, some painted in muted tones, others bright and distracting. The children's room is a riot of colour and toys and books. The witness suite is where, day after day, sometimes for weeks on end, grieving relatives will come to follow the trial that will (or won't) bring them closure. Here frightened witnesses, old and young, find refuge and courage.

I am told Sughra is already in the video link room. She is anxious to get started. There are a number of these video rooms, each equipped with a television screen that links to a court. These rooms have no windows, no pictures or posters or magazines or toys, nothing to distract the witness. There is only a table and chair facing a large television, and seating for the usher who will oversee the proceedings, and perhaps for an intermediary or interpreter as the case demands. I find the child sitting, staring at the blank screen as if she can will it into life. When she sees me she jumps up. So do the usher and intermediary. With five of us standing, there would scarcely have been room for Bryson Haig even if he had wished to come.

The child has large, serious eyes that study me carefully.

'Hello, Sughra. Why don't we all sit down?' I say.

We do. When she is settled, I ask, 'Do you know who I am?'

'The judge.' Her voice is soft and clear. She points to my wig as if that is determinative.

'I am.' I set the wig on the table.

She stares at it, where it sits like a sleepy cat.

'Do you want to hold my wig?' I ask.

She hesitates, then nods.

I give it to her. 'It's made of hair from a horse,' I say.

She considers this. 'Which horse?' she says.

'I wish I knew. Then I could take it some sugar lumps to say thank you for sharing its hair with me.'

She reflects, nods gravely and gives me back the wig.

'Sughra, do you know why you are here?'

I am sure it has all been explained to her but it's sensible to cover the ground again before she comes face to face with Mr Haig.

'You remember talking to police officers and they recorded the things you said? Have you had a chance to see those recordings?' I know she was shown the recordings yesterday, in accordance with the procedure for 'refreshing her memory'. 'You know there are some gentlemen who are going to ask you questions.'

'The barristers,' she says.

'That's right. The barristers have seen the recordings too, and now they want to ask you some questions just to check that everything you told the police is right and there are no mistakes in it.'

'Mistakes?' She looks quickly towards the door. This is the first sign of anxiety I have seen from her. It's as if she fears these unknown men with their questions are about to come in, and this little room which has been a place of safety won't be safe any more. Perhaps it was better, after all, that the barristers didn't come with me. Mr Haig would be mortified.

'They are in another room. A courtroom. When I leave here I'm going to that room too. But we will be able to see and hear you on the television' – I point to the screen – 'and you will be able to see and hear us.'

This is true, but what she sees and hears will be carefully controlled. I will permit the camera to point only to the person asking her questions. She will not see her parents sitting in the dock nor anyone in the public gallery. She will not see anything that might distract or distress her. Everything will be done to allow her to concentrate on the task in hand.

'The gentlemen will ask you questions, but I will be there to make sure they only ask you fair questions. Is that OK, Sughra?'

'Yes,' she says.

'Is there anything you'd like to ask me?'

There is not. She seems quite calm again and more than ready to do what she has to.

5

Back in the courtroom, Mr Haig will be first to cross-examine. This is because his client is first on the indictment. It is the choice of the Crown in what order they place defendants on an indictment. It can be an important tactical decision, for it dictates the order in which the barristers cross-examine prosecution witnesses, call their own evidence and make their speeches. Sometimes the Crown will choose to put the less likely wrongdoer first in the hope that material will emerge with which the prosecutor can, in his turn, cross-examine the more likely criminal.

Where there is pre-recorded evidence-in-chief (as in the ABE interview), the prosecutor will probably have no further questions to ask his witness. And so it is for Mr Haig to begin. It is tough for a barrister – without a jury to play to, without evidence-in-chief emerging just before he gets to his feet – to strike the right note, but Mr Haig has no doubt where to pitch his questioning. He is as ready as Sughra. The difference is that he knows what he is about and she doesn't. He is on home territory and she is in an unknown and alien world.

The link system is turned on. Her face fills the screen. The intermediary and usher look small in the background. I have decided she is old enough and her understanding developed enough to justify her making a formal promise to tell the truth, which she does. I instruct the intermediary to raise her hand if she thinks any ground rule is being broken, the usher to do the same if there are any problems with the link or if anyone tries to enter the room. We are ready to begin. I incline my head to Bryson Haig and he rises to his feet.

'Sit down, please, Mr Haig.' He looks startled. He has forgotten that witnesses in the remote witness room are questioned from a seated position. 'If you stand, Mr Haig, Sughra will see nothing but your waistcoat buttons.' Am I childishly gratified that he has made this mistake? I do hope not. Mr Haig scowls and sits. He glares into the screen at Sughra, who stares back at him.

'Are you a truthful little girl?' he demands.

Oh, good grief. If it starts like this, how will it end? Sometimes the better part of judicial discretion is to keep silent, but not here, not now. 'No, Mr Haig.'

'No she isn't truthful, My Lady?'

'No you may not ask that question, Mr Haig. I am sure it could not have been approved at the Ground Rules Hearing. It is a question of philosophical proportions that would challenge an academic. It is entirely unsuitable for a nine-year-old.'

Mr Haig bristles. 'It is central to the issue in this case.'

'It is irrelevant to the issue. The issue isn't whether the child is a truthful child in general, it is whether she is truthful about these matters. If you wish to introduce her general character you must make a specific application under a specific section of law.'* I don't add 'as you very well know'. I don't say, 'Push me at your peril, Mr Haig.' But our eyes lock and it might as well be horns. It is always like this with Bryson Haig.

'You are perfectly at liberty,' I continue, 'to ask whether her account in the ABE is a truthful account. If you like, I'll ask it myself.' I try to sound helpful. I ignore the hiss of pent-up steam that comes from him. Meanwhile, Sughra continues to stare across the screen.

* Section 100, Criminal Justice Act 2003.

Is she . . . can she be . . . taking his measure? Perhaps not, but she has the air of someone who has come to do a job and intends to do it. Good.

In the dock, Mrs Ibrahim keeps her head down but her husband watches Mr Haig with large eyes that darken moment by moment.

The barrister's job is generally to challenge the accuracy or truthfulness of the witness's account and to put his client's version of events. Mr Haig challenges with a will, but he puts no alternative case. Perhaps his client hasn't given him one. Perhaps he doesn't feel it appropriate with so young a witness. Whatever the reason, he satisfies himself with testing and probing to see if any part of her account will yield to him.

'Sughra,' he says, 'after your sister went out, you went to bed.'

The child looks at him, expectant, waiting for the question.

I sigh. 'Questions not statements, please, Mr Haig.'

He looks at me as if I am a new offence in the criminal calendar but all he says is, 'Sughra, after your sister went out, you did go to bed, didn't you?'

'No tag questions, Mr Haig.'

His cheeks darken dangerously. I truly hope he gets it right this time. I don't want to be responsible for a haemorrhagic stroke.

'Sughra, after your sister went out, did you go to bed?'

'Yes,' she says.

'Did you go to sleep?'

'Yes.'

'What woke you?'

A moment's pause, then, 'The shouting. Baba was shouting and so was Kubra.'

'But not your mother.' Mr Haig, defending Mrs Ibrahim, is only interested in her; but on each side of him the other barristers stiffen.

Sughra pauses, thinks. 'No,' she says, 'not my mother.'

'What did you do then?'

'I tried to go back to sleep.'

'And did you go back to sleep?'

She shakes her head. 'I couldn't. I listened to the shouting. Then I got out of bed.'

'Where did you go?'

'To the top of the stairs.'

'And then?'

She hesitates. Her little hand creeps up to pull at the end of her hair. Poor child, I think. She doesn't want to go where he is taking her. But Mr Haig is determined to drag her there.

'Answer my question, please,' he says brusquely.

'I went . . . I went down the stairs, and . . .'

'And?'

'And into the front room.' I can hear her mouth is dry. So can the intermediary, who pours a glass of water and places it on the table in front of her.

Mr Haig has got her where he wants her and is on home territory now – he will test her ability to see what she said she saw. He will go through light, distance, angles . . . and Sughra, being asked to recall what must be the most terrifying thing that has ever happened to her in her whole life, doesn't want to do this. You can see it in the sudden deep lines running from cheekbones to the corners of her mouth, in the slump of her shoulders.

'Is there a ceiling light in the front room?' demands Mr Haig.

The child looks bemused.

'Mr Haig,' I say, 'if you are changing subject, please do so in accordance with the ground rules and set the context for the witness.'

Mr Haig looks mutinous but says to Sughra, 'I'm going to ask you about what you could see, how you could see it . . .'

She nods reluctantly.

'So,' he says, 'is there a ceiling light in the front room?'

'Yes.'

'Was it turned on?'

She pauses, thinks. 'No.'

'So how could you see?'

Her shoulders tense but she answers quickly enough: 'Because the lamp was on.'

Counsel and I look at the bundle of photos which the Crown has provided.

'The tall lamp beside the chair in the corner?'

'Yes.'

'Where was Kubra?'

'Behind the mosque.'

We look again at the picture, at the low coffee table pushed to the left, the dome and white spires so carefully put together now knocked askew. Still you can see how perfect the symmetry was, with what patient love the detail had been recreated. I look from the screen to the dock, at the man who built it. A person who can do this might be expected to have built the life of his family with the same patient love.

'Kubra was behind the mosque against the wall. Baba pushed the table to one side and it went . . .' She demonstrates with her hands how the model got damaged.

'Your father pushed the table almost up against the wall on one side and went through the gap on the other side to where Kubra was?'

She nods.

'He was standing over Kubra?'

'His hands were . . .' Again she hesitates – she is an admirably careful witness. 'Like this.' She demonstrates, hands to her neck. 'And Kubra was doing this.' Again she shows us the horrible clawing motion of Kubra desperately trying to pull something from her neck. It is a shocking thing to see. Even Mr Haig is silenced by it. But not for long.

'But that was your father, not your mother.'

'Baba,' she says. 'Not Ammi.'

Mr Haig should have stopped. Stopped right there, right then. But he can't resist asking one more question: 'Your mummy didn't do anything, did she?'

I can afford to ignore the statement-not-question, the forbidden tag at the end, because Sughra isn't deflected or confused. She says, 'Ammi didn't do anything . . .'

Mr Haig is already leaning back in his seat.

'. . . not until Kubra fell to the floor.'

Mr Haig hesitates, but Sughra doesn't. She speaks in a rush now as if she must get the words out before they choke her. 'Kubra fell to the floor and Baba bent over her and so did Ammi. And Ammi was holding Kubra.' She holds her own arm, showing us what she means. Her small fingers close just above her left elbow, just where (Mr Haig and the rest of us know it) the pathologist found the grip mark.

Mr Haig sits forward again. There is no way Sughra can have made lucky guesses about the position of the bruises on the arm, on the head. He knows he shouldn't have asked that last question but he can't go back. The only way is on, so on he goes. 'You didn't see these things,' he accuses. 'You are a liar.'

Sughra stares. Her eyes fill with tears, which hover on the edge of her lower lashes.

'Mr Haig,' I warn.

But Bryson Haig has a finely attuned sense for the kill. Man and child stare at each other across the screen. He frowns. He turns back to the photographs, studies them for a moment, then looks back at her. 'How tall are you?' he snaps.

She looks blank.

His voice is urgent. He almost shouts, 'Does anyone know how tall this child is?'

'Mr Haig, you will ask appropriate questions of this witness, or you will conclude your cross-examination.'

But Mr Haig is no respecter of judges. He turns on Sughra. 'You,' he says, 'aren't tall enough to see over the top of that mosque, are you?'

Is she? Now he has said it, it's obvious. She is not, and she knows it. Slowly, dumbly, she shakes her head.

'So how did you see what happened to Kubra when she was on the floor?'

She bites her lip, draws a strand of her hair into her mouth and chews it, says nothing.

'If you are telling the truth, if your baba and your ammi were standing in the space on the right-hand side of the table, and you couldn't see over the top, how did you see what you say you saw?'

Too many 'see's and 'say's and 'saw's . . . Mr Haig is breaching every rule, but he is on to something. You can see it in Sughra's eyes – the panic, the defeat.

'You didn't see it, did you?'

Oh, Mr Haig, can't you ask a question without a tag? Do you have to raise your voice? Do it once more and I will have to stop you . . . but I won't stop you just yet because you are defending a woman charged with murdering her daughter, and you are about to show that the prosecution evidence is based on . . . on what? A lie?

'Temper your tone, Mr Haig,' I warn. 'Sughra' – I try to speak calmly, neither accusingly nor the opposite, just seeking the information – 'can you tell Mr Haig how you saw the things you told us about?'

'I stood in the gap on the other side of the table?' She indicates the left-hand side, but her answer is in the form of a question . . . her last desperate gamble, and it will fail because we can all see the photographs. We can all see the table had been pushed too close to the left-hand wall for this nine-year-old to have stood in the gap. Bryson Haig has her.

'You're lying!' he roars.

That does it. 'Enough, Mr Haig.'

'But—'

'I said enough. You have made your point.'

The prosecutor is sitting stony-faced. On the screen the intermediary half stands, appalled. Blown big on the screen, Sughra's face breaks apart, tears pour down her cheeks. I would put an end to this immediately but she is trying to say something, trying very hard to form the words, and she must be allowed to say what she needs to. The usher gives her a tissue which she scrunches into a ball and scrubs across her eyes.

'I lied,' she sobs. 'I lied. I lied.'

It's enough. She lied and that is an end of it. Or it would have been, but Mr Haig cannot resist it. He just never learns.

'Why did you lie?' he shouts.

The child looks straight into the camera. 'Because the lady said . . .' She sobs, gets control of herself. 'The lady said we could only tell what each of us saw, and Ata wouldn't.'

There is a silence while we digest this, while the prosecutor's face turns from stone to something softer, and Mr Haig's hardens. In the dock, Sughra's mother and father look at each other. It's left to me to ask it.

'What are you saying, Sughra?'

'Ata,' she weeps. 'He saw it. He told me. But he wouldn't tell the lady with the elephant, and I couldn't tell her what Ata told me because she said I was only allowed to say what I saw myself. So I pretended it was me who saw it, but it wasn't.' Her voice trails away.

'Not you?'

'Not me,' she whimpers. 'Ata.'

6

I tell Sughra we are going to take a little break. I give instructions that she is to be kept in the children's room in the witness suite. When the link has been turned off, the prosecutor rises to his feet.

'My Lady, may I . . .?'

Yes, you may. You may have a short adjournment. You may go and talk to the CPS and the officers who dealt with the children. You must, because there is still Kubra to think about. And justice. Careful thought must now be given to the questioning of Ata. Some four-year-olds are perfectly capable of giving a truthful and accurate account of what they have seen. The courts have taken evidence from witnesses as young as three. But it's a big ask of this small boy and it must be done only after consultation with experts who can assess him, his capacity and needs. And things must be done quickly because every day when the children are together risks Sughra saying something that might contaminate Ata's account.

'Two o'clock,' I say to the prosecutor, 'for an update on what you propose should happen next.'

Lunch is miserable beyond the haddock kedgeree, which heaven knows is a matter for misery in itself. I can't put out of my mind the little girl who tried so hard to do the right thing for her dead sister, and who has failed. Who has been failed by the system. Whom we have all let down.

At two o'clock we are back in court. Mr and Mrs Ibrahim are in the dock again but – I'm surely not imagining it – they are not as they were before. They are sitting forward, waiting tensely, their eyes on the prosecutor as he rises to his feet.

'My Lady . . .' he says.

He is going to tell me that the Crown wants to re-interview Ata, the beloved son in whose small hands the key to this case now seems to lie. He is going to say that with more careful thought and the input of a child psychologist to help plan the ABE interview, there is a chance, a good chance, that Ata will give the account which Sughra tried so hard to give for him. The Crown will need some time to do this, during which, what will happen to Ata and Sughra? I will, of course, give him the adjournment he needs because my job is only to see the guilty brought to justice, the innocent acquitted. But, oh, the consequences of what is playing out before me. If Ata does give the account which Sughra says he can, then what happens to these two children? And if he doesn't? Then, since neither parent can be identified as a killer and both may be acquitted, the children may go back to the house where their sister was murdered, back to the parent or parents they know were responsible for her death. And Ata will go through his life carrying his silent burden.

The prosecutor is waiting patiently. All right, I think, make your application. Ask for your adjournment. But he doesn't. Instead he says, 'My Lady, may the indictment be put again to Mr Ibrahim?'

I blink in astonishment. This can only mean one thing.

Counsel for Mr Ibrahim is standing now. 'Yes, My Lady. We would ask that Mr Ibrahim is re-arraigned.'

I am beyond words, but a nod suffices. My clerk stands. Mr Ibrahim does the same. For a moment he is unsteady on his feet but then he is himself again, more himself than I have yet seen him. He is once again head of his family and sure of his place in the universe.

'Akhi Ibrahim, you are charged with murder,' says my clerk. 'The particulars of the offence are that on the thirteenth of May 20—you murdered Kubra Ibrahim. Do you plead guilty or not guilty?'

Mr Ibrahim doesn't hesitate. 'Guilty,' he says. He speaks as if it is his duty to say the word.

I have to force myself to turn from the man in the dock because the prosecutor is explaining something and requires my attention. He is telling me that in the light of Mr Ibrahim's plea of guilty, the Crown accepts that Mrs Ibrahim was only trying to help her daughter and will not proceed further against her.

So this is the deal that has been done. The father pleads guilty to murder. The mother goes free. I can't know if Mr Ibrahim was indeed the murderer, and if he was, whether he was the only murderer. I can't know if the killing was a spontaneous moment of mad fury or a calculated act to stop what the family somehow perceived as wickedness by poor little Kubra. I can't know if he offered up the life of his elder daughter to his beliefs, or if he is offering up himself for his family. But this I do know. Neither he nor his wife is prepared to offer up Ata.

7

How to understand the Ibrahims? How to follow where these parents have gone – the killing of one daughter, the preparedness to let another be tortured for trying to tell the truth?

No one can think the killing of a child is anything other than wicked. But how can a court like mine really understand the tensions at work here? What must it have been like for this family? A husband and wife whose religious and cultural roots were the foundation of their very view of life. Kubra, a girl on the verge of womanhood who had grown up both in their world and another beyond their household. Sughra, the bright and brave little girl who was guided by none of them but only her own sense of justice. And

Ata. Little Ata, who, too young to make any decision of his own, had knowledge he did not want thrust upon him.

The wickedness that has been done cannot be undone. Nothing can bring Kubra back. Nothing can fill the hole in Sughra's heart. But perhaps (and perhaps I hope this is so) no punishment I can give Akhi Ibrahim will be worse than the daily punishment he will from now on inflict upon himself.

The criminal law is at its weakest when it is dealing with domestic violence. It is too blunt an instrument to cut through the thicket of emotions that lie at the heart of family relationships. And the criminal courts are at their most fragile when dealing with the evidence of a vulnerable child witness. The courts are bound by rules which can conflict with each other and which require honesty and integrity to disentangle. So, for example, all barristers have an overriding duty to the court to act with independence in the interests of justice, and not to knowingly or recklessly mislead the court. The defence barrister also has a duty to act in the best interests of the defendant by all proper and lawful means, which may include cross-examining vulnerable and intimidated witnesses about matters which are very distressing to them. The judge has a duty to ensure that witnesses can give evidence to the best of their ability. But it is also the duty of the judge to ensure that no defendant is ever convicted unless the jury is sure of his or her guilt. Guilt should only ever be proved after a scrupulously fair trial. But both sides – prosecution and defence – are entitled to fairness. This is the struggle which every judge faces.

A while back I told Sughra that I would only allow the barristers to ask fair questions . . . but what is a fair question? It is easy to stop questions that are irrelevant or merely offensive. It is easy to stop questions that breach ground rules about clarity and simplicity. But it is much more difficult when it is the tone or the attitude of the questioner which is offensive or intimidating. Does a fair question become unfair by reason of the way in which it is asked? Bryson Haig, after all, got to the truth. And so it is the job of the judge to watch over all these matters, to decide when to intervene and when not to. Decisions have to be made and there is no one else to decide them. The Bench can be a lonely place.

TRIAL FIVE:
The Good Soldier

LONDON WAS HOT as hell. Four days with the mercury pushing high into the thirties, the fourth stifling night. It was nothing new to him. Iraq had been hot. Afghanistan had been hotter. Syria . . . best not to think of Syria. No one could sleep in this heat. He reckoned he could cope better than most, but four sleepless nights was enough to get anyone down. She had opened all the windows but there weren't many of them. The flat was small, high up. He closed his eyes and perhaps he dozed because he was suddenly high up in another small place. A tent on the side of a mountain. Here the air should be blessedly cold, so the heat that was suffocating him must mean something, must mean danger, must mean gas-attack or they have set a fire or . . . He threw off the sheet and got up.

She was still asleep. He was glad of that, at least. He couldn't bear her sympathy, though he recognized there had been less of that recently. He thought of how, earlier, she had confronted him, had said it couldn't go on . . . as if he wanted it to go on. As if he wouldn't have stopped it if he could. As if he courted this torture. He stared at her, at her breasts rising and falling, at the hair across her face that stirred with her steady breathing. She fussed too much, he thought. He couldn't bear the fussing. He had enough of that with the psychiatrists.

He hated the psychiatrists. He couldn't understand why they poked about in minds when they could have worked with bodies. God knows, there were enough bodies needing help. Think of Iraq. Think of Afghanistan. Think of . . . no, don't think of Syria. They said they understood what was going on in his mind. They gave it a name. PTSD, they said. It's common, they said. Not just soldiers, they said, but battered wives and abused children and all sorts. They knew what it was, but they couldn't make it go away. Years of it behind him. Years of it ahead of him. Endless torment.

At least they had given him the tablets. Perhaps he'd take one. Outside in the London night a siren sounded and took him back to a place that wrung his heart. Yes, he'd take a tablet. She kept them in the kitchen drawer. Counted them. Regulated his taking of them. Shouted at him when he took too many. Shouted she would leave him if he couldn't control himself. Said she cared about him too much to bear what he had become. But she was asleep now.

He padded across the bedroom and into the kitchen. The ghost of moonlight shone in. He didn't turn on the light. He didn't want to give them any clue where he was. Caution was the watchword. They could creep up on you in a moment. He felt for the drawer and slid it open. His hand closed around the tablets. With great care he pushed the wrapping to release the capsule. The foil cracked with a sound that made sweat spangle his forehead and drip into his eyes. Another siren screamed past and the sense of danger was so acute he thought he might vomit.

He went to the sink, found a cup and ran some water. You could torture people with water. He swallowed the tablet. He realized he was shaking and leaned against the work surface to steady himself. In front of him he saw the dark shape of the knife block. He pulled out the meat knife. It felt cool in his hand. A blade is a good thing to have against danger. Best to keep a blade close. After all, they could be anywhere, everywhere. He began to make his way round the kitchen with slow care, peering into corners, opening cupboards, bending to look under the little table.

When he was sure the kitchen was safe, he went back into the hall. He felt his way to the cupboard, put his ear to it, thought he caught the drawing of a ragged breath behind it. One hand held the knife. The other he placed gently on the cupboard door. He steeled himself and then with a sharp movement pulled it open. The little light inside came on. He stared at the suitcase. It lived on a shelf at the back of the cupboard and someone had moved it. He bent down and tested its weight. Heavy. Full. Slowly he opened it. It took a while for him to understand what he was seeing – her clothes, her washbag, a book she was reading. On the top, a picture of him as he had been in the army. Beneath that, a sheet of paper. 'Dear Josh . . . ' – her large, looping hand spread across the page – 'so very sorry . . . I don't seem able to help . . . only till you are better and I am more able to cope . . . just need some space . . . school holidays seem a good time to get away . . . only for a while . . . love.'

Love! He put the paper on the floor and ripped it through with the point of the knife. He spent a moment or two considering the coldness that had settled inside him, despite the heat. Then he closed the cupboard door and went silently back to the bedroom.

For a while he watched the shape of her on the bed, listened to her breathing. Sweat dripped down his arm so that the knife was slick in his hand. He made himself focus on every tiny sound. He wanted to be sure they weren't too close. When he was satisfied, he lay down beside her. For a moment he couldn't think what to do with the knife, then he slid it down by his side and it felt cool against his skin.

Beside him she slept on. It wasn't fair that she slept so easily. He thought about the unfairness of it. Then he thought about what she had written. Surely she wouldn't leave him. And if she did? If she deserted him? He thought of deserters, of those who left their comrades to suffer and die. They had to be punished. It was only right. The punishment for desertion in time of war was death. Another siren. He was drenched in sweat now and his stomach heaved inside him. His heart pounded. He thought of the blood flowing through him, flowing through her. He thought of its redness. Red for danger. There was danger everywhere, and it was inside and it had to be let out. His hand closed on the knife.

1

It took a long time to get Joshua Goodall's case heard. On five
separate occasions he was brought to court, each time accompanied
by two nurses and a psychiatric report. At first he was deemed 'not
fit for trial', diagnosed with – among other things – severe depression related to trauma and bereavement. That raised eyebrows in the
press-box and public gallery. 'Run that past us again' said the eyebrows. 'A man kills his wife and gets depressed because he is
bereaved? Are you serious?' It was apparently serious enough for
prison doctors to transfer him to a psychiatric hospital for the period
of his remand. And that raised eyebrows too. Before she became her
husband's victim, Joy Goodall had been a much-loved and respected
daughter, sister, aunt and teacher. Sympathy was in short supply for
her killer. Still, with or without the sympathy, two doctors including
one for the prosecution had found him 'Pritchard unfit'; that is to say,
he could not properly follow and participate in the proceedings.*

Ten months and some interim hearings later, he is back before
me again. The doctors have decided he is now fit enough to stand
his trial but he doesn't look fit for much else. He has lost muscle and
grown gaunt. His hair is shaggy and unkempt in a way neither the
army nor Joy would have countenanced. Still, he stands or sits as
directed, answers to his name, and seems to be listening to counsel
and myself. He appears as normal as many others who come before
me – except when he places his hands over his eyes as if to hide
himself from us. Each time he does this, his nurses gently urge him

* See Appendix L, pp. 302–3.

to lower his arms, and each time he does so I see his eyes are large and liquid with fear. It's as if the glass partition around the dock is to keep us out rather than to keep him in.

He is defended by Stella Camden KC. She is a canny and experienced silk, used to representing people charged with homicide. She has sat many times in a tiny cell in the bowels of this and other courts, face to face with a killer. She knows her job. She needs to. Defending in a murder case where an accused has mental health issues is difficult. As well as the ordinary range of defences, entirely different ones need to be considered. The fact that Joshua Goodall may have mental illness doesn't mean he must be guilty of murder; and it doesn't mean he can't be innocent for the same reasons any accused might be. Like any defendant, his case might be:

- 'I wasn't there', or
- 'I was there but I didn't do it', or
- 'I did do it but it was an accident', or
- 'It wasn't an accident but my act, though deliberate, was only done in self-defence', or
- 'I only did it because I lost my self-control'

However, a defendant with mental health issues might also be raising a psychiatric defence:

- 'I did it but I didn't know what I was doing or that it was wrong because I was insane at the time', or
- 'I did it but my responsibility for doing so was diminished because of my mental state'*

* See Appendix M, p. 304.

I have known optimistic defendants try to run more than one defence at the same time, their case being something like this: 'I wasn't there, but if I was I didn't do it, and if I did, it was an accident, and anyway insanity runs in the family.' As a judge once memorably put it, 'good luck with that one'.

If you had a choice of defences, you wouldn't pick the psychiatric ones. Both come with serious difficulties. First and very unusually, each shifts the burden of proof away from the prosecution (where it usually is) and on to the defence. Generally the prosecution must make the jury sure a defence does not apply, but with a psychiatric defence the defendant must satisfy the jury on a balance of probability that it does apply. Not an easy burden to bear.

The psychiatric defences are not ideal in another way too. Even if they succeed, neither of them leads to a straightforward acquittal. After a verdict of 'not guilty by reason of insanity' a judge often sends the defendant to a hospital where he may remain for many years before it is deemed safe to release him. A verdict of diminished responsibility is, from the defendant's point of view, even worse because while it leads to a verdict of 'not guilty of murder', it involves the alternative 'guilty of manslaughter', which may (and generally does) lead to a long term of imprisonment.

Some defendants may be spoiled for choice, but Joshua Goodall isn't. The evidence makes clear that he was the only person in the flat with Joy, that she was asleep in bed when she died, that it was his hand and no other that held the knife, and that the neat and fatal cutting of her throat was no accident. That leaves Stella Camden with the psychiatric defences. The defence of insanity requires her client to have parted company with reality in a way that she cannot hope to prove. All that is left is diminished responsibility. If she cannot argue that her client was not responsible for Joy's death, she can at least try to persuade the jury that he wasn't *fully* responsible for his actions because he was mentally ill. This is the mast to which she has pinned her colours – and she makes no bones about it.

'My Lady,' she says, 'my client is charged with murder, which he denies. However, he accepts he killed his wife. His defence to murder rests on his state of mind, which we will argue diminishes his responsibility for the killing from murder to manslaughter. If the prosecution will accept a plea of guilty to manslaughter, there is no need for a trial.'

Neil Selwyn KC is on his feet. 'My Learned Friend well knows the Crown does not accept that defence applies here. We say this is murder, and if the defendant doesn't accept that, there will be a trial, and the jury must choose between murder and manslaughter.'

Miss Camden and Mr Selwyn glare at each other – two perfectly nice and reasonable people fighting other people's battles with as much venom as if the battle were their own.

And so when Neil Selwyn opens the case to the jury he tells them, 'The Crown will call evidence about how Joy Goodall died, at whose hands, where and when. Very little of this will be disputed by the defence. Rather, they will invite you to conclude that when Joshua Goodall slit the throat of his loving wife, it wasn't murder because he had a mental illness which diminished his responsibility. We for the prosecution do not accept that – and if the defence call psychiatric evidence to this end, we will challenge it and rebut it with psychiatric evidence of our own.'

Mr Selwyn is a peaceable man not given to theatrical outpouring, but Joy was a good woman and before the trial started he spent time with her grieving family. Besides, he knows the public gallery is full of her friends and colleagues, all looking to him to express their hatred and contempt for the man who took her from them. Of course it is no business of the prosecutor to express any such thing, but, after all, Neil Selwyn is only human.

2

Having opened the case, the prosecutor begins to call his evidence. He concentrates on painting a picture of Joy Goodall. His kindly manner conceals a steely determination to make her life and death a real thing to this jury, and that's not as easy as it sounds. In a murder trial it can be a struggle to keep the dead alive. Faced with the physical presence of the defendant and the absence of the deceased, a jury can lose the fact that what is now 'the body' was once as real as they are, was a person who could have sat beside them on a bus or in a coffee shop or even in another jury-box. Mr Selwyn, however, does a good job of making Joy live for us. Her photograph is at the front of the graphics bundle, next to one of the defendant – the two of them, head-and-shoulders, side by side. That of Joy shows her leaning a little towards the camera, eyes large and bright, lips wide in a smile. Her hair falls in clusters of curls. It is a kind face, a compassionate face. It is the face of the woman she was – a nursery-school teacher, well used to providing plasters for small hurts and comfort for larger ones. The invisible subtext for the jury reads: 'This is the sort of person to whom you entrust your own children, because this was a good woman.' Beside her, the photograph of Joshua in his army uniform is unsmiling and stiff. 'Don't be fooled by the man in the dock' is the subliminal message, 'because this is who he really is. He is a soldier. He is a killer.' It is the job of the prosecution to make the jury sure of the facts that prove guilt . . . but you can't overestimate the impact of emotion on what a jury finds – that, at least, is what these photographs seem to prove.

The evidence that follows only strengthens the impression. For three days the prosecution builds its case, brick after brick, nail after nail. It begins with Joy's last evening. At 8 p.m. she had phoned her sister. They had chatted, planned a shopping trip. Neil Selwyn is an experienced KC who knows what he's about, and he calls the sister to give evidence. He doesn't need to. Her statement could be read. But with the appearance of her sister, Joy is before us. The woman in the witness-box has the same eyes that look out at us from the jury bundle; when she speaks it is with the same lips. Grief hangs palpably about her as she describes the last time she spoke to her sister.

'Joy was so worried about him . . .'

Mr Selwyn doesn't press her, only says gently, 'About . . .?'

'Him.' She shoots a bitter glance at the dock. Joshua Goodall lifts his head to stare back at the face so like the one he gripped, the neck so like the one he slit. The jury stiffens. He is a step closer to conviction.

Next, Mr Selwyn takes us to the 999 call. At three o'clock in the morning Mrs Abella May, in the adjoining flat, phoned the police. Such calls are always recorded and this one is now played to us.

'There's a noise,' says the disembodied voice of Mrs May. 'It's been going on for an hour. It's . . . well, it's not a screaming, not a weeping, but a sort of keening. It's not right. Listen for yourself.' She must have taken the phone to her balcony because the courtroom is suddenly filled with the sound she was unable to describe, and which had caused the operator without hesitation to send police and ambulance.

When Mr Selwyn has finished with this he presents the jury with another recording, this one even more distressing. The images have been captured by a body camera worn by one of the officers who went to the scene. We see the police car draw up, the officers get out. We are with them as they go to the entrance to the block. They have a little difficulty getting in, but soon we are in a narrow lobby, with a narrower staircase. Their footsteps thud and echo on the stone steps. The darkness is broken only by occasional and inadequate wall lights, high up behind grilles. On the fifth floor they leave the staircase and now we are looking down a corridor with doorways on each side. One of the doors opens and a man appears. He is bare-chested, bare-footed, holding out his hands which are dark with blood. Before the officers can say anything he comes towards them.

'I killed her,' he says. 'I killed my Joy.' The voice is flat, a bald state-ment of fact.

The jury don't know what they would sound like if they were mak-ing such a confession but – says the collective look on their juridical face – it wouldn't be like this. It wouldn't be so cold and distant. They would at least have the grace to weep and show remorse.

'Ladies and gentlemen,' says Mr Selwyn, 'would you kindly open your jury bundles at divider two.'

We do, and find ourselves inside the flat itself. Together we look at the photographs of the bedroom where Joy died. The body has been removed, exposing to the camera the tangle of sheets with their terrible stains, the knife caught up in them. In the kitchen, the photographer had taken pictures of the knife block, the empty slot; in the hallway, the cupboard, the little suitcase, the torn halves of the letter she had so carefully written for Josh. Nothing escapes the camera lens.

We move on to the post-mortem and the pathologist who has examined Joy's body with the same care and thoroughness. He found bruising to her back and a broken rib consistent with the defendant having knelt heavily on her. There was fingertip bruising round her jawline where he had forced her head back, and a gaping wound across her neck like a smiling second mouth. The knife had cut straight through the jugular vein, the thyroid and the trachea. It would not have been an easy death, blood pouring from her as she struggled to suck in oxygen through a severed airway. It would, says the pathologist, have taken some minutes for her to collapse into unconsciousness and death. And she had known what was happening. She must have been woken from sleep and struggled to fight him off before he overcame her, because her hands and fore-arms bear the marks of defensive injuries. I ask the pathologist to explain these injuries.

'You get them in cases of knife attack,' he says, 'when the victim sees the blade coming and raises her arms to ward it off, or grabs it in an effort to stop it penetrating her face or body.'

A silence as the jury takes this in, pictures the man in the dock, knife in hand, breath hissing with the effort of holding down another human being, ripping the knife through her with quick, irremedi-able movements.

Next, Neil Selwyn takes us to the police station where CCTV footage shows Joshua Goodall in the custody suite. 'Good Christ,' the custody sergeant is heard to say, 'what's happened here?' We are by now all thinking much the same thing. The defendant stands before the police officer. His eyes are sunken hollows in his face. There is blood across his naked torso and stiffening his hair. He is all grey and red. He is a figure out of Dante, out of Milton, out of Hell.

Finally, the prosecutor plays for us the police tape recording of the interview with their suspect. The proper procedure had been followed: a doctor had certified him fit for interview, a duty solicitor had been called to help and advise him, police had dis-closed what he was to be questioned about, and time was given for a consultation. Then the solicitor, suspect and police officers had sat down in a room equipped with recording devices. All this is very usual. What was not usual were the solicitor's next words.

'Before you start,' he said, 'I want to make it clear that, in my view, my client is unfit to be questioned.'

'That's not the view of the medical officer,' says the police officer.

'Then' – the solicitor's professional voice is momentarily replaced by one of bemusement – 'your medical officer needs to take another look.' Professional again, he says, 'I have advised my client not to answer any of your questions.'

Perhaps the solicitor was right, because his client seems not to have understood the purpose of the advice he has been given. While he obediently gives no answers to the questions asked, he does – regularly, and in a mercilessly clear voice – say, 'I killed her. I killed my Joy.'

This is not how it is supposed to go, and after some minutes of it, the officer's nerve breaks. 'Interview terminated,' he says.

And so Joshua Goodall was charged with murder. He was remanded in custody and – the solicitor really may have been right – within a few weeks the prison medical team shipped him out to a psychiatric hospital. There his medical record is long and convoluted. The one thing that is clear is his repeated insistence that he had killed his Joy.

Three days of evidence, and Stella Camden has barely asked a question. She challenges nothing and only speaks to clarify a detail here and there. In the dock, Joshua Goodall sits, arms hanging limp, head down as if the weight of his thoughts is too much for him to bear. The jury look at him, and look away. Are they seeing a frightened and pathetic man or are they seeing a killer? For killer he certainly is. He has been trained to do it and he is good at it – at least, he made a very thorough job of killing Joy.

Three days of evidence, but it's not perhaps the evidence that will ultimately matter because we all know – have known since Mr Selwyn's opening – that the real question here will be a psychiatric one. The real drama is yet to come. The leading actors are still in the wings – or, to be precise, they are in the row of seats behind counsel, where Dr Parker and Professor Frick sit listening and making diligent notes in their files.

3

Psychiatrists, being experts, are a more exotic breed of witness than your common-or-garden variety. Ordinary witnesses can only tell the jury what they saw or heard, but experts have specialized knowledge and experience which allow them to offer an *opinion* in their field of expertise. The purpose of such evidence is to provide the jury with findings and opinions in areas of science, medicine or other technical matters about which they could not be expected, without assistance, to form conclusions. At least, these are the words (or something like them) with which a judge must explain experts to jurors.

Historically, there was the pathologist who dealt with the body, the psychiatrist who dealt with the mind, the fingerprint expert who speaks for himself, and the blood-splatter man who . . . isn't it interesting, the things that people choose to make their life's work? But times have changed and custom cannot stale the infinite variety of expertise which the courts have gradually come to accept. Nowadays, experts in DNA and telephonic communications are commonplace. Experts in CCTV images and foot- and shoeprints turn up regularly. From time to time experts in fabrics, fire, insects and flora, handwriting and voice recognition appear in my court. Occasionally I see readers of gait, facial-mappers, and specialists in the mores and argot of street gangs. Then there are the rare birds – the hypnotists, and those who know all there is to know about ear prints . . . seriously. There are hundreds of categories of expertise but, among them all, many of us still consider psychiatry one of the most arcane.

Forensic psychiatry most commonly deals with men, but there are plenty of woman and child offenders with mental illness. It most commonly deals with violence, but addiction disorders like drugs or gambling can lead people to steal; and emotional or personality disorders can lead to sex offending. The strangeness of the science of psychiatry is its 'untouchability'. The cause of a physical illness or injury can be identified – bacteria, virus, wound or poison. But the cause in the brain of a mental illness is often unseeable and, perhaps, unknowable. The psychiatrist can tell you what events may have precipitated a mental illness, what symptoms result, what medication might help, but in the courtroom we don't see the hurt bit of the brain as we see the severed aorta or crushed trachea. Psychiatrists don't tell juries what a brain with PTSD looks like or how it differs from a brain without PTSD. Instead they identify the illness by the symptoms. And as with anything that is difficult to observe, grasp hold of and test, even experts may form very different and fiercely held conclusions. I have rifled through the Digital Case System and read the reports of Professor Frick and Dr Parker. I know we are in for a classic Battle of the Experts.

This sort of conflict is always difficult for the jury, for how do they choose which expert is right? The answer, I fear, is that they will be persuaded by whoever is the more persuasive. The way in which psychiatrists present the evidence, the way in which they can engage and get a jury to follow their arguments, may make the difference between a defendant being convicted of murder or not.

I said that Dr Parker and Professor Frick sat making diligent notes, but in fact Dr Parker is less diligent than Professor Frick. He comes and goes, nodding to ushers and others, for he is a familiar figure at the Old Bailey, sometimes giving evidence for the Crown, sometimes for the defence. He is probably popping into other courtrooms to tell other juries about a psychosis here, a schizophrenia there. His neat black three-piece suit demands our trust in his professional judgement. His measured tones tell us we can have faith in him. I know from his report that Dr Parker takes a dim view of

Joshua Goodall's defence. 'The man may have symptoms of PTSD,' it says, 'but that doesn't mean he isn't a murderer.'

The expert sitting behind Miss Camden is very different. She's a woman I haven't seen before. She sits through every word of the evidence, a large bag beside her and a large pad of paper in front of her. The bag and pad echo her general largeness. And her brain must be sizeable too because the qualifications set out in her report occupy most of its first page. She is clearly not used to the Old Bailey and looks about her with innocent and frank interest. Miss Camden is taking a risk to put Professor Frick up against one of the most experienced forensic psychiatric witnesses in the business. But the professor is an expert in a particular field – the very one with which we are concerned, that of PTSD in soldiers. She holds more than one university post. She has studied endless cases of PTSD and written about them. She has no doubt had very many patients. She knows what is to be known about her subject; but her subject is not the courtroom. I watch her scribbling furiously, passing a drift of notes to Miss Camden, who bears it with fortitude. Dr Parker – when he is present – watches this too, lifts his left eyebrow, smiles. This is going to be interesting, and I am looking forward to it. It should follow hard on the heels of Mr Selwyn closing his case – unless Miss Camden is going to call her client.

If Joshua Goodall is to give evidence, he must do so before the expert. I look again at the man in the dock, whose head is still down. If I were Miss Camden, would I call him? I wouldn't want to. I would think he'd do himself little good in the witness-box. On the other hand, it is his case and if he wanted to talk directly to the jury, I wouldn't stop him. His choice. Her problem. So when Mr Selwyn closes his case and sits down, I turn expectantly to Miss Camden. Will it be Joshua Goodall or Professor Frick whose name she speaks? Slowly she rises to her feet.

'My Lady . . .'

Frick or Goodall? One or the other. But Miss Camden calls neither. Instead she asks for a break.

'A break?' I say.

'Time for the jury to have a cup of coffee.'

'Now?'

'Now if you please, My Lady.'

'Ten minutes,' I tell the jury. They leave the courtroom. I remain. I don't believe for one moment counsel cannot go ahead without a shot of caffeine. I am right.

'My Lady, may we detain you for a moment?'

It is Mr Selwyn who is now on his feet. Whatever are they up to?

'My Lady, Miss Camden and I have been discussing the course the trial will now take. I understand she has not yet finally decided if she will call her client into the witness-box, or whether she will embark upon the psychiatric evidence . . .'

Miss Camden acknowledges this is where she is at.

'Well, she had better make up her mind,' I say – caffeine deprivation is apt to make me spiky – 'because she only has ten minutes to decide.'

'It may be rather longer than ten minutes,' says Mr Selwyn gently.

I narrow my eyes and prepare for trouble. It transpires that both barristers think it would be helpful if I were to give the jury directions about murder and diminished responsibility at this stage. Normally the judge gives such 'directions of law' at the end of all the evidence, preceded by counsel's final speeches and followed by a summing-up of the facts. But in more recent times it has become common for some directions of law to be given at an earlier stage in the trial if this will help the jury follow the evidence. It is a sensible thing to do where the law is particularly complicated. It allows jurors to recognize and focus on the areas of evidence that will really matter to the decision they will ultimately have to make.

'The issue for the jury will be one of diminished responsibility,' he says. 'It can be difficult.'

It certainly can.

'We thought that if Your Ladyship gave the jury the direction on murder and manslaughter by reason of diminished responsibility at this stage, it would enable them to follow the psychiatric evidence more clearly.'

Dr Parker, who has reappeared, nods judiciously. Professor Frick looks as if she has no idea what we are talking about.

The barristers are asking me to give the jury a written document. It will set out the questions the jury must ask themselves, the steps they must follow to reach their verdict. It requires me to reduce into a form that a layman can understand an area of complex law that taxes most barristers. Although the law of murder is always the same, the document headed 'Steps to Verdict' contains different aspects of the law according to the issues that arise in the particular case. Each time the 'steps' must be crafted to meet the needs of the case. Sometimes a trial will involve consideration of whether defendants acted together either as 'joint principals' or 'aiders and abettors' or in other ways. Sometimes the defence rests on general principles, for example 'accident' or 'lack of the necessary intent'; sometimes it rests on what a defendant specifically avers, for example 'self-defence' or 'diminished responsibility' or 'loss of control'. The burden of proof most often rests on the Crown, but in some situations it is on the defence. In the former, the Crown must make the jury 'sure of guilt'. In the latter, the standard of proof is usually 'on a balance of probabilities'. The drafting of any set of Steps to Verdict in any murder case is a laborious business. Miss Camden will have plenty of time to decide how she will proceed with her case.

'A little forewarning would have been helpful, Mr Selwyn.'

Mutely he bows his head.

So Professor Frick must wait and I must cancel an evening

engagement and . . . 'Very well. It is three o'clock now. I will send the jury away till half past ten tomorrow morning. Counsel and I will sit an hour before that to review the matter.'

4

Next morning, when the jury is brought back into court, the usher hands each of them a copy of the document I have produced.

'Ladies and gentlemen,' I say, 'before we embark on the defence case, both counsel think it would help you to follow the evidence if I explain to you the nature of the defence advanced on behalf of Mr Goodall. Normally I would do this after the evidence is completed and as part of my summing-up, but it can be done at any stage, and I am going to do it now.'

The jurors are each given a copy of my legal direction. They look at it. They look at each other. The trick is not to give them time to panic.

'You will see,' I continue quickly, 'it's headed "Steps to Verdict", and that is exactly what it is – a route map which you must follow, asking yourselves the questions in the order they are set out, following where your answers lead you. In this way you will do what you each promised at the beginning of the trial, which is to reach a true verdict according to the evidence.'

Twelve pairs of eyes stare at the document held in twelve pairs of hands. Over twelve faces there passes an expression of disbelief, anxiety, dismay. I try not to let my own face mirror theirs. I am about to try to explain some very complicated law to twelve laymen.

'It looks difficult,' I say, 'but we'll go through it together and it will become clear.' At least I hope it will become clear. This job of explaining complicated principles of law to non-lawyers is one of the daily tasks of a judge. If only those who create such difficult law had to do the explaining.

The document I give them is set out below. Before you look at it, can I beg you to bear this in mind: if you lose patience with it, you are in the happy position of being able to skip it. Not so my jurors. They have sworn to bring in true verdicts, and to do so they have to apply this route to verdict. And to do this, they have to understand what is being asked of them. And I have to make sure they understand. Because if I fail to make this law clear, I make it impossible for the jury to succeed in their job. If I fail in this, there can be no true justice.

Steps to Verdict

Murder: Before you may convict the defendant of murder you must be sure of the following:

1. That he deliberately killed Joy Goodall.
   - The defence accepts it was he who killed her.
   - 'Deliberately' means not accidentally. The defence does not suggest the killing was accidental.
   - Go to step 2.
2. That the killing was unlawful.
   - Such a killing is unlawful unless it was done in lawful self-defence.
   - The defence does not suggest this killing was done in lawful self-defence.
   - Go to step 3.
3. That at the time he killed, he intended to kill or at least to cause serious bodily harm.
   - The prosecution submits that if a man draws a knife across the throat of another, what else can he intend but to cause at least serious injury. However, this remains a matter about which you must be sure.

- If you are not sure he intended to kill or cause at least serious injury, he is not guilty of murder. If you reach this conclusion, that is your verdict and you need go no further through these steps.
- If, however, you are sure he intended to kill or cause at least serious injury, go to step 4 and the defence of diminished responsibility.

I break off from the 'script', give them a moment to digest what I have said.

'Now, before we look at this defence of "diminished responsibility", let me say a word about it. Firstly, if you find it proved, it does not lead to a complete acquittal. But it does reduce "murder" to a lesser offence of "manslaughter by reason of diminished responsibility". Secondly, whereas murder is only proved *if the prosecution has made you sure* of all the elements set out above, diminished responsibility is only proved if the *defence satisfy you on a balance of probabilities* of all the elements set out below. Thirdly, the elements required for "diminished responsibility" involve you considering psychiatric matters such as "abnormality of mental functioning" and "recognized medical conditions". You haven't heard about these yet, but you will, and in detail. It is the defence's intention to call an expert psychiatrist, after which it is likely the prosecution will call one too. These experts will give you evidence about the matters which will enable you to make your decisions on the next series of steps I am about to give you.'

Both the jury and I take a deep breath as we pick up the document where we broke off.

Diminished Responsibility: Has the defence satisfied you on a balance of probabilities (i.e. that it is more likely than not) of the following:

4. That at the time he did the killing, the defendant was suffering from an abnormality of mental functioning which arose from a recognized medical condition.

- If not, the defence fails and he is guilty of murder; that is your verdict and you need go no further through these steps.
- However, if you are satisfied on the balance of probabilities that he was suffering from an abnormality of mental functioning which arose from a recognized medical condition, go to step 5.

5. That the medical condition(s) substantially impaired his ability to
a) understand the nature of his own conduct and/or
b) to form a rational judgement and/or
c) to exercise self-control.

- When considering the word 'substantially' ask yourself whether, looked at with common sense, any impairment of his ability to do one or more of these three things really made a significant difference. If there may be some impairment but it was not something that really made any great difference, then this requirement is not proved.
- If you are not satisfied of this, the defence fails and he is guilty of murder; that is your verdict and you need go no further through these steps.
- However, if you are satisfied on the balance of probabilities of this, go to step 6.

6. That the matters(s) in steps 4–5 provide an explanation for his act of killing.

- An abnormality of mental functioning provides an explanation for a defendant's conduct if it causes or is a significant contributory factor in causing him to carry out that conduct.

- If you are satisfied on the balance of probabilities that the requirements in steps 4–5 are met and these things provide an explanation for his act of killing, then the defendant's responsibility for the killing is diminished, and he is not guilty of murder but guilty of manslaughter. If you are not satisfied of this, then he is guilty of murder.

I am constantly amazed that juries are able to work their way through this morass, but they are and do. Their verdicts in case after case show this. My jury currently look as if I have just lobbed a grenade at them. But everything will fall into place, I hope, once we hear the psychiatric evidence. So . . .

'Miss Camden?' I incline my head invitingly.

She rises to her feet. 'I wonder if the jury would like another cup of coffee?' she says.

5

When the jury are gone I turn back to her. 'What is it this time?'

'My Lady, I intend to open my case to the jury.'

Really? Well, I wasn't expecting that. It so rarely happens. I look at Professor Frick, who seems to be receding into the distance before my eyes. There is no chance of hearing from her until I sort out this new problem.

The defence wants to open its case. It's possible, of course, but there are strict rules. The normal order of events in a trial is this:

1. The Crown's barrister 'opens' the case to the jury, telling them the facts from the prosecution point of view. This should include

an indication of what the defendant says and the matters in dispute between the two sides. If the defence barrister doesn't think prosecuting counsel has made it clear, he should (at the end of the opening) stand up and in a sentence or two explain the nature of his defence to the jury.

2. After that the prosecution calls its witnesses one by one, and the defence can cross-examine them.

3. After the Crown case closes, it is the turn of the defence. If they believe the Crown has failed to make out a case at all, they can ask the judge to stop the trial. If they succeed in this submission, that is the end of the matter. If they fail, it is time for the defence case.

4. The defence is allowed to 'open' its case if, and only if, it is calling a witness (other than or as well as the defendant himself) who can speak to the facts of the allegation. Even when the defence is calling such a witness, very seldom does it choose to open its case . . . why risk setting out a stall when your goods might not meet expectation? But sometimes there are good reasons to do it. One such reason (as in Joshua Goodall's case) is if defence counsel feels so on the back foot with the jury that she wants to recover a little ground before calling evidence.

Stella Camden wants the chance to talk directly to the twelve people whose minds she is trying to engage. But the law only permits her to open her case if she is calling a witness 'as to the facts'. An expert is a witness as to opinion, not fact. And what possible witness to the facts can Miss Camden have? This is what Mr Selwyn is asking himself, and receiving no answer, he asks her.

She listens. She nods. She says, 'My Lady, Mr Selwyn would like me to tell the court who my witness is. I'm happy to do so. It's Mrs Abella May.'

'The neighbour?' says Mr Selwyn.

'The neighbour,' confirms Miss Camden.

'But that's *my* witness,' splutters Mr Selwyn. He is on his feet now. 'My Lady, Abella May is my witness.'

'No, she isn't,' says Miss Camden. 'You didn't call her. You called the emergency services – at least you played a recording produced by the emergency services. She happened to be speaking on that recording. It is true that she made a statement to the police, but you haven't relied upon that.'

Neil Selwyn raises his eyes upwards and moves his mouth as if praying to the God of the Ceiling Lights. Poor man. How is he supposed to keep in mind all the statements which police have accumulated in the course of their investigation? The CPS will have reviewed them and picked out those which seem to advance the case. Any which might help the defence must be disclosed to them. The rest of the statements disappear in files, never again to see the light of day. And here is one of them popping up like a rabbit out of Miss Camden's hat. To open her case, Miss Camden needs a witness 'as to fact'. She has come up with Abella May. And why not?

'There is no property in a witness, Mr Selwyn,' I say mildly. 'You don't own Mrs May. The Crown may have brought her witness statement into being, but you haven't called her and she is available to Miss Camden now.'

'But what can she say about the facts which is not already before the jury in her 999 call?'

Good point. I raise an eyebrow in the direction of Miss Camden.

'Clearly,' she says, 'My Learned Friend does not recall the exact terms of Mrs May's statement.'

'I'd be amazed if he did. Until thirty seconds ago he had no reason to think it was of any significance.'

'The rule does not require the evidence to be new,' she says. 'It only requires it to be admissible. This "keening" which went on for so long must relate to events in the flat and must therefore be admissible.'

'My Lady,' says Mr Selwyn, 'the only person who could have made those noises was the defendant – this is all part of his psychiatric defence . . .'

'Of course,' says Miss Camden. 'But it is still evidence of the events that were happening. It would be wrong to bring down an artificial barrier on those events at the moment of death. The Crown has not done that. They have called evidence of the defendant's conduct in the immediate aftermath of the police arriving. I merely wish to call evidence of his conduct in the period before that. It clearly relates to the incident and Mrs May is a witness to it.'

Neil Selwyn shakes his head, finds his better nature, and courteously indicates he will not maintain his objection.

'Quite right,' I say. 'I cannot stop Miss Camden calling a witness as to fact, and if Mrs May's account is not evidence as to the facts, I can't think what it is. So Miss Camden may call her witness and accordingly she may open her case. Now' – I fix her with what I hope is a gimlet eye – 'can we get on with the trial?'

And so we do. The jury is brought back. Miss Camden gets to her feet and turns to them. She pauses, and takes in the arms crossed over chests, the tightened lips, the narrowed eyes, the collective signs that say, 'Well, Miss Defender, and how do you think you can explain away this mess?' They have been told not to come to conclusions till they have heard all the evidence, but they know that the defendant killed a thoroughly decent woman and at present they are not minded to listen to any excuses. Miss Camden was right to want to open her case. She needs to stop them closing the door on her defence long enough at least to give Joshua Goodall a hearing. She can see it will be an uphill battle but she shrugs her gown about her, takes a moment to engage the eyes of the jurors, then – she sighs. She allows the sigh to hover and sink. She shakes her head.

'I suppose,' she says, 'you hate Joshua Goodall. And why shouldn't you?' She gives them a moment to digest this. 'If you think I'm going to give you reasons why you shouldn't hate him, you're wrong.'

This has its effect. Foreheads lift, heads turn towards her just a little. The jury begins to listen.

'He has done something unforgivable and I am not going to ask you to forgive him. I am only going to ask you to bring in the right verdict. I am only going to ask you to convict him of the right crime. And convict him you will' – jurors' eyes widen, focus on her – 'because this man is guilty of either murder or manslaughter. There will be no other verdict available to you.'

They really are listening now, and she knows it.

She leans a little towards them, drawing them to lean towards her. 'The prosecution,' she continues, 'seem to think Joshua Goodall is guilty of murder, and in this they are certainly right because, as the judge has already explained to you, manslaughter "by reason of diminished responsibility" means he has committed murder – but it also means there is an additional factor, his mental illness, which reduces his responsibility for that murder, so that the right verdict is manslaughter. We for the defence will try to show you that is the case here. We will call an expert witness – a psychiatrist – who will explain to you what was going on in Joshua's mind.'

Miss Camden will never call her client 'the defendant' – she will not dehumanize him. She will seek to present him as a person, in much the same way Mr Selwyn has so successfully presented Joy as a complete human being.

'I am not going to ask you to excuse him,' she says, 'but I am going to ask that you give him a little of your time – enough to properly consider his side of the case.'

A few heads nod. Are they thinking after all that is only fair, and fairness is what they are here for?

'You know that so far in this case I have asked almost no questions and challenged none of the evidence. That is because none of it is in dispute. We have spent three days looking at the prosecution case but in truth it could have been presented in three minutes because I would happily have admitted all that Mr Selwyn has so far proved – that during the early hours of that fateful night Joshua Goodall left the bed in which he slept with Joy Goodall and went to the kitchen to take some medication. While there he picked up a kitchen knife and took it to the bedroom. He got back into bed and at some point in the time that followed he attacked Joy and slit her throat. None of that is in question.'

She makes it sound as if somehow Neil Selwyn has been wasting the jury's time and concealed from them what they really need to hear. Juror number one looks at juror number two. They both look at Mr Selwyn and frown.

'What Joshua did is not in question,' continues Miss Camden. 'The question is what made him do it. What was going on in his mind during the time he lay beside Joy with the knife in his hand, and as he finally acted, as he cut her throat, as he watched her struggling to draw a breath and saw her blood pouring over his hands and spreading about her? What was he thinking? What was he feeling? Scrutiny of this is your job. But how can you scrutinize the inside of a man's head? Of course I could call him to give evidence of what he was thinking. But that would be the account of a man who has every reason to lie.'

I think, 'Ahhh, perhaps she's not going to call him into the witness-box'.

'But there is a way of understanding what is going on in someone's mind. There are people who spend their lives doing just that. They are called psychiatrists. I will call before you an expert and eminent psychiatrist who has studied this case and will tell you that, in her opinion, Joshua Goodall is a sick man. She will tell you how and why she believes he became a sick man, and what effect that had on his thought processes and actions that night.'

Stella Camden sits down. A good opening. It has had its effect. Jurors have uncrossed their arms, have pulled their pads towards them as if ready to take a note of the evidence that is to come. One has even picked up his pencil. They are ready to go on a journey that will take them into strange places where we will be considering the making of Joshua Goodall's mind. It will be a long journey because a man is a long time in the making. And it will determine the verdict in this case.

'Miss Camden, are you ready to call your first witness?' I ask.

'I am.'

So, will she call Joshua Goodall? If a defendant is to give evidence, the rule requires he is called before other witnesses. Miss Camden turns to look at the dock. Joshua Goodall half stands. You can see now that he is a big, shambling man, hair falling thin and grey on to his shoulders, though he can't be past forty. He is very different from his photograph. The muscles have turned to sagging flesh. The smart, soldierly back stoops. You can barely see the one man in the other. This is what he has become in the ten months since the night he killed his wife.

At this point I must ask Miss Camden a series of formal questions. Is she going to call her client? And if she is not, does he realize this is his opportunity to give evidence? Does he understand that if he doesn't, the jury may draw an inference against him from his failure to do so? Understanding this, is it still his choice not to give evidence? But before I can embark on any of these questions, Miss Camden answers them.

'My Lady, I do not intend to call my client. Mr Goodall understands this is his opportunity to give evidence and that, although it is his right not to, if he doesn't the jury might hold it against him – though I hope, given his mental state, they will not do that.'

She has, albeit breathlessly, encapsulated in a sentence all the matters I would have raised, culminating in the adverse inference – and then got in a plug for not drawing it. Nice one, Miss Camden.

'Very well. Then who is your first witness?'

The absence of the defendant from the witness-box brings the psychiatrists a step closer to it, but still we must wait. Still there is the witness of fact to be dealt with. Mrs Abella May is called. She is a decent woman who was fond of her dead neighbour and who looks towards the dock with such distaste that the jury mirrors her action. Neil Selwyn, decently in the circumstances, manages not to look as if he has scored a point for the prosecution.

Mrs May is as surprised to find herself giving evidence as the rest of us, but she is willing to do her best. She describes the sounds she heard.

'Not shouting, not crying, a sort of wailing . . . not really a wailing, more a keening, like—'

'Like grief?' suggests Miss Camden.

'Don't lead,' says Mr Selwyn.

'Like grief, I suppose,' says Mrs May, then adds, 'or not. But whatever it was, it went on and on right up till the police came.' In cross-examination Mr Selwyn satisfies himself with eliciting what a lovely woman Joy was. Mrs May leaves. She really hasn't said an awful lot. Would Stella Camden have called her if she hadn't been desperate to find a witness of fact to justify her wish to open her case? Certainly not. But the law is the law, and if Miss Camden wants to use it in this way, no one will stop her.

With Mrs May gone, I wait for some other interruption. I wait for counsel to get to their feet and ask for the jury to leave again. I wait for whatever matter of law they have now dreamed up for me to deal with, but no. When Miss Camden gets to her feet again, it is to call Professor Frick, and we have finally arrived at the moment that matters.

6

I have had plenty of time over the past days to familiarize myself with Professor Frick's report. It is as unconfined as she is, and full of learned words and Latin terms which I only hope she will turn into simple English for the jury. When her name is called, she rises. It is the first time I have had the opportunity to really focus on her. She's big-boned and loose-limbed. She is looking round as if she is missing something and can't quite think what it is; then she remembers, rummages under the desk, and surfaces triumphant, clutching a large bag. She gets herself and bag out of the row, out of harbour, and steers a course towards the exit doors where she is headed off by the usher who leads her towards the jury-box. There she trips up two steps and, holding her bag to her as if it might contain a baby or a bomb, finds she has arrived. The jury gapes. The barristers look down. Dr Parker looks bemused. Only I am facing Joshua Goodall. Only I can see the curtain across his eyes draw tighter, shutting us all out.

Meanwhile, Professor Frick, oblivious of the impression she has made, gazes round the court. Brought back to the moment by my usher, she shakes her head at the proffered selection of religious books and chooses to affirm. She takes from her large bag a small pair of glasses which she balances on her nose. She reads aloud the words in a clipped and heavy accent, originating somewhere in Eastern Europe.

Miss Camden, no doubt in an effort to put her expert at ease, says, 'Would you like to sit? I'm sure Her Ladyship would permit it.'

Her Ladyship would, of course. But Her Ladyship doubts this would be a wise course. Her Ladyship is remembering what Miss Camden is not – that the folding seat built into the witness-box is a tiny one and there is a lot of limb about Professor Frick.

The professor considers the lip of wood, applies her considerable brain to the matter and, with commendable dignity, says she would prefer to stand.

Can something like this affect the outcome of a case? Of course it shouldn't, but it can. Two experts will lay their opposing views before the jury, who must decide which of the two (if either) it trusts. Dr Parker knows this. He will do nothing, say nothing to undermine the jury's trust in him . . . and his opponent? Well, we shall see.

Miss Camden has had enough of this. She grasps the reins and regains control. She begins with her expert's qualifications. They are impressive, so much so that I am beginning to wonder how it is that I have not seen this psychiatrist, so eminent in the field of PTSD, in my courtroom before.

The answer becomes clear when Mr Selwyn half rises and says, 'My Lady, it is customary to deal with experience as well as qualifications – I wonder if Miss Camden would be kind enough to set out her witness's experience in giving a jury the sort of evidence with which she is . . . enlightening us today.'

Before Miss Camden can stop her, Professor Frick lowers her spectacles the better to fix her gaze on Mr Selwyn, and says, 'Certainly, sir. I have given evidence to a jury on eleven previous occasions.'

'Eleven,' says Mr Selwyn, his mouth closing over the word as if it is a golden plum. 'Well, fancy that.'

Behind him, Dr Parker suppresses a grin. Over the years, he has given evidence before me on far more occasions than that – and I am one judge in one court. He must have written a thousand reports on homicide cases. Mr Selwyn sinks into his seat, gratified.

There is no doubt, however, that Professor Frick's brain is bigger than the average psychiatrist's. She has studied the defendant's history, and now pulls from the depths of her bottomless bag a wodge of papers to prove it. She spreads them in front of her and jabs at them from time to time but barely needs to look down: his career in the army, the war zones in which he fought, the traumas he underwent, his friends dying beside him, the constant fear of dying himself – all nestle in the folds and curves of that great brain, effortlessly interweaving with her knowledge of her subject.

'He was,' she points out, 'diagnosed with PTSD by an army psychiatrist and invalided out of service and there is no doubt that he was still suffering from this condition at the time he cut his wife's throat. Post traumatic stress disorder is, you will appreciate, a recognized medical condition, as your law requires for the defence of diminished responsibility. He suffered flashbacks, intrusive thoughts, difficulty in sleeping and, when he slept, nightmares. These things were deeply distressing to him so that his heart would race, he would sweat and shake, and feel nauseous or dizzy. He would panic and become easily angry or aggressive. He could become hypervigilant and find it difficult to concentrate on the everyday things about him.'

The jury blinks hard but there is no moment when Miss Camden can get Professor Frick to pause, to clarify, because the good doctor is mid-lecture and we are her students being taken where she wills.

'The brain,' she declares, 'will try to protect itself from horrible recollections by detachment leading to an emotional numbness.' She waves her arms to demonstrate the brain in isolation from its surroundings. 'He would feel safe nowhere. Nowhere. No – where!'

Before we can reflect upon this, she is off again.

'He would feel headache and dizziness' – she stabs at her head. 'Chest pain and stomach ache' – she stabs at her torso. 'Malfunction' – I hold my breath, wondering which part of the anatomy we are going to now, but no, she only declares 'everywhere' and demonstrates with her arms her impression of confusion and pain and malfunction.

So great is her effort to convey knowledge to the bunch of ignoramuses before her, something must give in the struggle. It proves to be her grasp of English pronunciation. Professor Frick's 's' and 'th' merge into an all-purpose 'z'. Her 'w's turn into 'v's. The jury make a heroic effort to follow where she is taking them, and fail. When the professor pauses to draw breath, Miss Camden opens her mouth, but not quickly enough.

'Hormones,' declares Professor Frick. 'Cortisol. Adrenaline. Fight. Flight. Freeze. You see?'

We don't.

'This man' – she jabs a finger in the direction of Joshua Goodall – 'this man, when he was a good soldier in danger, would have produced these hormones, and his body has continued to produce them ever since. He may see again full or partial images of the things he witnessed in war zones, he may relive the sounds and smells – even the tastes. He will feel again the emotion, the pains, the trauma.' She delivers the final word with such force we all reel back in our seats.

She nods hard. She is done.

By now I have reached a firm conclusion about Professor Frick. She is a fine psychiatrist but she is a far from fine witness. Miss Camden may be thinking the same thing, because for a long moment she says nothing. Then she draws a breath and steadies herself. She has to get this untameable witness to confirm the elements of her defence.

'Professor Frick,' she says, 'let us please apply all you have told us to the legal defence of diminished responsibility. Firstly, in your expert opinion, at the time he killed Joy Goodall, was Joshua suffering from a recognized condition, namely post traumatic stress disorder?'

'Obviously,' Professor Frick answers.

'Was there an abnormality of mental functioning?'

Professor Frick looks at Miss Camden as if it is she who is in need of psychiatric help. 'Madam, a man whose mind is functioning normally is hardly likely to get up in the middle of the night and slit the throat of his partner.'

Miss Camden smiles weakly. 'Did the mental condition substantially impair his ability to understand the nature of his own conduct and/or to form a rational judgement and/or to exercise self-control?'

'Certainly it substantially impaired his ability to exercise self-control.'

'And did it cause him to do what he did?'

'In my opinion, yes. It is not only PTSD. Often with this comes depression, anxiety, dissociative disorder. Often comes self-harm and suicidal thoughts. Especially comes suicidal thoughts. He is a sick man.'

Miss Camden has done what she can. It is now for Mr Selwyn to cross-examine. He gets quickly to his feet.

'A sick man who has killed his sleeping wife.'

'That is not a question,' Professor Frick says. 'I am here to answer your questions not confirm your statements.'

'Very well. Then let me ask you a question. You have come to the conclusion the defendant's responsibility was diminished, but you know that Dr Parker disagrees with you?'

She nods briefly, dismissively – as if to say, let Dr Parker have his opinion if he must, but I have mine.

'You,' says Mr Selwyn, 'have considered the question of diminished responsibility eleven times before, in eleven previous cases. Do you know how often Dr Parker has considered this question?'

'I do not.'

'Would it surprise you to know he has prepared for the courts over nine hundred reports on this and similar issues and given evidence many hundreds of times?'

It clearly does surprise Professor Frick, who, expert as she is in her subject, probably can't imagine the world of the Central Criminal Court, its forensic tactics and the intricacies of the law.

Mr Selwyn reckons the expression on Professor Frick's face is enough for him. He sits down. Professor Frick gathers up papers, glasses and bag and shuffles herself back to the seat behind Miss Camden, who does not spare her even a sympathetic nod. It can be a cruel world.

It is now Dr Parker's turn, and before Mr Selwyn can get back to his feet the prosecution expert has stood up, smoothed the non-existent creases from his expensive suit, run a hand across his immaculate hair and walked to the witness-box. He is more than a decade younger than Professor Frick and looks another decade younger than his age. He is an able doctor, a good witness, and he is, he knows, about to make mincemeat of a colleague. He places in front of him a neat file of papers and repeats the words of the affirmation without assistance from the prompt card. Mr Selwyn barely needs to take him through the evidence. He has only to point the good doctor in the right direction and let him go.

Dr Parker tells us that there is a fundamental flaw in Professor Frick's application of the law relating to diminished responsibility – probably, he says with a touch of Schadenfreude, because she has so seldom been called upon to apply it as a legal defence. He gently points out that a man can have PTSD (as he agrees Joshua Goodall does) but it doesn't mean his crime was committed as a result of that PTSD. 'A man may have the condition,' he says, 'but quite apart from that, he may have a temper. His PTSD only provides a defence if it is the disorder and not the temper which is the cause of his crime. If the illness is only the setting, the background for the killing – if the real cause is a character flaw such as readiness to anger, a tendency to jealousy or possessiveness, an inability to respect the rights of others above his own needs . . . if such things as these are the cause of his crime, why then the PTSD is not the cause.'

Dr Parker has the law at his fingertips.

'It is, of course, a matter for the jury to decide' – he pauses, and nods respectfully towards the jury-box where twelve pairs of eyes are fixed in fascination on him – 'but I would point out that the defendant had PTSD for a long time without slitting the throat of his partner or anyone else. He only killed her when he discovered her packed suitcase and her letter declaring her intention to leave him. I see no correlation between the discovery of the suitcase and a war zone, but I see a strong correlation between the discovery of the suitcase and a jealous anger that he did not control. The jury might conclude that this man is a trained killer and in anger he killed.'

'Not diminished responsibility?' asks Mr Selwyn.

'Not diminished responsibility,' says Dr Parker.

And so it is Miss Camden's job to cross-examine the witness. She cannot immediately see where to go with him, what to ask. For a moment she remains in her seat, eyes narrowing. Diminished responsibility is of course one of the rare defences in which the burden of proof lies on her rather than on the Crown. And Dr Parker is such a persuasive witness. And Dr Parker is so comfortable giving his evidence. And—

Miss Camden's gown is yanked from behind with a force that pulls her back in her seat. Professor Frick's mouth is clamped to the advocate's ear where she whispers earnestly and at length. Finally Professor Frick gives Miss Camden an encouraging shove to her feet. Miss Camden turns to the witness-box.

'So, Dr Parker,' she begins, 'is it your view that at the time Joshua Goodall killed his wife he intended to kill her, having simply lost his temper?'

'That is more than possible.'

'Most people lose their temper without slitting throats.'

'Most people,' says the doctor, 'aren't trained killers.'

'But since Joshua Goodall is a trained killer, if he has such a temper as you describe, would he not have lost it on many occasions in his life before?'

'Perhaps he has.'

'I think we might have noticed if he'd left behind him a trail of slit throats. Isn't it more likely that if he lost his temper before killing Joy, this was a rare occasion on which he lost it while in the middle of a flashback and an active episode associated with his PTSD?'

The psychiatrist hesitates. 'You mean not just PTSD and not just temper but a combination of both?'

'Of both, and perhaps with symptoms of what so often goes with PTSD – anxiety disorder, dissociative disorder, self-harm or actions that are destructive of self as well as of others.'

In the seat behind Miss Camden, Professor Frick bounces gently and mouths, 'Exactly so.'

Dr Parker frowns. 'I don't know about "more likely" but . . .' He is, after all, an expert whose duty is not to one party or the other but to the court. 'But . . .' He is, after all, a doctor whose knowledge should be used in pursuit of scientific accuracy. 'But I suppose it is possible.'

Normally 'possible' would be good enough for Miss Camden, but she must prove the defence was more likely than not. 'Possible,' she repeats. 'And you said you do not know if it is more likely than not. You cannot express an opinion on that crucial point?'

'It was a turn of phrase,' says Dr Parker, allowing for the first time a testiness to his tone. 'But since you ask, I can only say that it is not a matter for scientific opinion. Such a thing could happen. Whether it did or not is a question for the jury.'

Miss Camden appears to reflect. 'So, it is not in dispute that he got out of bed that night and went to the kitchen. It is not in dispute that his medication is kept in the kitchen drawer. It is not in dispute that the drawer was opened, and by him. If he got up to find his medication, doesn't it suggest he was suffering an episode that made him want it?'

Professor Frick emits a hiss of agreement. Dr Parker contents himself with, 'It might.'

'And if in the midst of such an episode he came across the suitcase and letter – even if it did lead him to become angry and resentful – surely the illness would be at least a significant contributory factor to the extreme way in which he reacted.'

Dr Parker stares hard at Professor Frick, who has opened her hands as if to welcome him into her fold. 'That,' says Dr Parker stiffly, 'is a matter for the jury.'

Miss Camden has done more than one might have thought possible. Mr Selwyn rises, considers, shakes his head and says, 'No further questions, My Lady.'

And that is it. The evidence done. Tomorrow, counsel will make their speeches, each urging the jurors to see things from this point of view or that. Then I will give further directions of law and attempt to sum up the evidence in a balanced way. The jury will leave the courtroom with their heads full of Professor Frick, of Dr Parker, of the complexities of diminished responsibility; they will attempt to disentangle it all, to get inside the head of this man who has, throughout the trial, shut us out. It is hard to say how he has done it but somehow Joshua Goodall has sat in the dock utterly removed from us. The one person who perhaps really would have understood what was going on in his world is the one person who can't tell us. Joy won't be telling anyone anything any more.

7

This whole trial has been about whether a defendant is guilty of murder or of manslaughter. I have no idea what the jury might decide and it doesn't help to speculate. Anyway, both offences are desperately serious so does it really matter of which he is convicted? In one way it certainly does. If Joshua Goodall is convicted of murder the only sentence I can pass is life imprisonment. I must then fix a minimum term to be served before he can apply for parole. In this case the starting point would be fifteen years. Joy's vulnerability and the fact she was attacked in her own home in the middle of the night aggravate the offence and increase that starting point. If the jury convict of murder, they will have rejected the psychiatric defence, so though I can make some allowance for his undoubted illness, it won't be a lot. I am likely to order that he serves a period between fifteen and seventeen years, after which the Parole Board may or may not release him. If the board decides he still presents a danger to the public, he could spend many more years than that in custody.

On the other hand, if convicted of manslaughter by reason of diminished responsibility, different sentences are open to me. If he is deemed treatable, I could send him to a psychiatric hospital till he is well enough for release, or till he is well enough for transfer to prison, or I could send him straight to prison. The prison sentence for this sort of manslaughter, with its aggravating and mitigating features, may justify a sentence of perhaps fifteen years' imprisonment* but from that I would deduct up to a third because he has always said he would plead guilty to this offence. And of the remaining ten years he would likely serve two thirds and almost certainly be released after serving six years and eight months from the time he was first remanded in custody. In short he would spend another five and three-quarter years in prison instead of something like another fifteen years or more.

In this way, it matters a lot whether it is murder or manslaughter. But in other ways it makes no difference. Nothing the law can do

* See Appendix N, p. 305.

will bring Joy back; nothing can mend the broken hearts of her mother, her sister, her family and friends. Nothing the law can do will end Joshua Goodall's illness – and, after all, whatever the jury's verdict, both psychiatrists agree he is a sick and suffering man. Perhaps it is also worth stating that his mental disorder was caused by his exposure to war in the service of his country.

Cases like this leave us all helpless. Nothing can resolve the human tragedy that underlies some trials. However grim, we must somehow see it through. We must just get on with the job. The law must be applied, the rules must be followed, because there is nothing else to be done. This is what I think as I make my way home that evening and what I am still thinking as I return next morning. But it turns out I am wrong. Someone has thought of another way through this tragedy, seen another ending to the one I am seeing.

In the long night, in the darkness of his hospital room, which isn't a cell but which soon may be, Joshua Goodall found another solution. He worked a hole in the edge of his sheet till he could pull the threads loose. It must have required care and determination but he kept at it until he could tear off a strip of linen. Perhaps he shivered and took his dressing gown from its hook on the back of the door and slipped it on. Did he pause, sit on the chair, and stare at the hook? Did he calculate the height against the length of sheet in his hand? You wouldn't think you could do what he had in mind, not with a hook and a bit of torn sheet, but it's surprising what can be achieved if you are determined; and Joshua Goodall was very determined. He had committed a crime he could not live with – and it doesn't matter whether you call it murder or manslaughter, because whatever its name it was unendurable to him.

Mental illness can be a wicked thing. It can eat you from the inside out. In past times people thought the mentally ill were possessed by the Devil. We know better now. But for the afflicted, hearing voices, seeing flashbacks, living in a world where everything is dark, it might as well be the Devil who has hold of them. For whose else is the voice that speaks to them in the night? Who else lives beside them in a world of horror no one else believes is there? So Joshua Goodall, his own judge and jury, passed his own verdict and sentenced himself to death.

And this is how it ends. Suddenly, with a jar, like a weight at the end of a rope. The jury is discharged, silent and shocked. Joy's family in the well of the court, her friends in the public gallery, stare in disbelief. Some will think justice has been done, others that justice has been snatched from them. Dr Parker has been called to another court but Professor Frick has come back. She sits beside Stella Camden, holding her hand. Neil Selwyn is very pale. Neither of the barristers will sleep easily, and then they will be too exhausted to stay awake. The events of a courtroom alter many people's lives but for those who make those events happen, cases come and go, and, after all, they are only cases – until something like this happens.

8

Between 2014 and 2017 the numbers transferred from prison to psychiatric hospitals fell from 1,061 to 936,* while the number of those in prison with mental illness was steadily rising. In 2017 there were ninety-seven self-inflicted deaths recorded in UK psychiatric hospitals, and in 2018 (a chilling coincidence) the same number in prisons in England and Wales. By 2019 the Institute of Psychiatry estimated that over half of prisoners had poor mental health

* www.mentalhealth.org.uk

including depression, post traumatic stress disorder and anxiety, with around 15 per cent having specialist mental health needs. In the year to December 2019 in prisons in England and Wales (including prison-operated immigration removal centres), 63,328 incidents of self-harm were recorded. In the year to March 2020, of 286 deaths, eighty were recorded as self-inflicted, three as homicides, and 180 as natural causes. Others were 'awaiting further information'. Some of those, one might think, are likely to add to the number of suicides.

I don't have to deal with all these needless deaths – the two thrown up by this case are enough to be going on with. I've already said some people will think Joshua Goodall's suicide is justice. I don't. It has, I suppose, produced a death for a death. But in my book that isn't the same thing as justice – and I think Joy, that loving and generous woman, would agree.

Our system of justice, as it is imposed by our criminal courts, is the application of statutory law as set down by those we have elected to govern us, and of the common law framed by our society over centuries. What is required of this law above all is that it is certain, so that we all know where the lines are to be drawn. The criminal law is there to serve us all. It is there so that we know there are rules to protect our lives, our health, our property. Society's need for this knowledge is why we designate certain behaviour 'criminal'. Having done that, of course, if the alleged wrongdoer disputes the allegation, there must be a system of adjudicating the issue. We wouldn't need the latter if we didn't have the former. And the former is all about making our society a safe, secure, viable place in which to live. But how does a wrongdoer – who, after all, is part of that society too – fit in with all this? Generally, if he has chosen to embark on criminal conduct, he has chosen to put himself outside that society and can't (or shouldn't) complain at the consequences. But what about a situation like Joshua's? For all the wickedness of his killing of Joy, he never set out to do anything wicked. How did he come to be the person who ended up in my dock, the person who killed the woman he (and so many others) loved? Who trained him to kill? Who exposed him to the experiences that made him ill? Who failed to make him well? Who failed to protect her from him, or him from himself? On whose hands is all this blood? It is no one's fault. It is everyone's fault.

TRIAL SIX:

Vengeance Is Mine

ANGELA BRIDGES CAME through the back door and into
the kitchen. She placed the bag on the table and looked inside
it at the black chiffon nestling in its folds of tissue. Charlie,
she knew, would like the way the dress skimmed her knees
and hugged tight at the hips . . . not bad hips for a woman of
forty-two. Charlie liked her clothes sexy enough to draw eyes,
classy enough to deter hands. That was Charlie.

The shops had been crowded and now she was tired. And
hot. Tendrils of hair curled damply at the nape of her neck.
Her mouth was dry. Best, she thought, to cool down before
she went to find him. At the sink she turned on the tap and
pressed the lever so that the water came out ice-cold. Charlie
had paid a lot of money for a tap that did this. She took a
glass, sipped the water. She opened the top buttons of her
blouse. Better still. She went into the hall to the mirror and
inspected her image. She allowed no grey in her auburn hair
and worked hard to keep her skin smooth. Charlie liked it
that way.

She walked past the dining room (she did like having a
proper dining room) and on past the downstairs cloakroom
(and how many people had one of those?) to the lounge.

'Charlie?'

He was sitting on the settee, the gun cradled against him.
He was rubbing it with a soft cloth, in small, loving circles, so
that it glinted softly in the sunlight.

'Charlie?'

He set down the cloth and transferred the weight of the gun from one hand to the other. A soft click as it opened. He reached for the small objects on the cushion beside him and slipped in the bullets – one, two, three, four.

'Charlie!'

He looked up.

'I thought . . .' She moistened her lips with her tongue so that she could speak. 'I thought you weren't going to use it again.'

'I'm not. It's only to frighten.'

'You don't need bullets to frighten.'

'Don't start, Angie.'

She knew she shouldn't. She knew she would regret it. But she couldn't help herself. 'You promised.'

'Just once more.'

'It's always just once more. One day you'll get caught.'

'Shut up,' he said, and lifted the gun in front of him, held it out, squinted to line it up with an object that wasn't there.

She thought about this. She thought about all she had been through, and about all she had and about all she had to lose. She thought about her fear and about her anger. She allowed these thoughts to fill her like air slowly filling a balloon, stretching her and giving her form. The heat of her anger evaporated her fear. How dare he risk everything.

'Charlie,' she pleaded, 'I've had years and years of it. Never knowing if you'll come home. And if you don't, never knowing if I'll find you in the morgue or the nick. I thought all this was over.' And she had. At least she thought she had. 'You'll get caught and we'll lose everything.'

'We wouldn't have anything to lose unless I did "all this".'

She stopped then, because it was true. But now they had so much . . . the house, the friends, the holidays. Now, surely, they could manage without . . . because it could all be gone, she knew, in the pressure of a trigger-finger. All that it had taken them a lifetime to build up could be gone, and some poor bastard dead and his wife and kids left and everything gone for them too, and they not even understanding why because they didn't even know Charlie.

She had always hated the gun. She'd always been against the violence. You could rob without violence if you planned it right, she thought.

'Please don't take the gun.'

'Shut up, Ange.'

'At least don't load it.'

'You're making me angry, Ange.'

She knew that it was bad to be angry when you were carrying a loaded gun. She knew it was dangerous, that it drew bad luck. 'You'll kill someone, Charlie. You'll take a life. And then you'll get life. We've got enough. We've—'

He set down the weapon and came towards her. She braced herself. The slap caught her round the side of the head and knocked her sideways. She knew he wasn't really angry because a slap wasn't a punch. It occurred to her that the reason he wasn't really angry was because he knew she was right. She turned on him. But he was gone.

She took a moment to steady herself; to think. She'd been doing a lot of thinking lately. About the slaps and punches. About the parties and the dresses. About the house with its separate dining room and the tap that ran water boiling or iced at the turn of a lever. Now she added to this thoughts about people who shoot and people who get shot. The anger, which had flickered and faded, flared back into life.

She could hear him in the dining room. She could hear the click of the drinks cabinet opening, the chink of whisky bottle on glass. She imagined him taking a sip, steadying himself, regretting that he had hit her – he always did regret it afterwards. She imagined him in . . . what would it be? A petrol station? A bookmaker's? The gun, the trigger, the explosion that would end it all. And she knew that something terrible was going to happen.

Charlie, she recognized with a sudden jolt of clarity, was a bad man. He was kind to children and dogs, but still he was a bad man. He was good to her, except when he wasn't; but still, he was bad. He hadn't killed anyone yet but one day he would and then he would be caught. And that one day was today, or might be. And the person he killed would be her, or might be. But even if it wasn't her . . . if it was someone else, once he was caught she would lose everything as surely as he would. And he had to be stopped, if only she could think how.

His voice came to her from the dining room, wheedling now. 'Come on, Ange. I've poured you a glass of wine.' And when she didn't answer, 'Come on, love. Come and have a drink. You shouldn't work me up like that. I know that . . .'

But what did he know? He certainly didn't know she had picked up the gun. He didn't know she was walking down the hall towards him holding it out in front of her. He didn't know that he would not carry out an armed robbery that night nor any night ever again.

1

TEATIME. WE'RE ON THE second pot and the best of the biscuits have gone when the list officer looks round the door.

'Sorry to interrupt,' he says, 'but I'm having a . . .' He hesitates.

'Crisis?' (That's H.)

'Moment?' (That's Q.)

'Surprise party?' (That's me.)

'I'm having a difficulty,' says the list officer. 'I have a murder which must be fitted in next week and I haven't got a judge.'

'You've got fourteen of us,' I point out. 'Three of us – H, Q and me – will finish our trials this week. What is this murder?'

'A shooting,' he says. 'Ballistics. Ricochets. The lot.'

He has our attention. We all like a shooting. Bullets and angles and maybe a little gunshot residue make such a change from stabbing. But there's something not quite right about the way he is offering us this desirable case. He has the air of a man whose Fabergé egg is cracked.

'What's the problem?' asks H.

'No problem,' he says quickly. Too quickly. 'It's a particularly interesting shooting as it happens. Woman defendant, killed her husband.'

'Who,' demands H, 'is defending?'

He's sharp, is H. He has put his finger on the nub of the thing. The three of us who are in line to inherit this so-interesting shooting look at the list officer. Please tell us it isn't . . . it's not . . .

H has gone very red. 'If it's Gloria Vaughan, the answer's no. The last time she was in front of me, I almost committed murder of defence counsel.'

Q, whose corporate manslaughter is rolling to a gentle close, and who could easily take on one quiet lady shooter, taps his chest. It is an apologetic gesture subtly indicative of regret and a heart that won't stand the strain of Gloria Vaughan.

The list officer looks at me. 'Please,' he says. 'Someone has to.'

This is how it starts. This is how I come across Angela Bridges. It's to be a short case – two weeks at most. A two-week case can't do much damage to my equilibrium, can it? It can't undo the beliefs I have built up over four decades in a system I know and trust . . . can it? Of course, I can't know, this first morning, what it can do. All I know is what I see – or what I think I see – in the case papers: a battered woman who has finally turned on her abuser and killed him.

Abusers are never nice, but Charlie Bridges appears to have been particularly nasty. Not in a personal way. When he wasn't battering his wife, he was – it seems – charming, generous, thoughtful. It was just that his charm came from behind a balaclava, his generosity was funded by robbery and his thoughtfulness generally arrived after he had committed the crime. As armed robbers go, he had undoubtedly done well. He had evaded charge on any number of occasions. Police had been pretty certain he was behind many offences – but 'pretty certain' is not the test for prosecution. Of the three occasions he had been brought into a courtroom, he had been twice acquitted. His single conviction had been twenty years ago, at a time when he hadn't yet honed his considerable skills. And even then, being young and having no criminal record, he had only served three years. Angela had been his wife since shortly after that, and having promised to stick by him for better or worse, seems to have taken her vows seriously. That she was a battered woman, subject to repeated domestic abuse over the years, I have little doubt.

It's an odd phrase we use. 'Battered woman' is such an anodyne couple of words for the catalogue of misery it covers. Typically, a victim of domestic abuse will endure escalating violence over a long period of time. It may begin with pinches and slaps then develop into punches, kicks and the vicious twisting of limbs. Often it will involve sexual abuse. Victims suffer not only the trauma and physical pain of attack, but the mental anguish that goes with it. For months, years even, they live with the knowledge that at any moment they may be assaulted. They never know when it will happen. They never know what mood will fall over their abuser, whether they will be beloved or bullied. Stress, anxiety, depression, alcohol dependency can all be associated with existing under this strain. Most, though not all, who suffer such grinding misery are women. Indeed, in psychiatric terms, 'Battered Woman Syndrome' is a subcategory of 'Post Traumatic Stress Disorder'. Mostly it happens unseen, unknown, behind a closed door. Sometimes, though, everyone knows only too well. Sometimes police and helplines receive daily calls from alarmed neighbours, from the victims themselves or their frightened relatives. Some victims break free. Some never do. Some leave and return. Far, far too many are killed or commit suicide. A few, driven beyond endurance, end up killing their abuser. This last, it seems, is what has happened to Angela Bridges.

Of the relatively few women who find themselves in the dock after killing their partner, no two are ever the same. Sometimes a woman has killed in the course of fighting off an attack – and, like anyone else, if she can avail herself of defences of 'accident' or 'self-defence' is entitled to be acquitted. Sometimes she has been driven into a state of mind that allows her to advance a defence of 'diminished responsibility'* or 'loss of control'.† Sometimes she is plain guilty of murder.

* See Trial Five: The Good Soldier, p. 187.
† See later in this chapter, pp. 261–5.

Gloria Vaughan has made a speciality of defending such women. She has an undoubted and genuine desire to support the battered and beleaguered who have or may have been driven to kill. She has very considerable courtroom skills. Numbers of women over the years have cause to be grateful to her. But her desire to support her clients sometimes – how can I put it? – oversteps the mark. Or perhaps it doesn't. Perhaps it only seems that way to H and Q and me. I don't doubt that everything Gloria Vaughan does, she does with the best of motives; but to dress her clients in pastel sweaters with Peter Pan collars ... to hug them whenever possible, and especially if it can be done in sight of the jury ... well, many of these women have perfectly good defences that don't need hugs and pink sweaters.

How much Angela Bridges will have to rely on a sweater I will only know as the case unfolds, but I can make a start on the information in the Digital Case System. Women arrested for violence against a partner and taken to a police station should always be checked for injuries which they themselves may have suffered. After all, if a woman has been 'battered' she is likely to bear some signs of it. So I dig through the system until I find the forensic medical examiner's report. Angela Bridges has the classic signs of a victim of domestic abuse. The FME has noted a series of fading bruises to her left arm, on her left breast a barely healing scratch, and on the side of her head a reddened area consistent with a recent blow or slap. Her assiduous lawyers have obtained her GP records and can show – all properly set out in a statement – more than half a dozen occasions when the doctor recorded unexplained marks on her body. Not that she had gone to him because of these injuries ... her appointments had always been for other things. And when pressed she had explained that she was clumsy, she knocked herself, she bruised easily. Perhaps she was. Perhaps she did. But the GP was a careful man and he had made careful notes. And so it all seems to fit – so far, so horribly normal for this sort of case.

What is not normal, of course, is the gun. Abusive men are more commonly killed by a blow to the head from a heavy pan or a stab wound from a kitchen knife – but perhaps in the Bridgeses household a gun was as readily to hand as anything else. Anyway, the defence which Gloria Vaughan is advancing is 'loss of control' (of which, more – much more – later). And if a man will keep loaded guns about the house and beat up his wife, what can he expect . . .? Such is the thrust of the defence statement, all properly uploaded on to the ever-useful DCS.

All of which means I am primed for sympathy.

I should know better. Although these days the torture which so many abused women endure as part of their daily life is well recognized, it is no business of a judge to be judgemental. In a jury trial it is the jurors who will make the findings of fact. The judge's job is to manage the case, to rule on the law and to make sure the jury can do their job. In short, I should not be forming views. I certainly shouldn't be taking sides. A slap on the wrist for the judge.

The first inkling I have that this case isn't going according to my preconceptions, or Gloria Vaughan's, comes pretty much the moment I walk into court. The prosecutor, Mr Chester Fenniman KC – ah, the Crown has pulled out a surprisingly heavy gun for a battered wife – is standing in his place, a proper expression on his very proper face; but the seat reserved for defence counsel is conspicuously empty. The dock, on the other hand, is unusually full. As well as the regulation two dock officers and a defendant, Ms Vaughan has managed to insinuate herself there. Heaven knows how. It's against all the rules, but there she is. She has her back to me as she addresses the seated figure of her client in loud and urgent whispers. Her wig is askew. Her gown flaps. She is brought to the fact of my presence by a sharp poke from one of the officers. She gives a final shake of her head, clamps her wig into place and scuffles out of the dock and back to her seat, watched with undisguised interest by Mr Fenniman.

I take the opportunity to eye up Angela Bridges. I am trying to see what has so upset Gloria Vaughan. It can't be her client's clothing, which is in the approved Vaughan style. The hair and make-up, a shade brighter than Ms Vaughan's ideal, are nonetheless appropriate enough. She sits peaceably in the dock, apparently unmoved by her counsel's agitation. But *something* is definitely up in the defence camp.

Ms Vaughan arrives back in her place. 'I'm sorry, My Lady.' She manages to sound as if she isn't. 'I hadn't realized Your Ladyship had come into court.'

I can think of a number of responses to this, all of which are better not said, so I only ask the clerk to carry out the formal identification of the defendant. He asks the woman in the dock if she is Angela Bridges, and she indicates that she is. It sounds stupid but I have known the wrong prisoner be brought into court, and it won't do to try someone for murder when they have only been charged with handling stolen socks.

I haven't had time to read into this trial much, but that doesn't matter – sometimes it is best to let the facts come to you as they come to the jury. I'll hear the Crown's case set out in Mr Fenniman's opening, and then I'll hear the evidence as it is presented. In a relatively straightforward matter this can be the best approach. I am still, you see, thinking this is a relatively straightforward matter.

'Are we ready for a jury?' I ask.

'Yes, My Lady,' says Mr Fenniman.

'Ms Vaughan?'

She gives a worried glance in the direction of the dock but doesn't raise any difficulty. With Gloria Vaughan this is the best I can hope for, so I send for a jury panel.

2

The jury bailiffs send me eighteen potential jurors. They file into my courtroom and we begin the familiar process to select the twelve who will form my jury. It goes unusually smoothly. As the trial is not expected to last more than two weeks, and as jurors expect to serve this long, there are few applications to be excused. I soon have my twelve and they take the oath or affirmation without incident. Seven women, five men. They seem a relaxed bunch, already quite matey with each other. Nudges are exchanged. Whispers pass between them. It's impossible to tell yet what sort of people they are but they give the appearance of a reasonable group who will work well together.

Why do I think this? Perhaps because they present a homogeneous picture of blue jeans and fawn trousers, of checked tops and dark sweaters. I study them for differences – the characters who will stand out. There's a burly man who could comfortably fill the driver's seat of a heavy goods vehicle. There's a woman with heavy-rimmed glasses and a look that brooks no nonsense. There's a man under whose dark jumper a flowered shirt flourishes at neck and wrists. There is a good mix of ethnic background and (from the oath-taking) religious belief. What is it, then, that is giving me pause? I can't immediately put my finger on it. And then I do.

Normally I get a spread of ages within the permissible bracket of eighteen to seventy-five, but no one here looks much over fifty, no one much under thirty. Of course, given the random system of calling up jurors, from time to time this will happen. Experience has taught me that the broader the mix – especially of age – the better the jury, but this is what I've got, and they must do. And they seem bright enough. In fact they are showing a surprising independence of spirit, which is keeping my usher on her toes. She has to remove a smuggled coffee cup, reprove a texter, and get two of them to go back to their appointed seats after they exchange them for reasons not explained. However, they seem attentive enough when I give them the usual guidance about the way jurors should conduct themselves; and, surely, everything will be fine.

When Mr Fenniman rises to his feet, bows to me and turns to them, he has their full attention.

'Members of the jury,' he says, 'I am about to open to you the case for the prosecution. That is to say, I will set out the central features of the matter which the Crown brings against this defendant, and the issues that you will have to tackle.'

The twelve of them settle back with the air of an audience at a TV reality show.

'This case concerns the death of Charlie Bridges. He was forty-four years old when he died at the hand of his wife of twenty years, Angela. That she killed him, there is no doubt. Only she and he were there, in the home they shared, at the time he died.'

The seven women jurors lean forward. They may have been prepared for a husband who kills his wife, but not for a wife who kills a husband.

'How she killed Charlie Bridges,' says Mr Fenniman, 'is also not in doubt. Her finger pressed the trigger of a loaded gun which discharged a bullet into his head.'

The seven women blink. Even the men look at Angela with a new respect, while she sits in the dock, impassive in pastel sweater, looking modestly down.

Mr Fenniman gives the jury a moment to take her in before continuing.

'I will not pretend to you that Charlie Bridges was a good man because, as you will hear, he was not. He was, or was likely to have been, an armed robber who got away with most of his crimes. But the law of this land protects us all – the good and the bad. And if any of us are to live peaceful, safe lives, all must be protected by that law. However much we condemn Charlie Bridges for his way of life we must remember that Angela Bridges chose for two decades to share it with him, and to benefit from the proceeds of his crimes.'

The jury give this consideration. Someone makes a note then puts a line through it.

'The couple,' continues Mr Fenniman, 'moved home a number of times, climbing the property ladder, ending up in a detached house near Epping Forest. The defendant, as I have said, was apparently happy to stay with Charlie Bridges, spending the money he stole and sharing his life. However, we for the Crown no more suggest he was a good husband than that he was a good man.' Mr Fenniman pauses, looks from juror to juror, makes sure they are listening. 'We do not seek to keep from you the possibility that Mr Bridges was a violent man, not only in his criminal profession, but possibly at times in his domestic life too. At least it is the defendant's case that he was violent to her, and perhaps he was. But the prosecution, I am confident, will satisfy you so that you are sure her act in killing him was nothing but a deliberate and calculated murder.'

The jurors take a collective breath. They have forgotten coffee cups and mobile phones. They are too busy forming views. They shouldn't, of course. They haven't yet heard a word of evidence. But the subject matter is the stuff of drama. There is a beautiful woman – or at least an attractive one – and there is a bad man. There is a body, a gun and a mystery to be solved. Is the defendant a victim or is the deceased?

Mr Fenniman brings the jury back to earth.

'So, let us look in a little more detail at the evidence that will be presented to you in this trial. What was the first that anyone knew of the terrible events inside that house? On the day in question, at around 3 p.m. more than one neighbour heard a loud bang but it occurred to no one that it was the sound of a gun. Some few minutes later the defendant made a 999 call. It was recorded, as all such calls are, and you will hear it played. You will hear Mrs Bridges sobbing as she explains that she and her husband had been arguing and that – as he had done before in such circumstances – he came at her as if to strike her, but that this time he had a gun in his hand. She wept as she said that in terror she grabbed at the gun and tried to turn the muzzle away from her, that there had been a struggle, and that the gun accidentally discharged. You will hear her begging for an ambulance to be sent quickly, before it is too late. This was her account then, and this was the account she repeated when she was arrested and taken to the police station to be interviewed. It is a heart-rending story, is it not?'

It is.

'Sounds convincingly like a tragic accident, doesn't it?'

It does.

'You will think it even more so when I tell you that not only the fatal bullet, when retrieved and swabbed, yielded a DNA profile that matched the deceased – of course it would, for it had passed through him – but also the cartridge case bore DNA that matched his and not hers. This, of course, supports her account that it was he not she who loaded the gun.'

I don't know where Mr Fenniman is going but this is a very high-stakes tactic. He is casting before us the defence case as a fisherman casts a line, tensing its weight just below the surface, playing with it, and any moment – his tone suggests – he will tell us something that will snap the line and the defence will sink without trace.

'Such a convincing story,' he says, 'but that is all it is. A story. The Crown will show you that Mrs Bridges' whole account – to the operator on the 999 call, to the police in interview – is top to bottom, beginning to end, a fraud. A piece of acting.

'Firstly' – he lifts an index finger, showing this is only the start of his argument – 'her plea to send an ambulance before it was too late was clearly a sham. She must have known Charlie Bridges was dead. Must have. Good grief' – an advocate's abandonment of lawyerly language – 'the man's head was half blown away and his brains splattered everywhere.

'Secondly' – up comes another finger to join the first – 'the prosecution will call a ballistics expert who will give the lie to her story that the gun was discharged in a hand-to-hand struggle. It is the opinion of this highly qualified, highly experienced expert that her account is not consistent with his scientific findings.'

I would now expect the prosecutor to set out before the jury the existence of the expert for the defence, the differing expert views, the issue between them which the jury will have to resolve; but he does not. I look at Gloria Vaughan, who is studiously applying herself to her notebook. Surely she has an expert of her own to answer that of the Crown? Still listening to Mr Fenniman, I begin to run through the contents of the Digital Case System, searching for a defence expert report. There is none.

Meanwhile, Mr Fenniman has kept up the pressure.

'You will hear from that prosecution expert,' he says, 'and I venture to think you will find him convincing. At least the defence must have found him so because, as I understand it, Mrs Bridges' primary defence of accident has changed since that interview at the police station. Now it will be submitted on her behalf that because of her husband's violence to her in the past, she simply lost her self-control. If this is so' – he puts a peculiar stress on the word *if* – 'there is a defence available to her, one which the judge will explain to you in due course. It is a defence which can reduce murder to manslaughter, but cannot lead to an outright acquittal. However' – he strikes the desk with the flat of his hand – 'it is the prosecution's contention that there is no such "if" in this case. It is not so. This is not a case of manslaughter but of bare-faced murder.'

3

Mr Fenniman has opened his case for nothing less than a conviction on murder, setting the bar high. The question now is whether he can present evidence to match his opening. He sets about the task with a will. That afternoon he calls three or four neighbours to say they heard a loud report and thought it was a motorbike backfiring or some such thing. 'After all,' says one, 'you don't expect a murder in the middle of a summer's afternoon in the middle of a nice area like ours.'

'Quite so,' says Mr Fenniman.

Each witness has their fifteen minutes in the spotlight but Ms Vaughan does not seek to challenge their evidence. The day finishes with the 999 call. The jurors are given transcripts of it, although when we hear the recording, they don't need the written word. The call is so clear that if you closed your eyes you could imagine yourself beside Angela Bridges, breathing in the acrid smell of gunpowder, the iron smell of blood. Her voice, as she tries to explain the situation to the operator, is thick with tears. I can detect none of the falsity for which Mr Fenniman contends. But what do I know? The jury listens intently while the call is played twice through. They look at the dock. They look at each other. But I cannot tell what they are thinking.

Day two of the trial, and we get to the meat of the matter. Mr Fenniman calls the ballistics expert, Mr Travers. I know him of old. He has been doing this job for years and I have seen him in my courtroom many times. What he doesn't know about firearms isn't worth knowing. He is a smallish man, very neat about the collar. His hair is thinner than it was when I first came across him, but there is still enough for a parting sharp as a scalpel. He places his file of notes on the ledge of the witness-box, reads the oath and gives his qualifications and experience. He is a quiet man. It's hard to imagine him in the laboratory or on the test range among the bangs and the smells that go with his trade. But there is clearly a sterner side to him. He takes us, without even a frisson of distaste, to the post-mortem.

'The pathologist asked for my attendance,' he says.

'Is that common?' asks Mr Fenniman, knowing that it is.

'Oh, yes,' says Mr Travers. 'Of course, for the actual . . . ' – he hesitates delicately – 'the dissection, I defer to the pathologist. But I am interested to see the surface of the skin and any scorching. I am interested in the presence of particles of gunshot residue. I need to understand the path of the wound in order to assess its trajectory.'

Mr Fenniman doesn't want us to have all our sweets at once. He holds up his hand, and Mr Travers obediently stops. 'Were you able to see where the bullet had entered the deceased?'

'It couldn't be missed. It went in through the forehead. It passed downwards into his body at an angle of approximately thirty degrees. It emerged through his back.'

'Can you tell us anything about the way Charlie Bridges was positioned at the time he was shot?' Of course Mr Fenniman knows perfectly well the answer to his question – but he isn't the witness; he can't give the evidence. And anyway, the tension is building nicely. The jury are staring at Mr Travers as if he has come from a parallel universe about whose existence they have heard, but in which they did not until now wholly believe.

'Ah, yes,' says Mr Travers. 'The position of the deceased before he was, as it were, deceased. There I can help you.' He closes one file and opens another. 'I attended the scene.' Scrupulously he gives date and time. 'You will note that this was within twenty-eight hours of the shooting and nothing had been moved except the body. Crime scene managers had, however, marked up significant features. I noted the place where the deceased had fallen, the wall behind him and the wall to his left, and the table in front of him. I noted where the bullet had been found on the floor. Examination of the room confirmed that this bullet had ricocheted first off the wall behind the deceased and then off the one immediately to his left. I took the angle at which the bullet hit the first wall, which I calculated to be twelve degrees. I used this information, together with my measurements and observations during the post-mortem, to lead to my final calculations.'

'Have your calculations been provided to the defence?'

'Naturally.'

'And to what conclusions did your calculations lead you?'

'I have concluded that the head of the deceased was lower than the hand that pulled the trigger, and was bent forward, facing rather to the right.'

'She was over him?'

'I cannot tell you whether the shooter was male or female. I can only tell you the deceased's head was lower than the hand which pulled the trigger.'

Mr Fenniman looks meaningfully at the jury. Ms Vaughan doesn't.

'Let us now consider another question. Can you tell us how far from Charlie Bridges' forehead the gun was when the trigger was pulled?'

'Not precisely, but I can give some assistance. The gun was recovered from the scene so I know its exact measurements, particularly the length of the barrel and the length from end to end. I was also able to see at the post-mortem that there was powder tattooing around the entry wound. Using all this information, I estimate that the end of the gun's barrel was approximately eighteen inches from the victim's forehead.'

'Not closer?'

'Certainly not closer. Possibly a little further away.'

'So the shooter, with hand extended and holding the gun, must have been at least a couple of feet from the victim, and the gun pointing downward at his head?'

'That of course is a matter for the jury but it is what the science indicates.'

'Could this have been a shooting in the course of a hand-to-hand struggle between victim and shooter?'

'I don't believe so.'

None of us believes so. How could it be!

Mr Fenniman sits and, after a moment, Gloria Vaughan gets to her feet and faces Mr Travers. She has not looked at the jury. She certainly has not turned to look at her client. Does she have a killer point that will expose a flaw in Mr Travers' expert analysis? It seems she does not. She narrows her eyes and stares him down for a moment but the best she can manage is, 'You weren't there. How can you possibly know it wasn't an accident?'

And having delivered herself of this, she sits again.

I see two women on the jury look at each other, then at Angela Bridges in the dock – today's sweater is lemon – and finally at Ms Vaughan. But what else could she have asked Mr Travers? The science is the science.

We take a break, during which I consider the position. The fact that Gloria Vaughan has no one to respond to Mr Travers speaks volumes. If the prosecution is calling an expert, the defence will always be able to call an expert to refute him, *if* they can find one. However, in the UK, expert witnesses owe no allegiance to one side or the other. Their primary duty is to the court itself. They may only attest to an argument which properly arises on the science. They cannot make it up to please their paymaster. It looks as if Ms Vaughan has been unable to find one to support the proposition that the shooting was an accident.

I allow to run through my head the potential defences available in a case like this. Where there is no doubt that it was the defendant's finger which pressed the trigger, the options are:

- accident
- self-defence
- lack of intent to kill or cause really serious injury
- diminished responsibility
- loss of control

Only the first two can lead to outright acquittals but they can hardly be run together. To claim that the defendant's finger pressed the trigger accidentally is the opposite of saying she was forced to press it deliberately in order to defend herself. Besides, once she had the gun and he didn't, how could it have been necessary for Mrs Bridges to shoot her husband in the head? So, scrub self-defence. As to accident ... it seems that in the light of Mr Travers' evidence, Ms Vaughan doesn't think she can do anything with that either. Each of the remaining three defences could lead at best to a verdict of 'not guilty of murder but guilty of manslaughter'. However, 'diminished responsibility' would require supporting evidence from a psychiatrist – and clearly the defence no more have one of these than they do an expert in ballistics. I give some thought to 'lack of intent'. I suppose, if you were of an optimistic bent, you might shoot a man in the arm or leg without intending to do him serious harm, but you can hardly shoot him between the eyes without knowing the outcome is not going to be good. That leaves 'loss of control'.

It's the classic defence for a battered wife who has been pushed over time beyond endurance and who finally snaps. If I had been defending Mrs Bridges, this is where I would be, and it is clearly where Gloria Vaughan is. But is it where the defendant herself is? Suddenly I remember the argument I witnessed in the dock on the first morning of the trial. Not argument, perhaps, for it takes two to argue, and Angela Bridges had sat immoveable throughout, but I see now that it might have been about the nature of the defence to be advanced to the jury.

Is this where we are? Mr Fenniman is confident that the defence of 'accident' will not hold water . . . or will hold so much water that it is doomed to sink. Ms Vaughan agrees with him and wants to work with the alternative defence of 'loss of control'. But is Angela Bridges sticking with her first account, Mr Travers or no Mr Travers? Does she want vindication and the prison doors to open while her counsel thinks the best she can do is a verdict of manslaughter?

Not that a manslaughter verdict is to be sneezed at. Murder with a firearm is likely to yield a life sentence with something in the region of thirty years to be served before the Parole Board can consider release. Manslaughter in these circumstances might lead to a sentence of no more than twelve years, of which she would serve two thirds. Why would anyone risk a conviction for murder and serving thirty years if they have a chance of manslaughter and only serving eight? Unless, of course, they know that it *was* an accident. Unless they believe the jury will see that it was an accident. Back in the courtroom, I look narrowly at Angela Bridges but she is as unreadable to me as is this jury.

4

The trial is going fast now, almost as if it has a momentum of its own. That afternoon the pathologist tells us more about the body than some of us want to know. The crime scene manager explains what evidence he recovered from the house. But the excitement of their stories has been stolen by Mr Travers. On the fourth day we hear of events at the police station – the defendant's account to the interviewing officers that it was all an accident. Her reported words, read out to the jury, ring hollow after those of Mr Travers. There is still, of course, the forensic medical examiner's findings of the fresh and not-so-fresh injuries she had suffered to arm, breast and head, which the prosecution – in fairness – must put before the jury; but Chester Fenniman has taken the sting out of that by forewarning the jury of it in his opening. All in all, at lunchtime, when he says, 'And that, My Lady, is the case for the Crown,' things are looking very tidy for him.

I give the defence the afternoon to prepare, and so it is on the Friday morning that Gloria Vaughan says, 'My Lady, I call the defendant to give evidence.' And from the dock, neat in today's offering of apple green, Angela Bridges crosses the courtroom to the witness-box. She takes the oath on the Bible, using a pair of spectacles to do it. She looks about her with a little pout of the lips, then turns to her counsel.

'Are you all right, Mrs Bridges?' Ms Vaughan's opening question is not one recommended in advocacy training for those newly called to the Bar, but in the right hands – and surely Gloria Vaughan's are the right hands – it has the merit of setting the scene. 'Look,' she is saying to the jury, 'only look at how vulnerable my client is as she stands there in her apple-green sweater.'

But perhaps Angela Bridges hasn't read the script, for she only gives a wry smile and responds, 'I've been better.'

Ms Vaughan takes her client through the years of the marriage. After Charlie came out of prison, Angela Bridges tells us, she thought the criminality was all behind him. She thought he was working in asset management.

'That's one way of putting it,' says Mr Fenniman, not so *sotto voce*.

It was years, says Angela, before she realized the truth. And by then she was, well, he was her husband. She loved him. And besides, by then she was . . . She shakes her head. 'I never knew whether he would hug me or hit me. People always say why didn't you just leave, but they don't understand that you can love someone even if sometimes they are cruel to you. And then the cruelty piles up and you just don't know what to do at all.'

Ms Vaughan nods as if she understands – as if it's so obvious, we should all understand. Because obviously it is true that people can be overborne in this way. The issue here, however, isn't whether some women can be overborne. It is whether this woman was. And if she was, did she finally snap and lose her self-control because of what had been done to her. Sooner or later Ms Vaughan must tackle it, and after we have spent a considerable time on the history of the marriage, she does.

'So, Mrs Bridges,' she says at last, 'that final, that dreadful day. You had been shopping?'

Angela nods. She has pulled a handkerchief from her pocket and is twisting it in her hands. 'Charlie's friends had invited us out to dinner. He wanted me to wear something . . . new. I bought a dress I thought he'd like. I was going to show him. He was in the lounge, just sitting there. He had the gun.'

'The gun?'

'The same one he'd had for years. The one he took when he was going to . . .'

'You thought he was going to commit another robbery?'

'I knew he was. It was the only reason he would get out the gun. I told him not to take it, or if he had to take it, not to load it. But he wouldn't listen. He got angry. He hit me.' She puts her hand to the side of her head where the forensic medical examiner had found reddening. 'He hit me and left the room. I heard him go into the dining room.'

'And the gun?'

The smallest pause. 'I don't really remember but I suppose he must have taken it with him. A minute later, perhaps less, he called me. Maybe I shouldn't have gone to him. Maybe if I hadn't, he would still be alive.' She twists the handkerchief round her fingers, bites her lip, stops.

'Be brave now, Mrs Bridges,' says Gloria Vaughan in a tone which makes me glad for H that he is not sitting on this trial. 'Tell us what happened next.'

Angela Bridges looks up, her eyes full of tears. 'I went to him believing he was going to apologize for hitting me. He often did.'

'So, what happened?'

'I don't know,' she says. 'At least, I know he came at me with the gun. Perhaps he was only going to hit me with it, but I thought he would shoot me and I tried to grab it. I thought . . . I still do think that we struggled over it and somehow it went off, but the prosecution's ballistic expert . . .'

'Mr Travers?' suggests Ms Vaughan.

'Mr Travers says it couldn't have happened like that. So I don't know what to say. I genuinely believe it was an accident as we struggled over the gun.'

Ms Vaughan gives the jury a moment to absorb this. Angela Bridges has been allowed – and who could stop her? – to lay out her hopeless defence of 'accident'. Now Ms Vaughan sets to work on 'loss of control'.

'We all understand how you explain the accident,' she says gently.

'Not all of us,' mutters Mr Fenniman.

'But, if Mr Travers is right, can you explain how the muzzle of the gun might have been some eighteen inches from your husband when the bullet was fired?'

Mrs Bridges shakes her head. 'I can't. I was so frightened. I really thought that this time he would kill me. It's all a blur. If I did something . . .' She takes a deep breath. 'If I did what Mr Fenniman says . . . if I got the gun and pointed it at Charlie and deliberately shot him, I don't recall it, and it could only be because things had built up to such a pitch I couldn't bear it any more and . . .'

'You lost your self-control?' says Ms Vaughan.

'Don't lead the witness,' snaps Mr Fenniman.

'Perhaps that's it,' says Angela Bridges. 'Perhaps I lost my self-control.'

Gloria Vaughan can do no more. She hands over her precious client to Chester Fenniman, who receives her like a hunter given the freedom of the forest. He seems to expand as the opportunities open up before him. He is a fine advocate. Poor Angela.

'Mrs Bridges,' he says, 'let us start with your marital relationship.'

'My what?'

'You tell us you loved your husband.'

'Mr Fenniman' – she looks straight at him – 'I did. I do. I know you say he was a bad man and I know in many ways you are right, but I knew him better than you and I can tell you there were a lot of good things about him. He supported an animal charity. He gave presents to orphanages at Christmas time. He donated two computers to a local primary school. You have to set these things against him being an armed robber and a wife-beater.'

Oh, clever Mrs Bridges. Chester Fenniman finds himself wrong-footed.

And she has another card up her sleeve. 'It is cruel of you to doubt my love for Charlie. You have all been so cruel. You have given me no space to grieve for him. He was, you know, my husband of over twenty years.'

In another world, it occurs to me, this woman would have made a very good barrister. Perhaps Mr Fenniman thinks so too. He shifts his ground and his tone to one of sarcasm.

'You say it was an accident but that if it wasn't an accident then you lost your self-control. Perhaps you'd like to have a go at another defence too? What about self-defence? Does that one take your fancy, Mrs Bridges?'

This is unworthy of a fine advocate, and I can only assume Mr Fenniman has been shaken by the cleverness of her previous answers. I am about to ask him to move on but she is ahead of us both.

'I don't ask the jury to consider self-defence, Mr Fenniman, because that would mean I made a deliberate and calculated decision to kill my husband to prevent him from killing me. I made no such decision. Does that answer your question?'

Mr Fenniman has the grace to blush under her long gaze. Do I see, out of the corner of my eye, a juror give her a thumbs-up sign? Of course not. It must be a trick of the light.

'Let us go straight to the heart of the matter,' says Mr Fenniman. 'Let us look at this suggestion that you lost control of yourself. How do you suppose that happened?'

'I don't know,' she says. 'I was very frightened. When Charlie lost his temper he could be a very frightening man. I was thinking of all he had done and all he might do to innocent people; all he might do to me; all we stood to lose just because he wanted to do one more job. If Mr Travers is right and the shooting wasn't an accident, perhaps I did just snap.'

In her seat, Gloria Vaughan nods.

'But it's not how I remember it,' says the witness rebelliously.

Ms Vaughan stops nodding.

'If you pulled the trigger, the gun must have been in your hand.'

'I suppose so.'

'And at the moment you pulled the trigger, the muzzle must have been pointing at Charlie's head.'

'It must have been.'

'Are you used to handling a gun? To lining up the muzzle with the target? Are you a good shot?'

'No,' she says. 'No to all your questions. Perhaps it was just an unlucky shot.'

'Very unlucky for your husband,' observes Mr Fenniman, 'for you got him square between the eyes. Was that just bad luck or good aiming, Mrs Bridges?'

'Bad luck,' says the defendant.

'Then let's consider Mr Travers' next point. You not only seem to have taken aim at a most vulnerable spot, but to have had your victim at your mercy, being over him at the time you pulled the trigger.'

Ms Vaughan is on her feet. 'That is a most unfair way to put it,' she snorts. 'Mr Travers only said the hand on the trigger was higher than the forehead. There may be—'

'I'll put the matter another way,' says Mr Fenniman. 'Mrs Bridges, were you taller or shorter than your husband?'

She hesitates. 'Shorter,' she says. And before he can ask the inevitable next question adds, 'By some six inches, I think.'

'So, you had the gun. Your hand was above him, the gun pointing down at him. I don't suppose you were standing on a chair, were you?'

'Of course I wasn't.'

'Then should we picture him cowering before you?'

'Picture him how you like,' snaps Angela. Then, recovering herself, 'Because none of it happened like this.'

Mr Fenniman gives the jury a moment to see the image he has conjured up before he goes remorselessly on. 'You say you were in fear of violence from him, but if you had the gun, how exactly did you think he could hurt you?'

She shakes her head. She looks at her counsel as if to say, 'Is this your great defence of "loss of control"?'

She turns to the jury. 'Look,' she says to them, 'I know there are women abused as I was, who snap and do dreadful things. I don't know if I'm one of them because I don't remember any of the things

Mr Travers says happened. I believe Charlie and I struggled in a hand-to-hand fight over the gun and it went off accidentally.'

'All right,' says Mr Fenniman. 'Let's look at the possibility of this accident you describe.' He is using the voice of a man of utmost reason. Beware the advocate who adopts this tone. 'You went to the dining room believing your husband wanted to have a drink with you – to apologize as he often did after he struck you.'

'Yes.'

'And it looks as if that was his intention because afterwards crime scene managers found two glasses on the floor, both of which had contained alcohol. One was a shattered whisky glass, the other an unbroken wine glass. So, your husband has gone into the dining room and taken the whisky decanter—'

'Bottle,' she says.

'Taken the bottle, and he has also taken a tumbler. He has poured himself a drink. Then he has taken a wine bottle and a wine glass, and poured you a drink. The purpose was that you should drink together, a reconciliation, and there are the two glasses to prove that was his intention.'

She is suddenly very still. She can see where this is going. So can I. So can Gloria Vaughan. The jury hasn't yet got the point but they will any moment now.

'Let's picture it, shall we? Your husband has lost his temper and struck you. He has left the room and recovered his temper. He has poured you each a glass of something reconciliatory. As you come in, he offers the wine glass to you, inviting you to drink with him. If he is holding a whisky glass in one hand and a wine glass in the other, in which hand, Mrs Bridges, was he holding the gun?'

Angela Bridges does not crumble. Instead, she straightens her spine and turns away from Chester Fenniman to the jury, who stare at her, breath abated. She takes a moment to compose herself, then she speaks directly to them.

'My whole future,' she says, 'is in your hands. You will do what you decide is right. But I just want you to know this. I devoted all my life to Charlie Bridges. He was a bad man who did bad things, and I think I must have been a bad woman to go along with what he did. He hurt me, yet I stayed with him, and I suppose that was my choice.' She frowns as if she cannot quite understand how she ever came to make that choice. 'But I never went along with him hurting other people, because other people didn't have a choice. I just knew that his luck was running out and that sooner or later he was going to kill someone with that gun. I knew it was going to happen, and when it did, not only would I lose everything, so would someone else – and so would that someone else's wife and kids. Charlie Bridges deserved to die and there's an end to it.'

This is quite a speech. It has rocked the jury in their seats. It has caused Chester Fenniman's jaw to drop. He has cross-examined hundreds of defendants but he has never heard anything like this.

'Mrs Bridges,' he says slowly, 'are you saying you killed your husband because he deserved to die? Are you confessing to murder?'

She turns back from the jury to her tormentor. 'I'd be a fool to do that, wouldn't I, Mr Fenniman? There was a hand-to-hand struggle and in the course of it Charlie was shot. It was an accident.'

5

Poor Ms Vaughan. It happens sometimes. A defendant in the witness-box can lose it, can say things they don't mean to, that can't be unsaid. I am surprised that it has happened to Mrs Bridges because I thought she had a reasonable defence of loss of control and enough brains and composure to put up a better show – but there it is, and Gloria Vaughan can't undo it. She does what she can, putting before the jury the material from Mrs Bridges' GP. And then evidence is closed.

It is almost three o'clock on Friday – only the fifth day of the trial, though it seems somehow longer. I adjourn the case until Monday morning when counsel and I must look at the law and see what remains in the wreckage of the defence case. The jury will come back at 2 p.m. that day.

I spend the weekend mulling over what defences remain live. The law requires that I direct the jury on any available defence. A defence, however unlikely, is available providing there is evidence to support it. It is for the jury to decide what, of all the evidence, they accept and what they reject. After a deal of thought I set about drafting a Steps to Verdict document for the jury to follow.

Murder

Before you may convict Mrs Bridges of murder you must ask yourselves the following:

Step 1. Are you sure that she killed Charlie Bridges?
- She accepts that she shot him and that this shooting caused his death.
- Go to step 2.

This first step is simple enough. And uncontentious. The second step requires more thought. It concerns the defence of accident. Mrs Bridges, despite the better view of her barrister, has stuck with this throughout. The reason Gloria Vaughan was not happy running this defence is that it is unrunnable if the jury accepts the evidence of Mr Travers which precludes an accidental firing of the gun – at least in the way described by Angela Bridges. However, the jury must consider not just what he says, but all the evidence, including hers. They must decide if it is safe to reject her account because of the expert evidence of Mr Travers. It must be their decision, not mine. And so I draft step 2.

> Step 2. Are you sure that the act of shooting was deliberate, i.e. not accidental?
> - This is a central matter in dispute. Mrs Bridges says that her finger accidentally pulled the trigger in the course of a hand-to-hand struggle with the deceased. The Crown relies on the expert evidence of Mr Travers to say this could not be so.
> - If you conclude her act of shooting was or may have been accidental, she is not guilty of any offence and that ends your deliberations. If you are sure the act of shooting was not accidental, go to step 3.

> Step 3 is the more straightforward and familiar stage before anyone can be convicted of murder.

> Step 3. Are you sure that at the time she shot him, the defendant intended either to kill Mr Bridges or at least to cause him really serious injury?
> - If you are not sure of this, but are sure she intended to cause him some injury (short of really serious injury), she is not guilty of murder but guilty of 'manslaughter by lack of intent', and that is the end of your deliberations.
> - However, if you are sure she deliberately shot Mr Bridges intending to kill him or at least to cause him really serious injury . . .

Here I pause. Am I going to leave the defence of 'loss of control' to the jury or not? If I am not, the sentence above will finish 'she is guilty of murder'. If I am, I must tell the jury now to consider the final defence, i.e. 'loss of control'. As with any defence, the question I must ask myself is whether there is evidence of it. What is the evidence of 'loss of control'? It cannot be supplied by Ms Vaughan's wishing it so. It is there, or it isn't. And if it is there, it won't go away because I dislike drafting this direction – the longest, most complex and least comprehensible to any jury. That Parliament has legislated in such terms says a lot about its belief in the UK's elementary education system. In the end I decide to draft a direction for the defence, and to discuss the matter with counsel on Monday morning. Accordingly, I set out the following:

You should now consider the final defence of 'loss of control'. This defence applies in the following circumstances:

1. The defendant lost her self-control, i.e. lost her ability to maintain her actions in accordance with considered judgement or lost normal powers of reasoning.
- This involves a subjective examination of what was going on in her head.
- In considering this you are entitled to take into account:
  - all that you conclude happened between her and Charlie Bridges in the course of their relationship as well as on that last day
  - the period of time that elapsed between anything you conclude happened between them and the killing
  - any other relevant circumstances
- If you are sure she did not lose her self-control, she is guilty of murder and that is the end of your deliberations. However, if you conclude she did or may have lost her self-control, go to paragraph 2.

2. Consider whether the trigger for her loss of control was attributable to her fear of serious violence from Charlie Bridges.

- In assessing this, you should consider her state of mind, together with all the circumstances around the shooting, including the history that led up to it.
- Ask yourself if her fear was genuine even if mistaken. It is her case that he pointed a loaded gun at her. It is the Crown's case that no such thing happened.
- If you are sure the trigger does not apply, she is guilty of murder and that is the end of your deliberations. However, if you conclude the trigger does or may apply, go to paragraph 3.

3. Consider whether someone of her age, sex, with a normal degree of tolerance and self-restraint, and in her circumstances, might have reacted in the same or similar way she did.

- You should superimpose on her subjective position an objective test, asking how an ordinary person of her age, sex and circumstances might behave.
- You should take into account all of her circumstances except those whose only relevance is to reduce her self-restraint. This is because the law does not allow anyone to 'get away with murder' by saying I've got an unusually short temper or I'm unusually prone to losing my self-control. You should ignore any matters in so far as they may have reduced her self-restraint. However, you should take them into account if you find they have another relevance.
- If you are sure a person of the defendant's age and sex, with a normal degree of tolerance and self-restraint, and in her circumstances (excluding those whose only effect is to reduce her self-restraint), would not have reacted in the same or similar way she did, the defence fails and she

is guilty of murder. If you are not sure of this, she is not guilty of murder, but guilty of 'manslaughter by reason of loss of control'.

If I give the jury directions in this form, it means that while there is only one route to a conviction for murder – the long and tortuous journey through every step of the draft – there are two different routes to manslaughter, 'by lack of intent' or 'by loss of control'.

Armed with this, I return to court on Monday.

'Well?' I ask counsel. 'Am I to leave both "accident" and "loss of control" as issues for the jury to consider?'

'You must leave accident,' says Mr Fenniman, 'because the defendant has advanced it as her primary defence. However impossible it seems in the light of the unchallenged – I may say unchallengeable – scientific evidence, the Crown accepts this is a matter for the jury.'

Mr Fenniman is not being generous here. He is taking a purist view of the law. Besides, he knows he has nothing to fear from this defence for he's right when he says no challenge was put to Mr Travers' scientific explanation. Ms Vaughan also says 'accident' must be left to the jury to consider, but the real heart of the defence, she says, must be 'loss of control'.

'Where is the evidence of this?' I ask. 'The defendant doesn't say she lost her self-control.'

'She says she might have done,' says Ms Vaughan, 'and that is enough to at least raise the defence. It is then for the Crown to prove she did not.'

She is right. But she isn't finished.

'And Your Ladyship asks where is the evidence!' The exclamation mark after her words hangs in the air. Ms Vaughan has entered upon declaratory mode and it is fortunate for Q's delicate constitution that he is not presiding over this case. 'Have we not heard of the long history of domestic abuse?' she cries. 'Have we not seen the injuries to head, breast and arm, all apparently of differing ages and so bespeaking the ongoing course of that abuse? That, together with evidence from her GP, must give any jury the right to consider whether, under such an accumulated strain, the pointing of a loaded gun at her led her to snap and do what she would never otherwise have done.'

I turn to Mr Fenniman. He considers the matter. He is an experienced and usually fair prosecutor. Finally he says, 'It is the Crown's case that the deceased never pointed the gun at the defendant in the way she describes. But if the jury conclude he did or may have done, I accept that "loss of control" falls for their consideration.'

I agree. In the light of the evidence, both defences are paper-thin, but both must be left to the jury. Angela Bridges deserves that, at least.

So at 2 p.m., when the jury returns, Mr Fenniman makes his closing address to them. He lays out his material logically, building brick upon brick. It is a strong case. When he has finished, it is Ms Vaughan's turn. She makes an impassioned plea for battered women everywhere. She paints a terrifying picture of the build-up of fear over months or years, the final snap when the abused cannot support the strain any longer and turns on her abuser and kills him. She makes a good fist of it. She has done all she can. Now it is for me to sum up.

I begin with the Steps to Verdict as I have drafted them. The jury frown and blink over the complexity. So do I. I point out that there is open to them one route to a verdict of murder, and two different routes to manslaughter – 'lack of intent to cause really serious harm' and 'loss of control'. I explain to them that if their verdict is manslaughter, they will not be asked whether they have found 'manslaughter by lack of intent' or 'manslaughter by loss of control'. They do not have to agree on that point. It is sufficient if each, according to his or her oath, agrees she is guilty of manslaughter.

I give them further directions of law and then turn to my summary of the central features of the evidence. I emphasize that this is only a summary, and therefore I have had to make a selection of the material – but it is their view of the evidence that counts, not mine.

By mid-morning on Tuesday I have completed my job, and theirs is about to begin. I give them some final words about the need to work together, pooling their thoughts, respecting each other's point of view. I direct them to choose a foreman – any one of their number – to chair their discussions and return their verdict in due course. I point out that the foreman carries no more weight than any other of their number but has the duty of ensuring everyone's voice can be heard, and of keeping the discussions on track. 'You make the findings of fact,' I tell them, 'and apply the findings you make to the law as I have given it to you. In that way you will be true to the promise you made at the beginning of the trial, to give true verdicts in accordance with the evidence.'

And off they go.

6

Over the next days, for however long it takes, they will work in their jury room, examining the evidence, deciding what it means, seeing where it drives them. I may get notes asking for clarification of the law or for a reminder of some of the evidence, but otherwise this part of the trial is all in their hands.

You can never tell how long any jury will take to consider their verdicts, and this one has a lot to think about. The direction on 'loss of control' is one all judges hate giving because it is so complicated. It will, I think, keep them busy for a good while. So I settle down to wait, and occupy the time in considering possible sentences.

As ever, it is much easier to sentence murder than manslaughter. For murder there is only one sentence, that of life imprisonment. The task then is to find the minimum term that must be served before the prisoner can apply to the Parole Board for release. Had Mrs Bridges hit her husband over the head with a frying pan, the starting point for this term would have been one of fifteen years, but the use of a firearm raises the starting point to thirty years.* Of course, the starting point isn't the finishing point. Murder is always a heinous crime with irreversible effects not only on the victim but on his or her family and the wider community. But in one sense, Angela Bridges is the victim's family, and I suppose it could be argued that the wider community won't much miss Charlie Bridges. I am going to struggle with where in the sentencing bracket to place this one. And, of course, it's always possible the jury will find her guilty of manslaughter, where sentence may vary depending on which of the two forms of manslaughter applies.†

I am still thinking about the various sentences when, towards the end of the afternoon, the usher knocks on my door.

'Jury note, My Lady.' She offers me the folded sheet of paper.

I take it, expecting a question about the law, or about the evidence, or a request to go home early, or for the heating to be turned up, or down. I am not expecting what I see. I am so not expecting it that I have to read it twice to understand it. But here it is: 'We have reached a unanimous verdict.'

I can't imagine how they have given Mrs Bridges' case fair consideration in only four hours, with all the various steps they had to go through, but no one will ever question them about this. No one

* See Appendix O, pp. 306–7.
† See Appendix P, pp. 308–11.

should ever question any jury about their deliberations because it is a crime to do so.*

'Reassemble the court,' I tell the usher. 'Get counsel down. Get the defendant up. We have a verdict.'

Within ten minutes I am back in court. The two barristers sit before me. The defendant is in the dock. Members of the press are blocking the doorway. Others who have caught wind of a verdict are drifting into the public gallery. There is a low hum, like an unhappy light bulb, which stops suddenly as the jury are led back into court. The foreman – it is my Lady of the Glasses – takes the traditional seat in the jury-box closest to the judge. My clerk rises to her feet. She asks the defendant and the foreman both to stand.

'Madam Foreman,' says my clerk, 'on this indictment, have you reached a verdict upon which you are all agreed?'

'We have.'

'Madam Foreman, on the count of murder . . .'

In the dock, Angela Bridges looks straight at the jury, her face unreadable. Mr Fenniman gazes politely into the middle distance. Ms Vaughan stares down, bracing herself. Everyone who has ever defended in a murder trial will know what her thoughts are likely to be. She has worked hard on this case. She never believed she could get an outright acquittal, but she had really hoped for manslaughter, and here is such a quick verdict that she wonders if this jury have given any thought at all to her case. For her, it is disappointing. For her client, it is a disaster. For surely, surely her client was a battered wife and—

* Section 20D Juries Act 1974 makes it a criminal offence for a person intentionally (a) to disclose information about statements made, opinions expressed, arguments advanced or votes cast by members of a jury in the course of their deliberations in proceedings before a court, or (b) to solicit or obtain such information, subject to the exceptions in sections 20E to 20G.

'. . . do you find the defendant, Angela Bridges, guilty or not guilty?'

'Not guilty,' says the foreman.

Mr Fenniman carefully conceals what must be bitter disappointment. Ms Vaughan dares to look up, to stiffen her back, to give a firm nod. Of course her client is not guilty of murder. Angela continues to stare at the jury.

The clerk now has to ask the second question: 'Members of the jury, do you find the defendant guilty or not guilty of manslaughter?'

This time the Lady of the Glasses turns to the dock. She smiles. 'Not guilty,' she says.

'You find the defendant not guilty,' says my clerk, as if she can no more believe what she has heard than can the rest of us.

'We do,' says the foreman firmly.

'And that is the verdict of you all?'

'It is.'

Only Angela Bridges shows no sign of surprise.

7

I go back to my room and to the paperwork still spread on my desk. The Sentencing Act 2020 schedule 21 for sentencing murder with firearms, the Sentencing Council's Definitive Guideline on Manslaughter, the Coroners and Justice Act 2009 section 54 which created the defence of 'loss of control' – they all mock me. I don't know whether I'm dismayed or heartened. The result is clearly a wonderful one for Angela Bridges, but what does it mean for justice? The only proper way in which this jury could have reached the verdict they did is by accepting the defence of 'accident'. To find there was or may have been an accident means they must have found poor Mr Travers' unchallenged evidence unreliable. I don't believe for one moment this is what they have done. I am as certain as I can be that they have said 'a plague on your lack of intent and on your loss of control and on your endless drafting of endless law . . . here was a man who deserved to die and a woman who deserves her life back'. If this were written in a book, I might be cheering. But in the real world, what does it mean if people defy the law to impose their own sense of right and wrong? Because it rather seems that is exactly what Angela Bridges and her jury have done.

It is a shaken judge who makes her way down to tea. The system in which I have believed for my entire career as barrister and judge has been exposed as having a huge hole in its centre. My feelings must be evident on my face because when I enter the judges' dining room there are small exclamations of concern. Tea is poured for me. I am given the pick of the biscuits. When I explain what has happened, I am met with a range of different views.

'Look at it this way,' says S. 'If a battered woman is overborne by the abuse she suffers and loses control, she has a defence to murder, while if she is abused but not overborne, she doesn't, though the actions of both her and her abuser have been identical. Maybe it's the law that's wrong, not the jury.'

H is more robust. 'If the difference between an accident and a murder is eighteen inches, perhaps it doesn't matter,' he says.

But none of us believes these things, because we all believe in the rule of law, which has no defence of 'he deserved what he got'. People can't be allowed to go around killing others because they judge them unfit to live. If they did, the whole system would collapse and society would be chaos. This is what the Old Bailey judges believe. Fervently. And it is fundamental to this belief that jurors can be trusted to follow legal directions and bring in true verdicts according to the evidence.

'What do you think?' I ask S, arbiter of all good sense.

He pauses for a moment, then says, 'Come with me.'

'Where?' demands H, who hasn't finished his tea.

But S is already out of the door and we trail obediently after him. He leads us down the stairs and through the door that separates the judges' side of the building – the private side – from the public side. Happily, most people have gone for the day, and our passage goes unremarked.

S takes us from the bright modern side of the Central Criminal Court into the cool dimness of the part that was built in the earliest years of the twentieth century. Down here at ground level, the large hall, off which are Courts Seventeen, Eighteen and Nineteen, is a study in muted marble. The ceilings are relatively low with rounded arches. The pillars and pilasters give it a cloistered feel. S leads us to the far end, to the plaque on the wall which commemorates the events of a trial that took place at the Old Bailey in 1670.

William Penn (he of Pennsylvania fame) and his fellow Quaker William Mead were brought before the court for unlawfully preaching to people in the street and drawing a tumultuous company after them. The plaque isn't about the two Williams but about the courage and endurance of the jury who tried them. The jury found it hard to swallow an unlawful preaching in the street which only happened because soldiers had locked the door to the Meeting House; and when it came to labelling the God-fearing Quakers as tumultuous, they drew the line. The judge in those far-off days believed there was no proper route to an acquittal, and when the jury returned a verdict of 'not guilty' he sent them out again to reconsider. When they held fast to their view, he locked them up without food or water for two days. Still they were not to be swayed. Finally, he fined them. It took the intervention of the Lord Chief Justice to resolve the matter with an opinion that established the right of juries to give their verdict 'according to their convictions'.

'You see the point,' says S.

We do. There is no appeal against a jury's acquittal. There may be against a conviction if the judge gets the law wrong, but an acquittal is sacrosanct, because the jury is sacrosanct.

'It's the thin end of a very thick wedge,' says H, expressing what we are all reluctantly thinking.

S makes a small moue. 'Juries over the years have scarcely abused it,' he says, 'but the right of a jury to return a verdict in the teeth of the evidence survives. Think of Clive Ponting. Think of Michael Randle and Pat Pottle.'

We do.

In 1985, Ponting, a civil servant, was accused of leaking classified documents about the sinking of the Argentine warship the *General Belgrano* during the Falklands conflict. He admitted doing so, asserting he acted in the public interest because the documents showed that those in authority had lied about what happened, and that the *Belgrano* was heading *away* from the Royal Navy task force when it was hit. The judge had ruled there was no defence in law. The jury acquitted anyway.

In 1966, Randle and Pottle helped spring George Blake from Wormwood Scrubs where he was serving a forty-two-year sentence for passing secrets to the Russians. In 1990 they were unwise enough to explain how they did it in a book. In 1991 they stood trial at the Old Bailey for their admitted crime. They defended themselves, saying that, while they in no way condoned Blake's espionage activities for either side, a forty-two-year sentence was inhuman and hypocritical and in those circumstances they were right to break the law. The judge disallowed their defence. The jury acquitted.

'So, you see,' says S, 'perverse verdicts have a noble history.'

In 2001, as part of his review of the criminal courts, Lord Justice Auld concluded that although the perverse verdict had been an accepted feature of our jury system for a long time, seen as a useful long-stop against oppression by the State, this was wholly wrong. He said a juror who chose perversity broke his promise to bring in a true verdict in accordance with the evidence. He called the perverse verdict 'a blatant affront to the legal process'. He said jurors weren't there to substitute their view of the propriety of the law for that of Parliament or its enforcement for that of its appointed executive. He recommended 'that the law should be declared that juries have no right to acquit defendants in defiance of the law or in disregard of the evidence'.* Thus spake Lord Justice Auld. But he, as all judges must, has gone, while the perverse verdict remains.† And with it there remains the ultimate power of jurors – the people of this country randomly drawn from its ranks – to return a verdict which they believe to be right.

* The Auld Report, 2001.
† See Appendix Q, p. 312.

CONCLUSIONS

TODAY, SOMEWHERE IN THIS country, a murder will be committed. Almost certainly more than one. Day after week after month the bodies pile up. Each year hundreds of our community are unlawfully killed by those who live alongside them.

For all the wrongdoers about whom I have told you, there's no doubt each took the decision to act and each must bear the responsibility for that. There is, after all, *always* a choice. But if we think that is the end of the matter we are not just foolish, we are wickedly so. We are not just blind, we are closing our eyes to the obvious. Wrongdoers don't fall from the skies in the last shower of rain. They grow up in this or another society, they are formed not just by their capacities but by their experiences. Some – most – of those who come before the courts have had particularly difficult experiences in childhood and adolescence.

In some cases, if we are honest, we must accept we have allowed them to become what they are. Of course, everyone is different. No two people start the same and they won't end the same. But surely everyone is entitled to the same chances. If we want to empty our courts of the sort of crimes that currently fill them, we should reflect on that. After all, if significant numbers of young people feel disaffected from our society, we shouldn't be surprised if they create their own rules by which to live. If mental illness makes more of us vulnerable, then more of us will become both victims and perpetrators of crime. The internet allows those with perverted sexual thoughts about children to enter a child's bedroom. People stalk each other. The drugs trade destroys lives and breeds violence.

Day after day, defendant after defendant, case after case, each with its victims. Lives lost or irreparably damaged, families forever changed, friends indelibly scarred. For those caught up in it, each tragedy is wholly personal and individual. But each is played out in the same court setting, according to the same law, the same rules.

Who created these rules? The answer is *we* did. Every society makes its own laws. In so far as the most basic of these laws are the same, whether in dictatorship, democracy or theocracy, most societies across the ages have had the same basic needs. In so far as they diverge . . . well, needs develop and differ. 'Thou shalt not kill' and 'Thou shalt not steal' are concepts as central to the smooth running of modern society as they were when inscribed on Sinai stone. 'Thou shalt not commit adultery' and 'Honour thy father and thy mother' have become matters of morality not criminality. 'Remember the Lord's day to keep it holy', among others, is now widely regarded as no longer having either legal or moral force.

Our law these days is made largely by those to whom we have given the power of governing. Though we are still a common-law jurisdiction, our criminal law is mainly made in Parliament where statutes come thicker and faster than ever before. They lay out what behaviour is prohibited, what sentences are available, what rules of evidence apply. If the number of people in prison and the length of time for which they are there have increased exponentially (the prison population doubled between 1990 and 2017), that is a result of the acts of those we have elected, and the sentencing guidelines that have been created on the back of the legislation.

All those good minds trying to make good rules by which we can live good lives . . . it seems presumptuous to ask if we have got it wrong; but we certainly have got something wrong. We must have or there wouldn't be a 'day after day, defendant after defendant, victim after victim'. So, before you and I part company, let us think about that.

I suppose what is right and what is wrong depends on what we are trying to achieve. We want, of course, to proscribe acts and omissions so damaging to our society that they must be labelled crimes. So far, so good. Then, having identified those crimes, we want to stop people committing them; and it is here we seem to have lost the way. Historically we punished wrongdoers because punishment was their due. Then we did it in order to deter them (and others) from further offending. In more recent times we have embraced the concept of rehabilitation, the idea that if we show people who have committed criminal acts the error of their ways we can put them on the right path. And when that fails, we throw up our hands and say, 'OK, if they won't be rehabilitated and aren't deterred by punishment let's just lock them up so society is protected from them.' It's all perfectly logical. But – here's the problem – it just isn't working. It isn't stopping crime. It isn't even reducing crime. We are now in a position where we can barely accommodate all the people being sent to prison in accordance with the laws we have created. So maybe it's time to step to one side and reconsider.

Here's a thought. If what we want to do is to stop crime, maybe there's a fundamental flaw in the logic of all the above – because all of it requires a crime to be committed before any element bites. You only get rehabilitated or punished or excluded from society after the crime has been committed, after the victims have endured its consequences, after the offender has done what cannot be undone. Of course I'm not arguing against the need to rehabilitate and/or punish, but I do wonder how we have developed into a society in which so many young people grow up being prepared to offend against it in the first place. Maybe we should begin with questioning why people commit crimes at all.

The obvious answer – you might say – is that some people are greedy, dishonest, vengeful, angry, prepared to use violence to get what they want. Except that none of these things is really the answer. A person may be any or all of these things and not commit a crime, and many of us are. A crime is committed because when faced with a situation where he or she *could* steal, defraud, sell drugs, strike out and hurt or kill, the offender chooses to do so when someone else would not. Why is that? The situation provides the opportunity to offend. He or she doesn't have to take that opportunity, but the offender does. The idea for committing a crime occurs – he doesn't have to follow it through, but the offender does. Almost always offenders commit crimes because they choose to. That choice may be planned or it may happen on the spur of the moment, but still the choice is theirs to make or not. So why do some people choose to offend when others do not?

Knives, drugs, gangs . . . anything new and superficially shiny has the power to magnetize and draw people in. And of course the immature brain has a harder time making the best decisions, and so the young are particularly vulnerable to making poor choices. And of course there are those whose mental make-up or addictions render them more vulnerable to bad choices. But however well or badly life has prepared someone for it, still for every single offender, the choice is theirs. It isn't the job of society to make the choice for them. But – and it's a big 'but' – maybe it *is* the job of society to equip them to make the right choice for themselves. At the moment we lay down the law, and when people breach it we roll out a complex system in which we frown and sigh and wag fingers and rehabilitate or punish the law-breakers; but maybe we would do better if *before* they break the law we helped them not to.

Here's another thought. Like almost all societies, we have worked out that we survive best by making rules that strike a balance between doing what each of us wants to do and behaving in a way that gives others the same chance – a balance between rights and duties. If we all want to take from the social pot, we must all give to it, or the pot will be empty and no one will get anything. It's not a difficult idea to grasp once it's drawn to our attention. It's not a difficult idea to teach once it occurs to us that everyone needs to learn this lesson. But people will only sign up to it if they benefit by doing so. At the moment there are far too many people who feel they don't benefit by signing up to our society; that its benefits are for some but not for all, not for them. They feel our society only works against them and so they choose instead to sign up to a different one, a different tribe, like that of the street gangs, the drug dealers.

What happens if we put these two simple thoughts together and then try to do something about it? What if every child grows up feeling that they will do best, and become the person they'd like to be, by belonging within our society, within the rules? What if every child had the same opportunity to make the right choices? What if we recognize that a child who goes to school hungry, who is bullied or belittled or sexually abused or traumatized by domestic violence, does not have the same life chances as others – and what if we really do something about that? Maybe, instead of clapping ourselves on the back for the excellence of our criminal justice system, we should accept that the commission of any crime is a mark that somewhere, somehow, we have failed.

We'll never be able to stop all people committing all crimes. But surely we can send our children to school confident that a teacher cannot abuse another child like Ruth and go undetected. Surely our mental health services can be structured and funded so that people like Joy and Joshua do not die. And if we can make one boy reaching for a knife pause, think, recognize the consequences of picking it up, if we can make him choose not to, then we will have achieved something. If one youngster opens his eyes and sees that running with the street gang is to run down a dead end, and seeing this turns away, we will have achieved something more. If we can get one young man yearning for rolls of banknotes to see he can make good in a business not built on the misery and degradation of drug addicts, that he has other choices, other ways forward, we will have achieved a great deal. Because for all potential offenders who pause, think, change their minds, we save them the waste of their lives, we save victims a world of grief, we save society a huge financial cost, we make a better and happier life for everyone. What's not to like in that?

Appendices

APPENDIX A

This is the sort of document – tailored to the facts of this case – that I give the jury to work from during their deliberations. I ask them to follow the steps in the order in which they appear. Within each step is a series of subpoints to guide their approach to that step.

Steps to Verdict

Take each defendant separately and follow the steps below:

1. Are you sure the defendant you are considering was the stabber?
    - If you are not sure he was the stabber, go to step 2.
    - If you are sure he was the stabber, go to step 3.

2. Are you sure he participated in the stabbing, i.e. that he deliberately assisted or encouraged the stabber, e.g. lending support by his presence or by acting as a getaway driver?
    - If you are not sure of this, he is not guilty of any offence.
    - If you are sure of this, go to step 4.

3. As for the stabber, are you sure at the time he stabbed, he intended to kill Daniel or at least to cause him really serious injury?
    - If you are sure of this, he is guilty of murder.
    - If you are not sure of this but are sure he intended to cause some (short of really serious) injury, he is not guilty of murder but guilty of manslaughter.

4. As for anyone who participated in the stabbing in one of the ways described above, are you sure he shared the stabber's intent?

- If you found the stabber guilty of murder, are you sure this secondary party also intended Daniel would be killed or seriously injured?
  - If you are sure of this, he is also guilty of murder.
  - If you are not sure of this but are sure he intended Daniel should suffer some (short of really serious) injury, he is not guilty of murder but guilty of manslaughter. If you are not sure he intended Daniel should suffer any harm, he is not guilty of anything.
- If you found the stabber guilty of manslaughter, are you sure the secondary party intended Daniel should suffer at least some injury?
  - If so, he too is guilty of manslaughter.
  - If you are not sure he intended Daniel should suffer any injury, he is not guilty of anything.

—————— APPENDIX B ——————

This is what I would have said in court when I sentenced these defendants.

IN THE CENTRAL CRIMINAL COURT
BETWEEN:

Regina

-v-

Meshach, Abednego

SENTENCING REMARKS

Introduction

1.   I have to sentence you, Meshach, for the murder of Daniel Devon, and you, Abednego, for his manslaughter. He was fifteen years old when you killed him. The facts underlying those bald words are very terrible.

Facts

2.   In the past, Meshach and Daniel were friends. I have heard no real explanation why that friendship ended, but it seems Meshach took offence at something Daniel did and refused or was unable to let go of his anger. He ruminated upon the perceived wrong and decided to revenge himself. He drew his friend Abednego into his crime and tried to draw another young man in too. He planned an attack, armed himself with a weapon, arranged transport so he could arrive and leave unseen. He found Daniel and chased him into an alley where there was no one to help him, and no way out. He stabbed Daniel three times, aiming at the chest, driving the knife in hard enough to penetrate clothing, skin, fat, muscle and heart. He could have had no intention but to kill.

Impact

3.   I have read moving statements from Daniel's family and friends about the effect of his death and have taken full note of them all. I have seen his mother and grandmother day after day, dignified even in their distress. I sympathize with them as they have sat through this trial watching Meshach's self-interested efforts to shift blame and his apparent inability to understand the irreparable harm he has done. I have heard from him no word of remorse and he has given no explanation to ease the suffering of the bereaved.

Meshach

4.   Meshach, there is only one sentence for murder. For someone of your age it is called detention during Her Majesty's pleasure. It is a sentence of life imprisonment. You will begin today to serve a sentence from which you might never be released, and for which – if you are released – you will always be liable to recall. You will only be released if the Parole Board deems it safe for the public. My task now is to decide upon the least period you must serve before you may apply to the Parole Board to consider your case.

5.   For a defendant under the age of eighteen, the starting point is always twelve years. I must then reflect the taking of a knife to the killing. For an adult, the uplift for this factor from the starting point that would otherwise apply, is one of two thirds. Even if I apply a lesser uplift, I must arrive at a figure of no less than eighteen years. I am then required by the law to consider what features aggravate and what mitigate your case.

6.   The aggravating features I find are these:
   i.   There was considerable planning of this murder.
   ii. You have offended many times before, although never so seriously.
   iii. I note the appalling impact of the killing.
Taken together, these features increase the term you must serve before you can apply for parole to twenty-one years.

7. As to mitigation, the only relevant feature is your age. Of course, that is already reflected in the twelve-year starting point; however that starting point applies to all youths up to the age of seventeen. You were only fifteen at the time of this offending. The difference between fifteen and seventeen is very significant at a time when the brain is still developing, and judgement, self-restraint and understanding are very far from complete. I give full weight to this, and find that it more than balances out the aggravating features.

8. Accordingly the sentence of the court on you, Meshach, is one of detention during Her Majesty's pleasure. The minimum term to be served before you may apply for parole would be one of seventeen years. The time you have already spent in custody counts towards that, so I must reduce the minimum term by that which you have already served, i.e. 215 days, making the minimum term sixteen years and 150 days.

Abednego

9. I have to sentence you, Abednego, for a very different offence. The harm you have done is of the highest order, for what can be more serious than the taking of another's life. But your culpability is very different. The jury's finding indicates that although you intended Daniel should suffer some harm, you never meant it to be serious and certainly did not intend death.

10. Applying as I must Sentencing Council's Guideline on Manslaughter, I am entirely satisfied you went with Meshach that day knowing he had a knife and that he had a grudge against Daniel. You ran with him, trapping Daniel in the alley. You involved yourself in an unlawful act, which carried a high risk of death or grievous harm, which was or ought to have been obvious to you. If you were an adult this would put your offence in a category with a starting point of twelve years' imprisonment and a range of eight to sixteen years.

11. As to other aggravating features, I find you were either part of the pre-planning or lent yourself to it. In mitigation, you have very little by

way of previous offending and nothing at all for acts of violence, which I take into account in your favour.

12. Taking into account these features, had you been an adult I would have sentenced you to twelve years' imprisonment. However, you were barely fifteen years at the time of your offending, rather younger than Meshach, whom I have no doubt was the leader in the enterprise. I am bound to apply another Guideline dealing with young offenders, which I do. Making appropriate allowance for your very young age, Abednego, the sentence on you will be one of eight years in a Young Offender Institution. If things follow their normal course and you behave yourself, you can expect to serve four years of that sentence. The time you have already served will automatically count towards that.

Reporting restrictions

There is one last matter with which I must deal. Because of their ages, both Meshach and Abednego have up to now had the benefit of restrictions on the reporting of their identities. That order will remain in place until each reaches the age of eighteen, unless I make an excepting direction. I may do that only if I am satisfied the original order imposes a substantial and unreasonable restriction on reporting the proceedings, and that it is in the public interest to remove it. I bear in mind the facts of this case, the rights of both boys as children and the principles of juvenile justice. Very great weight must be given to the welfare of a child and the power to dispense with anonymity must be exercised with care, caution and circumspection. However the welfare of the child will not always trump other considerations. Reports of proceedings should not be restricted unless there are reasons which outweigh the public's legitimate interest in receiving fair, accurate reports of criminal proceedings and knowing the identity of those who are guilty and may present danger.

In this case I note the strong and justified public interest in the commission of knife crime by youths, which is a blight upon our society. I also note the need for deterrence of such crime and that identification of offenders has a legitimate part to play in such deterrence. Having borne in mind all the relevant factors, I have concluded the restriction should be lifted.

—————————— APPENDIX C ——————————

Infanticide Act 1938 as amended by the Coroners and Justice Act 2009

Section 1. Offence of infanticide

(1) Where a woman by any wilful act or omission causes the death of her child being a child under the age of twelve months, but at the time of the act or omission the balance of her mind was disturbed by reason of her not having fully recovered from the effect of giving birth to the child or by reason of the effect of lactation consequent upon the birth of the child, then, [if] the circumstances were such that but for this Act the offence would have amounted to murder [or manslaughter], she shall be guilty of felony, to wit of infanticide, and may for such offence be dealt with and punished as if she had been guilty of the offence of manslaughter of the child.

APPENDIX D

This crime carries a maximum sentence of ten years' imprisonment. In sentencing, the judge must apply the Sentencing Guideline for Child Cruelty, assessing the offender's culpability and the harm caused. There are three categories of culpability (A–C) and three of harm (1–3).

A High culpability is indicated by (among other features)
  - Prolonged and/or multiple incidents of serious cruelty, including serious neglect
  - Gratuitous degradation of victim and/or sadistic behaviour
  - Use of very significant force or use of a weapon
  - Failure to take steps to protect the victim from offending involving category A factors
  - The offender has professional responsibility for victim (where linked to offence)

B Medium culpability is indicated by
  - Use of significant force
  - Prolonged and/or multiple incidents of cruelty, including neglect
  - Limited steps taken to protect victim in cases with category A factors present

C Lesser culpability is indicated where (among other features)
  - Responsibility is substantially reduced by mental disorder, learning disability or lack of maturity; or the offender is a victim of domestic abuse
  - Steps taken to protect victim fell just short of what could reasonably be expected
  - The level of neglect was low or involved a momentary or brief lapse in judgement

Category 1 Harm
- Serious psychological, developmental and/or emotional harm
- Serious physical harm (including illnesses contracted due to neglect)

Category 2 Harm
- Cases falling between categories 1 and 3.
- A high likelihood of category 1 harm being caused.

Category 3 Harm
- Little or no psychological, developmental and/or emotional harm.
- Little or no physical harm.

Identifying levels of culpability/harm gives rise to nine sentencing options:

A1 starting point 6 years, range 4–8 years.

A2 starting point 3 years, range 2–6 years.

A3 starting point 1 year, range high-level community order – 2 years 6 months.

B1 starting point 3 years, range 2–6 years.

B2 starting point 1 year, range high-level community order – 2 years 6 months.

B3 starting point high-level community order, range medium-level community order – 1 year.

C1 starting point 1 year, range high-level community order – 2 years 6 months.

C2 starting point high-level community order, range medium-level community order – 1 year.

C3 starting point medium-level community order, range low-level community order – 6 months.

Taking the starting point, the judge must then move up or down within the range to reflect the aggravating and mitigating features which include the following:

Aggravating features:
- Previous convictions or offence committed while on bail, licence or post-sentence supervision, or in breach of current court orders
- Failure to seek medical help
- Commission of offence under the influence of alcohol or drugs
- Deliberate covering up of the offence or wrongly placing blame on others
- Failure to respond to interventions or warnings about behaviour
- Threats to prevent reporting of offence
- Offence committed in presence of another child

Mitigating features:
- No relevant or recent previous convictions and/or good character/ exemplary conduct
- Cooperation with investigation and/or remorse
- Determination and demonstration of steps to address addiction/ offending behaviour
- Sole or primary carer for dependent relative
- Serious medical condition requiring urgent, intensive or long-term treatment
- Mental disorder, learning disability or lack of maturity

For detail see Sentencing Council's Definitive Guideline on Child Cruelty.

APPENDIX E

Sexual Offences Act 2003 section 16(1)

A person aged 18 or over (A) commits an offence if –
    (a) he intentionally touches another person (B),
    (b) the touching is sexual,
    (c) A is in a position of trust in relation to B.
    (d) . . .
    (e) either –
        (i) B is under 18 and A does not reasonably believe that B is 18 or over, or
        (ii) B is under 13.

A person is in a position of trust if he/she looks after those under 18 receiving education at an educational institution. *For detail see section 21.*

The maximum sentence after conviction on indictment is five years' imprisonment. *For detail see section 16(5).*

—————————— APPENDIX F ——————————

Mr Newton was charged with sexual offences on his wife. Their stormy marriage was already foundering when he buggered her. He said it was with her consent. She said it was not. In 1982, the insertion of a man's penis in a woman's anus amounted to the criminal offence of buggery whether or not she consented but, obviously, if she did consent it made a huge difference to sentence. Mrs Newton said that her husband tried, against her will, to have vaginal sex with her but failed because he was drunk; that when she fled, he caught and assaulted her, then proceeded to insert his penis into every available orifice. He said his actions might seem a little bizarre to ordinary tastes, but it was how they liked it and how she wanted it. He appeared at the Old Bailey and pleaded guilty to buggery. He had to because, on either version, he had committed the offence. The judge had to determine on which basis he would sentence. The judge said that the law required him to accept the accused's version as far as possible. This is no more than the application of our old friend the 'burden of proof'. Generally this burden lies on the Crown, which means where any matter is unresolved, the judge must take the view most favourable to the defendant. The judge was indeed required to take the accused's version as far as possible. But perhaps he didn't find it possible. At any rate, he didn't do it. Rather, he sentenced on the account put forward by the Crown on behalf of Mrs Newton. Mr Newton appealed. The Court of Appeal said a judge could accept a defendant's account or he could hear evidence to test that account, but he could not simply accept the Crown's version. That judgement binds me, and all judges, now.

APPENDIX G

In Guardian News and Media Ltd v. AB & CD [2014] 6 WLUK 320, the Court of Appeal concluded that the Rule of Law is a priceless asset of our country and a foundation of our constitution. A hallmark and safeguard of it is open justice including criminal trials being held in public and the publication of defendants' names. Open justice is a fundamental principle of the common law and a means of ensuring public confidence in our legal system. Exceptions are rare, must be justified on the facts and must be necessary and proportionate. No more than the minimum departure from open justice will be countenanced. However, open justice must give way to the yet more fundamental principle that the paramount object of the court is to do justice. Accordingly, where there is a serious possibility that an insistence on open justice in the national security context would frustrate the administration of justice, for example, by deterring the Crown from prosecuting a case where it otherwise should do so, a departure from open justice may be justified.

APPENDIX H

This crime carries a maximum sentence of fourteen years' imprisonment, a minimum two years' disqualification and compulsory extended re-test. In sentencing, the judge must apply the Sentencing Guideline for Causing Death by Dangerous Driving. The causing of death always puts the harm at the highest level. However the judge must assess the seriousness of the offender's wrongful driving. There are three levels of seriousness (1–3).

Levels of seriousness

Level 1. Where the driving in question involves a deliberate decision to ignore (or flagrant disregard for) the rules of the road and apparent disregard for the great danger being caused to others, e.g. prolonged, persistent, deliberate course of very bad driving AND/OR consumption of substantial amounts of alcohol or drugs leading to gross impairment AND/OR a group of determinants of seriousness which in isolation or smaller number would place the offence in level 2.

Level 2. Where the driving in question creates substantial risk of danger, e.g. greatly excessive speed, competitive driving against another OR gross avoidable distraction such as reading or texting messages OR driving while impaired as a result of consuming alcohol or drugs, failing to take prescribed medication or as a result of a known medical condition OR a group of determinants of seriousness which in isolation or smaller number would place the offence in level 3.

Level 3. Where the driving in question creates significant risk of danger, e.g. driving over speed limit/at speed inappropriate for the prevailing conditions OR driving when knowingly deprived of adequate sleep or rest or knowing the vehicle has a dangerous defect or is poorly maintained or is dangerously loaded OR a brief but obvious danger arising from a seriously dangerous manoeuvre OR driving while avoidably distracted OR failing to have proper regard to vulnerable road users.

Level 1: a starting point of eight years' custody with a range of seven to fourteen years

Level 2: a starting point of five years' custody with a range of four to seven years

Level 3: a starting point of three years' custody with a range of two to five years

Taking the starting point, the judge must then move up or down within the range to reflect the aggravating and mitigating features which include the following:

Aggravating features:
- Previous motoring offences and/or other offences committed at same time
- More than one person killed and/or seriously injured
- Disregard of warnings
- Irresponsible behaviour such as failing to stop, falsely claiming the victim was responsible or trying to throw the victim off the car by swerving to escape

Mitigating features:
- Alcohol or drugs consumed unwittingly
- Offender seriously injured in the collision
- Victim was a close friend of relative
- Actions of victim or third party contributed significantly to the collision and/or death
- Offender's lack of driving experience contributed to the commission of the offence
- The driving was in response to a proven genuine emergency where the facts fall short of raising the full defence of 'necessity'

--------------------------- APPENDIX I ---------------------------

The Domestic Violence Crime and Victims Act 2004 section 5 as amended by the Domestic Violence, Crime and Victims (Amendment) Act 2012

Section 5(1) provides that where death or serious physical harm is inflicted on a child or vulnerable adult (V) by a person who is a member of the same household and had frequent contact with V, not only is the person who inflicts the harm liable, but also (if there was a significant risk of this occurring) anyone (i) who was, or ought to have been, aware of the risk and (ii) who failed to take such steps as he/she could reasonably have been expected to take to protect V from the risk and (iii) the act occurred in circumstances of the kind that he/she foresaw or ought to have foreseen.

Section 5(2) provides that the prosecution does not have to prove whether a defendant was the person who inflicted the harm or the person who failed to protect V against the risk of harm.

Section 5(6) provides that 'child' means a person under the age of sixteen, and 'vulnerable adult' means a person sixteen or over whose ability to protect himself from violence, abuse or neglect is significantly impaired through physical or mental disability or illness, old age or otherwise.

Section 5(7) and (8) provide maximums at present of fourteen years' imprisonment for causing or allowing a victim's death, and ten years for causing or allowing a victim to suffer serious physical harm.

For detail see section 5 of the 2004 Act.

APPENDIX J

Youth Justice and Criminal Evidence Act 1999

Sections 16 and 17 identify witnesses who are eligible for special measures to help them give evidence.

Section 16 covers all those under the age of eighteen at the time of the hearing AND all those the quality of whose evidence the court considers is likely to be diminished by reason of the witness suffering from mental disorder, or having a significant impairment of intelligence and social functioning, or having a physical disability or disorder.

Section 17 covers all those where the court is satisfied that the quality of their evidence is likely to be diminished by reason of fear or distress in connection with testifying in the proceedings. The section sets out matters to be taken into consideration, e.g. the nature and circumstances of the alleged offence, social, cultural and ethnic origins of the witness etc. There is automatic eligibility for complainant witnesses in respect of sexual offences or offences under section 1 or section 2 of the Modern Slavery Act 2015. There is automatic eligibility for witnesses in a wide variety of offences including many offences of violence where a firearm or knife was or was believed to be involved. *For a full list and details see YJCEA 1999 schedule 1A.*

The quality of evidence referred to above includes its completeness, coherence and accuracy.

By the Youth Justice and Criminal Evidence Act 1999 sections 23-30, the special measures referred to above include:

- screens to shield the witness from the defendant and others
- a live link so evidence can be given from outside the courtroom

- visual recordings (a) made before the trial as the witness's evidence-in-chief and (b) made earlier in the process of cross-examination and re-examination
- removal of wigs and gowns by judges and barristers
- aids to communication, e.g. an intermediary, a communicator or interpreter, or through a communication aid or technique
- exclusion from the court of the public and press (save for one named press representative) in cases involving sexual offences or intimidation by someone other than the accused

APPENDIX K

Barristers these days must undergo a certain number of hours of specific training each year in order to be allowed to practise. Amongst the available training, much is concerned with the best practice in dealing with child and otherwise vulnerable witnesses. The Advocate's Gateway (TAG) is an independent body which provides access to practical, evidence-based guidance on vulnerable witnesses and defendants in the form of 'toolkits'. The toolkits are widely accepted as setting out the proper approach to dealing with such witnesses in court.

APPENDIX L

Unfitness to plead: the Pritchard test

Mr Pritchard appeared before the courts on a capital charge in the 1830s and the law that emerged from his case still dogs us today. It arises whenever the court has to consider whether a defendant is well enough to stand trial. These days it almost always relates to his or her mental capacity, but Mr Pritchard's problem wasn't so much mental as that he was deaf and mute. Baron Alderson ruled thus (in Pritchard (1836) 7 C&P 303): 'There are three points to be enquired into: – first, whether the prisoner is mute of malice or not; secondly, whether he can plead to the indictment or not; thirdly, whether he is of sufficient intellect to comprehend the course of the proceedings in the trial so as to make a proper defence – to know that he might challenge any of [the jury] to whom he may object . . .' A prize for longevity is to be handed to the Baron because few rulings have lasted as long as this one. The matter has been reviewed over and over in the Court of Appeal, but 'Pritchard' – a little battered, a little reshaped by section 4 and 4A of the Criminal Procedure (Insanity) Act 1964 – still survives. However abnormal, odd or frankly weird a defendant's mind may be, if he is capable of instructing his lawyers, following the trial, and giving evidence, he is likely to be fit to be tried.

If there is expert psychiatric evidence that a defendant is unfit to be tried, but may become fit in a reasonable time, the better course may be to adjourn the case to see if he/she recovers. However, if the issue is to be dealt with, it is determined by the judge alone, hearing expert evidence. If the defence asserts the disability, it must satisfy the court of this contention on the balance of probabilities. If the Crown makes the assertion, it must prove the matter beyond a reasonable doubt. If he/she is found fit to be tried, the trial proceeds in the normal way. If he/she is found unfit, a jury is empanelled to decide if he/she did the act or made the omission alleged. There is no consideration of a defendant's state of mind at the time he/she acted, so in the case of Joshua Goodall the question would only be if he cut his wife's throat. Why he did would be irrelevant. If the jury does not find he did the act, there is an acquittal. If they find he did do the act, the prosecution is paused until such time (if ever) as the defendant is fit to plead, when a trial can in certain circumstances take place. In the meantime, a defendant is often ordered into hospital or placed under a supervision order. Because of the consequences of a finding of unfitness, where the defendant has a promising line of defence it may be better to delay trying the issue of 'unfitness' and allow the prosecution case to be presented, to see if that fails before the trial reaches the stage where the defendant might be called upon to give evidence. *For detail see section 4A of the 1964 Act.*

APPENDIX M

Psychiatric defences

The distinction between the psychiatric defences 'insanity' and 'diminished responsibility' is clear in principle but not always easy to spot in practice. Both are concerned with the state of the offender's mind at the time of the killing. The 'insane' equivalent of Mr Pritchard was Daniel McNaughten, who in 1843 tried to assassinate Robert Peel, then Prime Minister, but only managed to kill Peel's poor secretary. McNaughten, again a little battered by statute, also still survives.

Insanity requires that a defendant was labouring under a defect of reason caused by a disease of the mind so that he or she did not know the nature and quality of the act they were doing; or, if he did know it, that he did not know what he was doing was wrong. Diminished responsibility requires that he had an abnormality of mental functioning which arose from a recognized medical condition that substantially impaired his ability to understand the nature of his own conduct and/or to form a rational judgement and/or to exercise self-control. And this explains what he did, e.g. causing or significantly contributing to causing his actions. *For detail see Homicide Act 1957 section 2 as amended by the Coroners and Justice Act 2009, section 52(1).*

In short, if Joshua Goodall slit his wife's throat believing he was carving the Sunday roast, he could plead 'not guilty to murder by reason of insanity'. If he did the same thing believing she would be happier in heaven than on earth, he could plead 'not guilty to murder by reason of diminished responsibility'.

APPENDIX N

The Guideline on sentencing for manslaughter by reason of diminished responsibility provides that though the maximum sentence is life imprisonment, most sentences fall in the range three to forty years, of which a defendant would most usually serve two thirds.

The first task is to assess the degree of responsibility which the defendant in fact retained (high, medium or low). For medium culpability, the starting point is fifteen years with a range from ten to twenty-five years. The starting point moves up the range for aggravating features, e.g. relevant previous convictions, significant premeditation, causing unnecessary suffering. It moves down the range for mitigating features such as good character, remorse, or if the offender had made a genuine sustained effort to get help for the mental illness.

Thought must be given to the offender's future dangerousness. Also to whether a non-penal 'mental health disposal' rather than imprisonment is appropriate. Or whether, if a penal element is required, it should be preceded by treatment in hospital before transfer to prison.

For detail see Sentencing Council's Definitive Guideline on manslaughter by reason of diminished responsibility.

─────── APPENDIX O ───────

Sentencing Act 2020 schedule 21

2(1) If (a) the court considers that the seriousness of the offence . . . is exceptionally high and (b) the offender was aged twenty-one or over when the offence was committed, the appropriate starting point is a whole life order (i.e. one from which there is no release).

2(2) Cases that would normally fall within sub-paragraph 2(1) include:

(a) murder of two or more persons where each murder involves any of the following:
　　(i) a substantial degree of premeditation or planning
　　(ii) the abduction of the victim, or
　　(iii) sexual or sadistic conduct
(b) murder of a child if involving abduction of the child or sexual or sadistic motivation
(c) murder of a police officer or prison officer in the course of his or her duty . . .
(d) murder for the purpose of advancing a political, religious or ideological cause
(e) murder by an offender previously convicted of murder

3(1) If (a) the case does not fall within paragraph 2(1) but the court considers that the seriousness of the offence . . . is particularly high and (b) the offender was aged eighteen or over when the offence was committed, the appropriate starting point in determining the minimum term is thirty years.

3(2) Cases that . . . would normally fall within sub-paragraph 3(1)(a) include:

(a) in the case of an offence committed before 13 April 2015, the murder of a police officer or prison officer in the course of his or her duty
(b) murder involving the use of a firearm or explosive
(c) murder done for gain . . .
(d) murder intended to obstruct or interfere with the course of justice
(e) murder involving sexual or sadistic conduct
(f) murder of two or more persons
(g) murder that is aggravated by racial or religious hostility, or by hostility related to sexual orientation

APPENDIX P

As in all offences, the judge must determine the harm caused and the offender's culpability. In all manslaughter, since death has been caused, the harm will be of the utmost seriousness. The categorization of culpability depends on the type of manslaughter.

For manslaughter during an unlawful act without intent to kill or cause GBH the categories are:

A   Very high culpability may be indicated by
   - the extreme character of one or more culpability B factors and/or
   - a combination of culpability B factors

B   High culpability may be indicated by death caused in the course of an unlawful act
   - where the offender's intention falls just short of causing GBH and/or
   - which carried a high risk of death or GBH which was or ought to have been obvious to the offender and/or
   - where there is concealment, destruction, defilement or dismemberment of the body

C   Medium culpability may be indicated by cases falling between high and lower including but not limited to where death was caused in the course of
   - an unlawful act which involved an intention by the offender to cause harm (or recklessness as to whether harm would be caused) that falls between high and lower and/or
   - committing or escaping from a less serious offence in which the offender played more than a minor role

D   Lower culpability may be indicated where death was caused in the course of an unlawful act

- in defence of self or other(s) (where not amounting to a defence) and/or
- where there was no intention by the offender to cause any harm and no obvious risk of anything more than minor harm and/or
- in which the offender played a minor role and/or
- in which the offender's responsibility was substantially reduced by mental disorder, learning disability or lack of maturity

Applying the above categories will lead the judge to the following starting points and ranges:

Category A: starting point eighteen years, range eleven to twenty-four years
Category B: starting point twelve years, range eight to sixteen years
Category C: starting point six years, range three to nine years
Category D: starting point two years, range one to four years

For manslaughter during loss of control the categories are:

A   High culpability may be indicated by
- planning of criminal activity . . . before the loss of control
- offence committed in the context of other serious criminal activity
- use of a firearm (whether or not taken to the scene)
- where the qualifying trigger for loss of control is only just met
- concealment, destruction, defilement or dismemberment of the body . . .

B   Medium culpability may be indicated where cases fall between high and lower because
- factors are present in high and lower which balance each other out and/or
- culpability falls between the factors as described in high and lower

C Lower culpability may be indicated where the qualifying trigger represented a very high degree of provocation.

Applying the above categories will lead the judge to the following starting points and ranges:

Category A: starting point fourteen years, range ten to twenty years
Category B: starting point eight years, range five to twelve years
Category C: starting point five years, range three to six years

In all cases of manslaughter, as with all offences, the judge must take into account aggravating and mitigating factors.

Aggravating features include:
- Relevant previous convictions
- Offence committed while on bail or on licence or while under a court order
- Offence motivated by or demonstrating hostility based on victim's actual or presumed religion, race, disability, sexual orientation or transgender identity
- Offence committed against an emergency worker acting in exercise of his work
- History of violence or abuse towards victim by offender
- Involvement of others through coercion, intimidation or exploitation
- Significant mental or physical suffering caused to deceased
- Offence occurred when victim was engaged in public service or duty
- Offence committed while under influence of alcohol or drugs
- Persistence of violence
- Offence involved use of a weapon
- Offending put others at risk of harm
- Actions after event, e.g. attempts to conceal evidence

Mitigating features include:
- No previous convictions or no relevant or recent convictions
- Good character or exemplary conduct
- Remorse
- Intent to cause GBH rather than to kill
- Violence begun by victim or victim's history of significant violence/abuse to offender
- Serious medical condition requiring urgent, intensive or long-term treatment
- Mental disorder or learning disability
- Age and/or lack of maturity
- Sole or primary carer for dependent relative
- Plea of guilty

APPENDIX Q

Early in January 2022 Regina v. Skuse, Graham, Ponsford and Willoughby (the defendants collectively known as the Colston 4) were acquitted of criminal damage, accused of participation in toppling a statue of the seventeenth-century Bristol slave trader, defacing it, dragging it to the river and throwing it in. At their trial the defendants did not deny doing any of these things which constituted the crime alleged. They asserted, rather, that they were justified in their actions because the presence of the statue caused offence – which does not constitute any defence known to law. The jury acquitted.

The Attorney General has spoken of invoking her powers to refer the matter to the Court of Appeal to clarify the law, but on one view the law seems perfectly clear.

The rules seem to be that a jury has a right to break them. Vivat lex!

ACKNOWLEDGEMENTS

I AM SO VERY GRATEFUL for the many contributions from all those who have made the writing of this book possible. First and foremost, thanks to my agent Alice Lutyens at Curtis Brown, who insisted I should try to write about the day job and was generous enough to let me work out how best to do it. Without her endless prompting and encouragement, I should never have undertaken this book. And even if I had, I wouldn't have completed it without the massive support of the entire team at Transworld – Susanna Wadeson, Patsy Irwin, Emma Burton, Katherine Cowdrey, Viv Thompson, Richard Ogle, Jack Smyth, Dan Balado, Sarah Scarlett and Lucy Beresford-Knox – and, of course, dear Andrea Henry who kicked it all off. You have all been magnificent. Your unending care over every detail has been inspirational. How very lucky I was that you found me.

My thanks also to Anna Davies at Curtis Brown Creative who started me on the journey when she gave me a place on one of their courses. And to the local bookshop who stuck Anna's flyer in their window, tempting me to apply for that place. And to those who were on the same course – it only lasted six weeks, but their support and good companionship has lasted far, far longer: Aliyah, Geoff, Ian, Louise, Ziella – writers all.

My sister, Elizabeth Mills, has always been my first reader. My earliest scribblings were inflicted on her in childhood, and she has never lost the habit of firm, kind and constructive criticism. Thank you, Liz. No one could have been more generous with their time and help than you have been.

My husband, Iain Jay, has listened patiently, frowned or nodded as appropriate, and got on with keeping our lives in order while I have been distracted by the joy of writing. Without you, dearest Iain, I wouldn't have got past Chapter One.

My humble thanks to all those who have passed through the courtrooms with me over the past 46+ years – barristers, judges, ushers and clerks. Thanks also to the patient list officers and court staff, caterers and probation officers, cell and security staff, the jury bailiffs and those who work for nothing in witness support – and to all those at the Old Bailey who have filled my life and walked beside me. Finally, most of what I have been privileged to learn has come from those whom the court serves – witnesses and jurors, defendants and victims and their families and friends. You have opened my eyes and I am grateful.

Until March 2022 Her Honour Wendy Joseph KC was a judge at the Old Bailey, sitting on criminal cases, trying mainly allegations of murder and other homicide. She read English and Law at Cambridge, was called to the Bar by Gray's Inn in 1975, became a KC in 1998 and sat as a full-time judge from 2007 to 2022. When she moved to the Old Bailey in 2012 she was the only woman amongst sixteen judges, and only the third woman ever to hold a permanent position there. She was also a Diversity and Community Relations Judge, working to promote understanding between the judiciary and many different sectors of our community, particularly those from less privileged and minority groups. She mentors young people, from a variety of backgrounds, who hope for a career in law and has a special interest in helping women. *Unlawful Killings* is her first book.